DATE DUE

Demco, Inc. 38-293

Rosemond Tuve

A LIFE OF THE MIND

Rosemond Tuve in the 1950s. Courtesy of Connecticut College Archives.

ROSEMOND TUVE

A LIFE OF THE MIND

MARGARET CARPENTER EVANS

Peter E. Randall Publisher
Portsmouth, New Hampshire
2004

© 2004 by Margaret Carpenter Evans
Printed in the United States of America

Design by Peter E. Randall

Peter E. Randall Publisher
Box 4726, Portsmouth, NH 03802
www.perpublisher.com

Distributed by University Press of New England
Hanover and London

ISBN: 1-931807-20-5
Library of Congress control number:
2003113711

For

Richard, Jean, Mary, and Andrew

CONTENTS

⤳ PREFACE ⤶

There is only one everlasting monument: frail words.
Rosemond Tuve

A YEAR AFTER LEAVING CONNECTICUT COLLEGE, I wrote a letter to Rosemond Tuve asking her opinion of a book I was reading. I have kept her response to that letter ever since, folded in a small edition of Thomas à Kempis's *Imitation of Christ* which she suggested I read: It is a book "my father put in my way," she wrote. Since then, you have remained for me a living presence.

Your reply, Miss Tuve, typed on both sides of a sheet of typewriter paper, single-spaced, crammed to the edges, and written up and down the margins in your miniscule hand, was prompt. Was it the intensity and generosity of your response, your caring, that so overwhelmed me that *I never answered your letter?* It is too late now to erase what may have been your disappointment at my seeming indifference, my ingratitude. What distresses me now is the wasted opportunity to communicate with the person you were, and whom I have since come to know. How well I can identify with another student of yours who wrote to me: "Alas for the limited perspective and understanding of the nineteen-year-old who only barely realized what an extraordinary spirit it was hearing." Finally, almost fifty years later, I am responding, not without sadness that it was never accomplished in your lifetime.

In 1979 I returned to live near Connecticut College where you taught for twenty-nine of your sixty one years of life. No visible sign of you remains. I saw others' names, faculty and administrators, etched on stone dormitories, portraits hanging on library walls, or honored through large endowments. Only later did I discover how *your* memory is perpetuated.

First, and fittingly, I learned of a small, obscure, Renaissance book fund; second, and more permanently for me and others, you are still visible astride your antiquated bicycle, pedaling furiously up the hill to the library in your "number nines," books all but spilling out of the huge baskets hung on either side, skirt billowing, wisps of reddish-gold hair flying as though sparked by your thoughts. Suddenly an arm would rise, a long and graceful finger would signal your turn into Palmer Library, and you would coast to a halt, almost as if descending from aloft. Speaking in your soft, musical voice to a student you might meet on the path, you would enter the building. I think now how truly you exemplified the function of poetry. You remained, in the words of Sir Philip Sidney, "a speaking picture, with this end, to teach and delight."

ACKNOWLEDGEMENTS

D URING THE PAST TWENTY-FIVE YEARS, I have taken considerable pleasure in researching and writing this biography of Rosemond Tuve. I have been buoyed by her many friends and colleagues—too many to list by name. The experience and knowledge I have acquired from these "Tuveans" over the years has enriched and sustained me. Those of you who appear in the book will recognize yourselves; to you, and the others, I owe my continual gratitude.

In addition, Rosemond Tuve, herself, has been an enlivening presence for me in this endeavor, aided by a quotation from one of her favorite poets: "Who are we, that our time is too short to understand George Herbert?"[1] I believe that understanding Rosemond Tuve has been worth every step of the long road I have traveled, the notes I have amassed, and the hours of struggle.

I need to mention a few people who are not in the book, but who provided me with indispensable help and encouragement: Barbara Snow Delaney, a classmate at Connecticut College, who encouraged me to take my first step; Susan Minot Woody, for prodding me; Trudi Brink-Johnsen, for translations from the Norwegian; Teresa Marin-Padilla, for unwavering support; Jean Lawe, for her willingness to read the early manuscript; Brian D. Rogers, for his kindness and always courteous assistance in the Charles E. Shain Library and beyond; and Thomas D. Cornell, for voluntary hours of painstaking work copying and annotating the Tuve letters in the Library of Congress.

I wish also to express my thanks to Upton B. Brady, my editor, who sustained me over the final years with his valuable experience and belief in this book; and, as well to every archivist and reference librarian who gave unstintingly of their help.

And finally, my deepest gratitude goes to Mary M. Evans, who so generously gave of her time and skills to provide hours of copyediting; and Andrew H. Evans, for his inestimable time and expertise with the technical aspects of preparing the copy. Without your unremitting support I doubt this book would exist.

CHRONOLOGY

November 29, 1903. Born, Canton, SD.

1916–1918. Canton High School.

1919–1920. University High School, Minneapolis, MN.

June, 1924. Graduated cum laude, Phi Beta Kappa, University of Minnesota.

May, 1925. Awarded Master's Degree, Bryn Mawr College.

1925–1926. Fellow in the English Department, Bryn Mawr College.

1926–1928. Instructor in English, Goucher College.

1928–1929. Somerville College, Oxford.

1929–1932. Instructor in English, Vassar College.

1931. Awarded Ph.D from Bryn Mawr College.

1932–1934. Abroad to publish thesis, *Seasons and Months: Studies in a Tradition of Middle English Poetry* and transcribe letters of Horace Walpole.

1934–1963. Instructor, then Professor of English at Connecticut College.

1947. *Elizabethan and Metaphysical Imagery* published.

1949. Received the Rosemary Crawshay Award through the British Academy.

1952. Visiting lecturer, University of Minnesota, spring and summer semesters.

1952. Awarded Doctor of Letters degree from Augustana College.

1952. *A Reading of George Herbert* published.

1955. Received the $2,500 achievement award from the American Association of University Women.

1956. Visiting lecturer, Harvard University, fall semester.

1957. *Images and Themes in Five Poems by Milton* published.

June, 1957. Awarded Doctor of Letters degree from Wheaton College.

1957–1958. Senior Fulbright Research Fellow, Oxford.

April and May, 1959. Lecturer, Christian Gauss Seminars in Research, Princeton.

May, 1959. Elected a Fellow of the American Academy of Arts and Sciences.

June, 1959. Awarded Doctor of Letters degree from Mt. Holyoke College.

January, 1960. Received the American Council of Learned Societies $10,000 award.

1960. NATO Research Fellowship, University of Aarhus, Denmark, spring semester.

1961. Awarded Doctor of Letters degree from Carleton College.

1961–1962. Visiting professor, Princeton University; also Senior Fellow of the Council of the Humanities.

1962. Spring semester, abroad to study and write.

June, 1963. Awarded Doctor of Humane Letters, Syracuse University.

1963–1964. Professor of English, University of Pennsylvania.

December 20, 1964. Died, Bryn Mawr, PA.

1965. *Allegorical Imagery* published posthumously.

ROSEMOND TUVE

A LIFE OF THE MIND

Rosemond Tuve about age five.

1

IREMEMBER CONNECTICUT COLLEGE in the early sixties. Some of the young male faculty would stand around, embarrassed, happy, apprehensive, perhaps talking about football, the girls, or the view— something profound like that—standing there and suddenly having someone whack my back. I turned around and there was Rosemond Tuve—a cigarette in her hand, her hair fuzzy, her dress not quite straight. 'What d'yuh fellas think of Alexander Pope?' Suddenly we were whipped out of our light talk and challenged. What *do* we think of Alexander Pope? She wasn't grilling. She was just terribly interested. How can we be here as young English instructors without some opinion of that topic? You got hooked on Roz; you wanted to go see her again. But when you went to find her she had hopped into this slightly battered but large, powerful, Oldsmobile car and taken off. She'd drive night and day to get out of these damnable, pretty hills of New England and out to the open spaces in South Dakota and she wouldn't stop, apparently, until she got there. She was frequently asked why she loved South Dakota—it's so flat. 'Of course it's flat,' was her retort, 'that's why it's so beautiful.'"[1]

Near the end of her life, she wrote a friend: "I never care about living in the world especially long except when I get on a prairie, then I wish life could please last."

Rosemond Tuve was born in Canton, South Dakota, on November 27, 1903. Like the azure-eyed goddess Athena, who sprang from the head of Zeus bearing a shield and spear, she seemed to emerge from her father's head embodying all of his intellectual and moral strengths. Anthony Gulbrand Tuve had been president of Augustana College for thirteen years before her birth, and it was his values and beliefs that formed her mind and spirit. As she grew and her life evolved into that of an eminent teacher and scholar, her father remained a lodestone in her life. Her mother, Ida Larsen Tuve, graduated from Northwestern Conservatory of Music, in Evanston, Illinois, at the age of eighteen. A year later Anthony invited Ida Larsen to be "preceptress" of music at Augustana College. After two sons, Ida expressed her joy at the birth of a daughter in her choice of a name— Rosemond Theresa Marie. Rosemond signifies "rose of the world" and Rose was Anthony's nickname for his wife. In an attempt to prevent the harsh-sounding nickname Roz, Ida chose the variant spelling. But to her brothers she was often RTMT, and to her friends, Roz, which disappointed her mother.

President Tuve and Augustana College lived symbiotically. In 1890, after only one year as an instructor, Tuve assumed the presidency at the age of twenty-six. Three years later he married Ida Larsen and they set up housekeeping in the president's cramped living quarters on the second floor of the single college building. It wasn't until 1900, when the college building was moved to a larger campus on the northeast edge of town, that President Tuve began construction of his own home, within walking distance of his office. This meant that Rosemond would spend her entire life on or near a college campus.

George Lewis Tuve, the first child born to Anthony and Ida and always known as "Lew," was born in 1896 while Anthony and Ida were still living in the college dormitory. Shortly after their home was completed, Merle Antony Tuve was born, on June 7, 1901. This meant that Ida Tuve would relinquish her teaching duties as head of the music department at Augustana College and her position as organist for the Bethlehem Congregation Church. The following year the cornerstone for a new and larger college building was laid. It was completed the year Rosemond was born. Eight years and two months later, Richard Larsen Tuve arrived.

Anthony Tuve took extreme pains that his home would be substantial, spacious, and equipped with the most modern conveniences. It stood proudly between the town and the prairies beyond, facing north as if in defiance of the constantly gusting winds. It was a high-ceilinged, two-story clapboard home, with a small garret centered at the top. An ample bay window, several gables, cornices, and a cozy front porch provided comfort to a growing family and welcomed church and educational leaders. Missionaries often visited, stirring the imaginations of the children, in an era when travel was rare. O. E. Rölvaag, who entered Augustana College in 1899, and would later write *Giants in the Earth,* helped in the construction of the Tuve home in partial payment of his tuition at the school. It may well be that Anthony Tuve was an inspiration to this young Norwegian immigrant, for Rölvaag, quoted in a preface to his novel, acknowledged that "once at school, the fierce desire for knowledge, so long restrained, took him by storm."[2]

Undoubtedly, Ida supervised the Victorian furnishings of their new home: figured wallpaper, throw rugs, ruffled pillows, and lots of photographs. The focal point of the living room was the piano. Ida's training in piano and classical music influenced the entire family. She would accompany them as they sang the old Lutheran hymns or, perhaps, on a warm, summer evening, with the windows open wide, a Bach chorale would fill the air. Rosemond's mother taught her to play the piano and instilled in her a love of music that sustained her for life. Richard recalled that during his years as choir director of the Congregational church in Silver Spring, Maryland, Rosemond would often spend her Christmas and Easter vacations with his family: "Frequently she would don a gown to take the alto part at either a Christmas or Easter service, for she knew all the liturgy and music of any church she entered without needing a rehearsal."

Richard remembered his mother as a "tall, upstanding, handsome woman, who treasured the best in people." Formal and precise, she enjoyed her social position, and immersed herself in all the cultural, social, and educational opportunities available to a woman in a midwestern town in the early twentieth century. Ida belonged to several reading groups and presented papers to the members, and persisted in this effort for years. She subscribed to *The Mentor,* a magazine containing rotogravure reproductions from current art collections here and abroad, along with articles on the history and meaning of art.

Later, writing to a friend following a visit to Canton, Rosemond recalled the influence of the church and its allegorical figures: "We got in the church where I was confirmed and my father was buried . . . and saw its windows and altar there I used to puzzle over . . . (things like Alpha & Omega, and all the wild puzzles of my childhood, like the symbols of the Crucifixion & bits of Greek)."

In a speech at Augustana College in 1961, she recalled her first experience of school: "I do not suppose that I look out upon many who can claim that they went to Augustana during the FIRST half-century of its existence. Now I did; I entered it as a student, though not officially on the books, at the age of $4\frac{1}{2}$.

Indeed I went to classes in the old Canton buildings (one already famous to me at $4\frac{1}{2}$ because the house my eldest brother [Lew] was born in, when my father, as President, and my mother, as instructor in music, brought forth the only baby I suppose ever born in an Augustana dormitory). I was a student of Humanities, went to English classes, with a few other faculty children, designed to give some Practice Teaching to the girls training for teaching in schools. I well remember my father's mirth and teasing of the college students for their large phrases about the psychology of education, when after the first week no one had discovered that I could read, and were still pushing on the problem of arousing in me a desire to learn to do so, by entering into my childish concerns, at My Level. I think this is still one of the comedies of American college education—a full day of Stimulating-the-Desire-to-Study to each $1\frac{1}{2}$ hours of time left over to Study; take dissolved in Coca-cola."

Her speech continued: "But the chief way I went to Augustana was that I learned from its two faculty members who were my parents, before I was 8, all that I have since discovered to be the ideals of scholarship. My father was a mathematician *primarily* and a president second, and contrary to unthinking opinion nowadays, this is the order of importances which the best college presidents . . . still operate under. It was the rigour and the beauty of mathematical thought which, as a child, I saw captivated my father, and he could not but teach it as one of the humanities; but what I caught as one catches measles was the unswerving and passionate devotion to inquiry into the truth of any matter, and this is the aim of all the learnings, all *scientia*—not just Humanities: the universality of this common motive I learnt too."[3]

Learning to read at the age of four enabled Rosemond to complete the third grade in the Canton public schools when she was six. Two months after her eighth birthday, and a few days after having her appendix out, she wrote the earliest of her existing letters. On lined paper, in a clear, round script, she wrote:

> Sioux Falls Hospital
> January 26, 1912
> Dear Mama:
> How are you getting along? I am getting along nicely. Has the new baby come yet? I hope you can come and see me pretty soon. Minnie told me you were making dresses for the new baby. Will you name her Emily? I like that name so well.

The baby, the fourth child for the Tuves, was Richard Larsen Tuve, born February 1, 1912.

Rosemond continued:

> I had to smell of the ether before I had the operation, and sometimes the doctor got it too close to my nose, and I said it was too strong, but he would not take it any farther away from my nose, so I had to stand it. You know I had to smell of the ether so I could go to sleep while they took my appendix out. I have my appendix right here in my room in a bottle. I have seen them and they look awful funny.
>
> I have put them in one of those little bottles, like the one you put camphor in when I and Aunty Emily went to Grandma's, to use for my tooth-ache.

Four days later she wrote again. The letter is headed "Soo Falls Hospital, Jan. 30, 1912." Already she is playing with words, and giving a hint of the colloquial style of writing to come.

The Tuve Family, left to right: Merle Anthony Tuve, Ida Marie Larsen Tuve, George Lewis Tuve, Anthony Gulbrand Tuve, and Rosemond Tuve, about age six.

Dear Papa and Mama:

I thought I would write a few lines to you, since Aunty Lottie is sending a letter, too. I cannot find my pencil anywhere. I think when I let papa use it he stuck it in his pocket and ran away to Canton with it.

I am going to buy me a nickels worth of pen-points to put in my pen-holder, because I haven't anything but a stub-pen at scool, [sic] Lillie Graneng gave to me. I hope the cow will come in soon.

Rosemond

Rosemond recalled her father's influence: "My father said long passages of Shakespeare and Tennyson and the New Testament as we hoed the peas, or tried in the face of my stubborn docility to make me willing to do my arithmetic the 'prettier' way by algebra instead of following the book, and for years on Sunday afternoons told me a story (indifferently concerned with the fortitude of St. Polycarp martyr or the floods from which my grandmother rescued my uncles) which I was allowed to rework into a 'composition,' after supper."[4]

Rosemond remembered: "I was brought up on everyone in the family of six (but especially my mother) reading aloud to all the others who had 'things they had to do,' and vast terrains, summer and winter, of leisure that was completely unscheduled—except for Shakespeare 'on Chautauqua' in July."[5]

Canton was a small town in the early 1900s, about 2,600 people, but a surprisingly sophisticated community. By the turn of the century there was a courthouse, a church, two public school buildings, and Augustana College. Many farmers had moved into town, as a second generation had taken over the farming. They were ready to enjoy their prosperity and increase their social and cultural opportunities. Canton's position as an educational center, and its size, undoubtedly attracted the touring company of Chautauqua.

Chautauqua began in 1874, at Chautauqua Lake, New York, as a summer school to train Methodist sunday school teachers. By 1904, its programs had become so popular that traveling circuits blossomed out to remote parts of America, bringing music, lectures, drama, and other entertainment to a public starved for culture. Each summer the company set up its tents in any town large enough to support it. The festival lasted for a week or ten days. Plays, mostly by Shakespeare, lectures, and concerts of classical music, trios and quartets, were the usual fare. William Jennings Bryan, Madame Schumann-Heinck, Edgar Bergen, Alben Barkley and Enrico Caruso all appeared in Canton. Popular music and dancing were banned in Lutheran homes, so these performances would have appealed to young and old alike. It was an oasis in their lives in which the total otherness of music, literature, and the world of ideas was experienced. Rosemond discovered "what it means to transcend this small and transitory life, how a man can get past being 'confined and pestered in this pinfold here.'"[6]

Rosemond remembered "endless hot afternoons without sight of a person, 'staking the cow' along the road-edges where the grass outlasted the dry Dakota summer, and training her to stay content with one staking per chapter of a book."[7] There, where the earth extends to infinity, she read and reread the Arthurian legends. Later, it was Thomas à Kempis's *The Imitation of Christ,* a book "my father put in my way," she wrote, that gave "me a perception of something beyond what I understood, especially regarding union with something higher than one's petty self."[8]

Merle Tuve, two and a half years older than Rosemond, recalled their early life in Canton: "There was nothing stuffy about it. We weren't aware we were being exposed to culture except we were rather mystified by the lack of books, magazines, and papers in a lot of homes around us. I suppose we were snooty in a sense that that wasn't really a good way to live. The way to live was to be *connected* with things."

Yet all was not culture. Each child was assigned a chore. By 1910 the family had acquired two cows. This, of course, was the cheapest and best way to get milk for a growing family. Lew milked the cow, which he disliked. His mother, eager for him to learn business skills, encouraged him to raise parsley in their garden to sell to the Canton restaurants. The hotel paid him two cents a bunch for his parsley. And, of course, Rosemond helped her mother in the kitchen and supervising Richard. Occasionally, the entire Tuve family could be seen dining at the Rudolph Hotel on a Sunday noon, after church, enjoying beef, roast pork, or fricasseed chicken. Like the pattern of their lives, the menu rarely varied.

"As the third child among four," Rosemond wrote, "I chiefly did what my three brothers thought was important, such as learning the Morse code to take down their wireless messages, and playing in neighborhood gangs, but I learned without noticing it before I was ten to care about most of the things I have since thought or written about—and no doubt was equally inescapably made ready to miss the rest."[9]

Almost nightly, the dinner table was the scene of loud and impassioned arguments, and no one gave her less attention because she was a girl. In fact, it was Rosemond and Merle who took "hammer and tongs" to the floating fray. They were not angry arguments; mostly they illuminated things. "They didn't end up with disagreement—we had a debate," Merle recalled. At the end of his life Merle expressed it philosophically: "There are many facets of truth. Even a single truth looked at from different viewpoints is all the colors of the rainbow, it's so varied. And truth itself, if we talk about the whole truth, that's an infinite body of knowledge, most of which we haven't acquired."

What was implanted in Rosemond's mind was a way of looking at the world and its infinite body of knowledge.

In 1912, with the arrival of Dick Tuve, the family was complete. Their life fell into a comfortable rhythm, complemented by the changing seasons of the natural world around them and the ever-revolving academic procession of semesters. Enrollment had grown to 250 students in 1915, and there were now twelve members on the faculty. A majority of the students who graduated had taken most of their courses in the Normal School, a strong division of the college. President Tuve's focus had become a practical one, though he never forgot that "in both vocational and classical courses, students saw their subjects within the frame of reference of a theo-centric philosophy of life."[10]

In 1915, after twenty-five years as president, Anthony Tuve, now fifty-one years old, decided to unburden himself of the heavy duties of his presidency and return full time to his first love, classroom teaching. It was to Rosemond that he confided his plan to write what had been forming in his mind for many years—a book on algebra. Before the academic year was out he had tendered his resignation to the Augustana College Association. It was accepted only on the condition that he continue as president until his successor could be found and serve as treasurer of the school and principal of the commercial department. On June 2, 1915, President and Mrs. Tuve held a reception at their home for faculty, students, and alumni to mark the occasion of his twenty-fifth anniversary as president, and the couple's twenty-second wedding anniversary. This was followed by a banquet, given by the Augustana College Association and the alumni in honor of President Tuve, at nine o'clock at the Rudolph Hotel. By the fall of 1916, he had initiated a short business course of eighteen weeks for farm boys who could not attend college until the harvesting season was over.

By 1917 there were disquieting undertows beneath the ebb and flow of their lives. On the surface, also, there were gradual changes. Lew had left home two years earlier to attend the University of Minnesota; Merle and Rosemond were both excelling in high school; and Dick was growing under the loving care and guidance of his mother and Rosemond. However, it was this same year, in June, four hundred years after Luther had nailed his 95 theses to the castle door at Wittenberg, at the annual meeting of the general church body, that three synods—the United Norwegian Lutheran Church, the Hauge Church, and the Norwegian Evangelical Lutheran Synod—merged to form the Norwegian Lutheran Church of America. In 1889, the Norwegian Evangelical Lutheran Synod had established a school, the Lutheran Normal School, in Sioux Falls, South Dakota, for the purpose of training teachers. In the 1917 merger, both Augustana College and the Lutheran Normal School were brought under the control of the new synodical organization. A movement began within the newly created structure to combine the two schools, for political and economic reasons, at the Sioux Falls location.

On June 2, 1918, the day Ida and Anthony celebrated their twenty-fifth wedding anniversary, another festive party was held at the Tuve home, which by now was a town landmark and the social center of Canton. It was also to be a triumphant send-off for the former president and his successor, President Paul Glasoe. They were leaving for the general church assembly at Fargo the following day, filled with the confidence resulting from having raised a half-million dollars with which to persuade the synod that the college should remain in Canton. Again, Anthony Tuve and the citizens of Canton had struggled to keep the college in their town.

On the spacious lawn outside their imposing Victorian home, the many young trees planted fifteen years earlier were luxurious in their maturity and the rhododendrons abounded. Merle recalled this scene: "big, long tables, planks on sawhorses, gallons and gallons of ice cream, strawberries, and cake."

At seven o'clock on the morning of June 3, Anthony Tuve boarded the train for Fargo, having given his wife and children a confident farewell. But the machinations of church politics, and a few uncompromising individuals, were overpowering. Despite the fact that enrollment had now grown to 324 students; despite the enormous support and the dedication of the citizens of Canton; and despite Anthony Tuve's persuasive arguments, the synod voted to merge the Lutheran Normal School and Augustana College at the Sioux Falls site. The new institution, which opened in the fall of 1918, was named Augustana College and Normal School, but later was changed to Augustana College, which it remains today.

The strain on Anthony Tuve to preserve a life's work had a crushing effect, both emotionally and physically. He contracted what is now known as Asian flu. Returning home, he had to be removed from the train at Minneapolis and was taken to Fairview Hospital. For six weeks he struggled for his life, during which time he seemed to be recovering, when a new and more virulent virus struck—spinal meningitis. He succumbed as much to the despair he felt at the loss of "his" college and the life it symbolized as to his illness. On July 21, 1918, he died at the hospital.

Later, Eleanor Lincoln observed that for Rosemond, not yet fifteen, her father's death was a hideous "blow from which she never recovered." She had been devoted to her father, and he adored her. A simple entry in Merle's diary, written when he was twelve and Rosemond just ten, reveals the quiet intimacy of their relationship: "Went to the library and read with Papa and Rosemond."

Whatever bitterness Rosemond harbored against the church politics that so abruptly and cruelly ended her childhood, she remained a Lutheran and a friend of the college for the rest of her life. On the occasion of the centennial convocation of the division of humanities at Augustana College, in 1961, she was invited to give the keynote address.

2

WHEN ANTHONY WAS STRICKEN returning home from Fargo, Ida was called to his bedside to be with him during his last weeks. "Poor Rose," was all he could say. The funeral for Anthony Tuve was a terrible shock following so soon after the joyous celebration on the lawn of the family's home just seven weeks earlier. It was a somber cortege that proceeded to the cemetery on a sloping hillside, several miles west of Canton, overlooking the Sioux River and the bluffs of Iowa. There would be nothing but the simplest headstone to mark his grave, for as Merle noted, the family agreed that "Papa would rather have them eat" than spend money on a large stone. Eventually, the alumni of Augustana College raised funds for a large monument of Sioux Falls granite, to be etched, simply, TUVE. Thirty-four years later a new women's dormitory would be named Anthony G. Tuve Hall.

Another former president, Lawrence Stavig, in a founder's-day address, paid tribute to Anthony's love of the classroom, recalling his vision of a Christian college and how he had inspired the immigrants with his faith and his commitment. He concluded his remarks by describing Tuve as a "giant in the earth."

One decision was certain. Lew would remain at the University of Minnesota, where he had completed his sophomore year in the school of engineering. It fell to Merle, who was just seventeen, and had graduated from the Academy that June, to assume his father's role in the family. He recalled: "After my father died, it was pretty threatening. How do you get clothes? How do you work this? I went to work to be head of the house for a while, to keep the furnace going. I got a job at

Puckett's general store downtown. Groceries in one store, dry goods in the other. They assigned me to the dry goods department. I earned fifty dollars per month. After Christmas I saw my high school friends come back from college. They told about their experiences there and what they were studying, all those glamorous subjects. I couldn't stand the idea that I was excluding myself from all this. Up to that time I had no interest in scholarship or learning anything. Just get along. Oh boy, that gave me a boost."

Ida's life immediately moved from social pursuits to the most basic concerns. Dick recalled: "Mother was courageous. By damn, she was courageous. She would do the best by her children. She would scrimp and save so that we could experience things we needed in our lives. She would promote ideas that we could embrace. She was not self-centered at all, she was busy thinking about us and how to keep the family together." For years, Ida would kiss Tony's picture before going to bed at night.

Rosemond may have transcended some of her grief by lavishing her love on Dick, who was only six. From this time on she would attempt to mold him, taking responsibility for his intellectual and spiritual development. When fall came, Rosemond's life began to flow in familiar channels. She entered her junior year at the Academy, continuing to perform in school plays and operettas and in the debating club, which tackled the same subjects as the men's Monday-night Athenian Club.

The Tuves' tenuous struggle to survive in Canton lasted only eight months. Ida Tuve had learned of a house to rent in the industrial district of Minneapolis. Rosemond recalled: "When I was fifteen, some months after my father died, we hurriedly picked up the household in mid-year and moved to Minneapolis to put safely into the University of Minnesota my next oldest brother, now a physicist with the Carnegie Institution, to prevent him from saving the family fortunes by going on the boards with a Chicago opera company [the Hinshaw Opera Company]."[1] The haste was precipitated by the discovery that Merle wished to marry his voice teacher at Augustana, twenty years his senior, and run off to Chicago. Instead, he would enter the university, beginning at the third quarter. Enrolling first in the school of arts, which required less tuition, he soon switched to engineering. Merle recalled: "I don't know how mother managed it. It was too much to have three of us in school at the same time. She stretched the insurance money, thirty-nine hundred dollars after the funeral expenses, over a series of years. It was a cushion which took care of us when we got into any kind of jam. But she sure protected that. Rosemond and I sang in St. Mark's Episcopal Church choir. They gave us one dollar per Sunday. That was a marvelous experience. Singing 'Messiah' with all those brasses, and 'The Creation.' It was enough to take the edge off of your needs. Few dollars here, a few dollars there, we made things go."

For Rosemond, entering the University High School in Minneapolis in midterm meant expanding relationships, new connections, and important self-discoveries. She established herself at once as a serious student, much to to the dismay of Dick, who later complained: "I had to listen to my high school teachers extol her scholarly record."

At least one Canton classmate couldn't forget her. A postcard, written a few months after she left, was found among her papers after her death. It is dated July 19, 1919. "Dear Friend: This is to hope that you have not forgotten one of your fellow-debaters in the excitement of moving to another world and that you will condescend to drop him a line or two on the subject of how you like your new home. Do you intend to take up debating at the school you are to attend? I shall take one more year and then retire gracefully. (???) I expect you see new sights all the time and must be having one grand time. Well, remember the purpose of this note and write to Your friend, Ruppert O."

For Rosemond Tuve, who thrived on "new sights," it was less than "one grand time." Every moment that was not occupied with her high school studies or snatched so she could read was given to helping her mother or earning money. If singing in St. Mark's was exhilarating, waiting on tables in a downtown ice-cream parlor exposed her to the unsavory realities of life. Shocked and humiliated by overtures from male customers, who pinched or otherwise made advances, she eventually found the job intolerable. Almost sixteen, she had ripened into a naive beauty, and was understandably frightened by the crude conduct of men so unlike other men she knew. She fled her job to sit and stare at the Te Deum window at St. Mark's.

St. Mark's Cathedral in Minneapolis, where Rosemond and Merle sang for the love of God and the money to continue their education, is an imposing church in the heart of the residential area. A massive circular stained-glass window, nestled between two stone towers, surmounts the front door. "Te Deum Laudamus" (We praise thee, Oh God) is the full title of the wonderfully crowded window. Angels are scattered over the top, followed by the symbols of the four evangelists, then a cascade of worshipers—saints, prophets, martyrs, and finally Edward VI, in whose reign the prayer book finally came together. While Rosemond sat in her favorite choir stall on Sunday mornings facing this window, sunlight illuminating the stained glass, she was filled with awe and wonder at the colors and the significance of the iconography. These windows had a profound influence on Rosemond; later, she would mention them in letters over and over again, and would never tire of sitting and staring at stained-glass windows in cathedrals throughout Europe.

Within six months, Ida Tuve moved her family from their temporary house in the industrial district to a more suitable dwelling, closer to the campus and surrounded by the homes of university professors. It was a typical turn-of-the-century house, not as large as their Canton home, but the neighborhood was, like Canton, congenial. Friedrich Klaeber, the renowned *Beowulf* scholar, with whom Rosemond would form a lifelong friendship, lived across the street. Other students, friends of the family, came as boarders to the Tuve home, supplementing Mrs. Tuve's small income. Merle recalled: "We never knew if we would be able to finance another semester."

Lew joined the family and within two years he married Helen Fox. The young couple occupied the top floor, cooking on their own electric stove. Now the life of the Tuve family took on some of its old flavor, always enhanced by new ideas they were discovering or the anticipation of another symphony concert. The love of serious discussions by these argumentative students drew friends, and Rosemond, although somewhat diffident, was always popular.

Books, social issues, scientific experiments took precedence over the inconveniences of daily existence. It was the life of the mind that counted. Rosemond had learned from her father that the only way to be of real value in society was to be educated. What was important was not material possessions, for the Tuves knew real poverty, but rather the furnishings of the mind. She later commented on these early years of struggle: "We had less and less money but thought nothing of it. We understood that the one thing no sensible man occupied his head with was money, either making or keeping or spending it. Except of course for 'education.' "[2]

Years later the poet William Meredith, who was her colleague at Connecticut College, described her in this way: "It was just as easy for her, or just as hard for her, to talk to people in the grocery store, or the liquor store, or the custodian, as to talk to anybody else. She had no sense, or much less sense than most people in the profession had, of being removed from other persons by her specialty. I think she must have always been shy and awkward as a child and always full of an out-goingness that overcame that, but I don't think she felt that she was peculiar because she was a scholar, but she was peculiar because she was Rosemond Tuve. This is all there is in the way of peculiarity. It was not the isolation of the intellectual. She talked to the grocery clerk as well as she talked to a colleague, but the same distance was her privacy and her private world. It was not an intellectual class thing at all. I think she always thought of herself as coming from that South Dakota home."

In the fall of 1920, some months prior to her seventeenth birthday, Rosemond "went on like my two elder brothers into the university, paying for it mostly by a job in which I put three trees into three holes in a Christmas card of which inexplicable thousands were needed to satisfy the demands of the country."[3] Although she would never completely lose her family's early perceptions of her as "goldie locks," she was an equal to her brothers and their friends, sharing her adventures in literature with their scientific discoveries. She developed a sense that life had unlimited possibilities, a legacy from her prairie years, and that nothing was beyond her capabilities. Later, in a letter to Merle, she wrote: "You know I've never really come squash up against anything that was just plain 'too deep' for me, have you? I've always felt I could do it undoubtedly if I took the time. Wouldn't it be awful to find out that you 'just weren't an M.A. person?' Jiminy, I hate mediocrity. It would be awful to have to descend into it."[4]

Rosemond had almost reached her mature height of nearly six feet. Notwithstanding her long arms and legs, often the source of real clumsiness, her trim body was well proportioned and graceful. Softly waving reddish blond hair, which defied constraint, was drawn loosely into a bun at the back of her neck. One had the sense of its having been combed in the morning, without a second thought that day. Her clothes were quickly thrown on from whatever was at hand. Short wisps of hair were forever straying about her face, not just suggesting the darting movements of her mind, but also revealing a soft carelessness that gave a feminine beauty to her gently rounded face. Her deep-set blue eyes attracted and held you; a generous nose, full cheeks, a sensual mouth gave her a mature beauty. Her definite but softly rounded chin finished the contours of a face not quite symmetrical, but instead giving evidence of the many facets of the person within. She was then, and would remain, fascinating to both men and women.

For Rosemond, recognition of her father's values meant the rejection of any role identified with her mother. They would clash all their lives on *modi operandi* and what was important in life. Formerly, Ida Tuve had used her energies for community activities; now they were consumed by the urgency of providing for her family. This left little opportunity, or perhaps she even lacked the capacity, to share her daughter's emotional life. Rosemond's intense feelings must often have exasperated her. Later, Rosemond would astonish her friends and colleagues with what was the "cross-rough" of her life, her wide swings from her "little girl act" to a demonstration of her "towering intellect."

One of Rosemond's first college essays, entitled "What a College Student Reads for Amusement," expresses her early awareness of her uniqueness. After criticizing the shallowness of magazine articles and current novels that students read for recreation, she admits that "perhaps I am not typical of the body of students as a whole, *but* I *am* a student. Something moves me to investigate *Nicholas Nickleby* and become interested in *Cyrano de Bergerac*. I read them to amuse myself because someone has called my attention to them and my interest is aroused."

Another early college paper that she saved until the end of her life, filed under the heading "Papers Written in Childhood," was titled "Allegorically Speaking." It was a parable about a man who wanted to teach the "beautiful and worthwhile things" he had learned. Clipped to this paper was a newspaper article reporting that state funds to the University of Minnesota would be cut. It was her first experiment with allegory. Allegory would become for her another language and the focus of her life.

For a course called "Bible as Literature," Rosemond wrote an essay on the "Humanity of the Bible." She asserts that the Bible "makes you refrain from using heart-cutting remarks, thereby keeping joy in one more human heart." In her vivid imagination she saw the "Hebrew patriarchs" not as "white-haired and long-bearded," but rather with "all the youth and fire they ever had." She complains that their vitality was lost, "vanished under the dampening influence of centuries of theological corner-trimming." Confidence in her own critical sense appeared for the first time. Rosemond believed that we should read the text, not the interpreters, for our own images are apt to be as vivid and true as those that the critics present to us. This was to become a major critical tenet throughout her life.

Her favorite biblical character was Peter. Later in the essay she wrote: "We love him the more for the loyalty, hot headedness and human pugnaciousness (I have always felt that Peter was the original Irishman) that impelled him to cut off the ear of the soldier who was seizing his Christ." No plaster saint was Peter. Better to see "the perfect character that we ourselves may become, painfully and human-ly evolve out of the small and discouraging beginnings that we ourselves are. And after all, if the Bible is to be a force in the character building of the race—which is the best reason for its permanence—isn't it more effective to build ideal men out of human material than to start with a little angel and end up with an impossible saint?"

At the end of Rosemond's sophomore year, the Tuve finances had reached a precarious level and she could not continue on into her junior year. That summer, when she was eighteen, she enrolled in the

Southern State Normal School (now the University of South Dakota at Springfield) to prepare for her teacher's certificate. For the first time she would be away from her home and family.

Summit Hall, where Rosemond stayed that summer, is a handsome building, newly constructed of Sioux Falls jasper and finished throughout in birch. It housed ninety-one young ladies. For six weeks Rosemond studied arithmetic, geography, drawing, and practice teaching. She received her highest grade in practice teaching. Yet she learned something even more salient that summer, something that supported her own beliefs and helped in her guidance of Dick. In a letter to Merle, she wrote, "Encourage Dick to go to concerts, study his violin, go to the Art Institute, read those 'Mentors' & lots of books because it's worth sixteen times his school work. I saw so many people at Springfield that were absolutely devoid of any background of either experience or general information that I would rather have him flunk arithmetic than be that way."[5]

Carl G. Lawrence, who first entered the Tuve family's life when asked by Anthony to teach Latin and history at Augustana College, was now president of the Southern State Normal School. His home had formerly been across the street from the Tuves' and his son, Ernest Orlando Lawrence and Merle had spent their youth experimenting with electricity in the Tuve basement. In a reply to a letter from Merle that fall, Carl Lawrence spoke of Rosemond: "We enjoyed having Rosemond with us for a while this summer. She is a fine girl and was very popular with the students here."[6] Just before the end of the school term, Rosemond wrote to Merle:

I just thought of something—will you please go up to my trunk in Lew's dinning room & take out my Minnesota memory book & untie that string & remove 1 of the 1st sheets that has places for autographs & signatures on it. I want 1 page to make the kids here sign their names because I'll never see them again & want their names. Put it in a documentary envelope & mail it to me just as fast as you can so I get it before schools out next Tues. A.M. Lots of bother but I'll do something for you some day.

Love, R[7]

Merle had been corresponding with his friend Ernest Lawrence, urging him to come to the University of Minnesota to work for his masters degree under Francis Gray Swann (who unfortunately died that summer) and Anthony Zeleny. In a letter to Merle, Ernest wrote: "Rosemond surely has developed into quite a girl—very capable, I believe."[8] Later, after she had received her "first grade" certificate, she was invited to stay with the Lawrences while awaiting final confirmation of a teaching position for September. In another letter Ernest wrote to Merle: "She is so much like you that it is exhilarating to just know she is around. You see Springfield is barren of anyone interested in my work and R of course is. Nevertheless I am sure I bore her because I want her to do all the talking."[9]

Merle succeeded in persuading Ernest to come to Minneapolis. He boarded at the Tuve home. Now the two friends would have another year together, not with bells and whistles in yards and cellars, but working in the university laboratory with advanced equipment and professional guidance. Often the two young men were seen attending concerts of the Minneapolis Symphony, for which Merle regularly ushered. But it would be something akin to musical chairs for Rosemond. While Ernest undoubtedly moved into her room as a boarder, Rosemond left for Toronto, South Dakota, to occupy her cousin Art's room while he was away at St. Olaf's College. Rosemond found a position teaching fourth and fifth grades in the Toronto school, and was able to live with her uncle Ole Tuve, her father's brother, and his wife, Anna Lovre. With great difficulty she left behind the excitement of university life, the stimulating discussions of Merle's and Ernest's work, and the cultural opportunities she had come to love that had sustained her more than she was then aware.

Toronto is an isolated, tiny town in a particularly bleak area of the state. It lies about one hundred miles north of Canton, surrounded only by treeless, windswept plains, and the winter chill is biting. The Toronto public school, where Rosemond had her first experience teaching, was built in 1902, almost a miniature of the new Augustana College building started the same year. This reddish brown, boxlike structure with a cupola perched on top to house the school bell combined the grammar and high schools. Rosemond's fourth-and-fifth grade classes were in one room. Gail Storey, the town historian, remembers her as strict and demanding, but asserted that her students "learned more in one year than ever before."

Not long after arriving in Toronto, Rosemond betrayed some homesickness in a long letter to Merle, but characteristically did not dwell on complaints. She wrote:

"Leiber Bruder—two days of it, and I feel as if I had never done anything else. Peculiar sensation—I feel as tho I were Methusalah and had taught all the 969 years. I like it, tho.

"If I ever have any children I'm going to begin teaching them at the age of 3 how to turn to page 10 when they're told. Please tell Dick—because it's the most provoking thing in the world."[10]

Looking back on her own experiences of the same subjects, the same books, with only "one interesting idea per week & that uninterestingly presented," she doesn't see how she had the interest to "stick thru 8 grades." Again, concerned with Dick, she wrote to Merle: "I think you better take Dick out & let him take regular courses & then really *take* them."[11]

She remained in touch with many of the activities in Minneapolis and was aware that Archibald MacLeish's play, *J.B.,* was soon to be given there. She hoped Merle wouldn't miss it, and urged him to "make Mama go." Feeling deprived, she went on: "I'm going to welter in music when I come Christmas. Do you think Avery [Stanley Avery, the choir director] will let me sing the Messiah with them? I'll be just sick if I can't. Oh boy, to sing 'Surely' under Phillips again!" She asked Merle to send some news of the university, "even if you just copy the names of the buildings out of the catalogue. You don't realize what a rich life we were living up there, if we were poor as church mice. Bum paradox. If you aren't stuck up over this letter, you ought to be. There's no other man but what I'm tickled pink when I get to the end of the first sheet & have an excuse to stop. If you don't write me after this epistolary caress you are a base ingrate." As an afterthought, she concluded: "Say send me your picture, also Lew's and Mama's & a Kodak of Dick. Gotta have a paper family, anyway".[12]

Rosemond was a "self-starter," and had the confidence and skill to conduct Toronto's church choir. Although she found within herself the resources to enlarge the scope of her small world, she longed the entire year for spiritual beauty. She was appalled at the lack of taste or cultural refinements around her. She wrote to Merle:

> The ceiling and walls [of the Church] are of that fancy tin stuff like the ceiling in Dan Brogstad's shoe store. Woof! And the choir sings "those old Baptist hymns—Holy Roller things... Finally stirred them up to order some Christianson & that booklet of carols. I just love to conduct. But they're as unresponsive as a herd of cows, because they never look at me, being too occupied in reading the notes.

And then she exploded with, "I just long for the sight of that Te Deum window!"[13]

Although men were attracted to her, and someone called "Prof" would invite her out, she found him offensive. She wrote to Merle:

> Honestly, I'm afraid you and I will never go the way of the common mortal. I simply can not think of any man, boy or bachelor I have ever met that I could endure more than 6 dates with. They all seem so "ishy" and simpish after I've been out with them a few times that I haven't even got the pep to give them any encouragement. Their neckties, or hair, or vocabulary or manners always get on my nerves after 3 exposures. I am weary, weary, . . . But, seriously I'm afraid it will be cats and toast as the family has predicted.

No man could hope to equal her father or brother. "Oh well," she added, you get your Ph.D. and I'll get my M.A. and we'll live together in single blessedness, on Bach, Shakespeare and Gothic art, with occasional treats of fried cabbage and rutabaga."[14]

As the Christmas vacation approached, she wrote Merle with high hopes that school might let out one day early. "Oh bliss! I could take wings when I think of the luck that bro't Damrosch there at the same time I come. I'd like to go Jan. 4 in St. Paul & then to the same program in Mpls. Jan. 5—I've always wanted to do that! I feel always

as tho a symphony were half wasted because a person doesn't understand it enough to fully appreciate it." Getting fat on "auntie's" food,
she asked Merle to "tell Mama I want fried oatmeal & vegetables for
every meal." Never forgetting Dick, she urged him to go to concerts,
attend the Art Institute, and study his violin, and then offered a bribe:
"If he'll read Oliver Twist I'll take him to the movies."[15] Dick was now
ten years old.

Ideas about teaching methods were swirling in her head, and not
just at the fourth-grade level. They had begun to form at the university, and they were becoming crystallized as she thought, read, and
developed her own style. While reading history or a historical novel,
her mind was alive not only with the romance of travel abroad, but
also with the importance of history for the humanities. It was to
Merle, again, that she freely expressed herself:

> I'd like History—I read it for fun down here (by the
> way—Wm Stearns Davis—Minnesota man—our Hist.
> Dept.—writes positively fascinating books—nothing like his-
> tory to give you that balanced feeling of knowing something
> about something) but the blamed old History Dept. up there
> makes the subject nothing but a bunch of outlines & scads of
> reading notes, & outside reading with your eye on the num-
> ber of the page. It ought to be more leisurely, with time for
> assimilation, and all the fat women profs with bloomers
> kicked out. I've always had a theory that all fat people had
> dulled aesthetic and intellectual sensibilities, and woe, I'm
> getting fat myself. I believe it's a judgement on me for ridi-
> culing other fat people. I exercise 20 minutes every night and
> try not to eat, but you know auntie's food. Rich as Croesus.[16]

In yet another letter to Merle, she wondered:

> What will I do when I get out? Teach in some fool little
> High School like this, and just pass away, & spend one year
> after the other, waiting for Fridays and payday? Oh dear, such
> monotony! I never heard of Fellows in the Eng. dept., and

how on earth else can one start teaching in Colleges? I'd like
to skip to France or Germany & teach Eng. Lit. over there,—
you would be very imposing as a Herr Professor at Heidelberg
or Göttingen.

She suggested to Merle:

> Read Stevenson's 'Inland Voyage,' & 'Travels with a
> Donkey,' & you'll get the fever   too. I'm looking forward to
> that cycle trip—oh boy!! Just think how much fun we'll have
> chasing around from 1 town to the next. We'll travel by dawn
> & by moonlight and be thoroly crazy—& the beautiful part is
> that being related we can do any blamed fool thing we please
> . . . . we really shall have to lite for the continent and take
> a walking trip, or travel on a donkey or a canal-boat trip or
> something crazy, in some old country, & stop whenever &
> wherever we please. Why not live an eventful life—not a
> made-to-order-one![17]

After Christmas vacation, when she "wallowed" in music, and
"soaked up good things like a *sponge*," she returned to Toronto armed
with the materials for a university correspondence course in German.
This would add four credits toward her degree and end the indecision
about a minor. She had expressed to Merle her hesitation about
French, which was "pretty pepless, so polishedly useless," and
German, which "makes me feel as tho I had sauerkraut sticking out of
my ears."[18]

Easter Sunday she wrote to Merle: "I wish it were 8 weeks from
now. Church this a.m.—choir sang 'God so loved the World' & that
Easter 'Alleleuia' hymn they always march in on at St. Mark's." The
previous Sunday she had been asked to "lead 15 minutes of congregational singing—hymns—I took old ones and talked a little about
sources etc, but I suppose most of them thot, 'That big Tuve girl I
wonder what she thinks she is, slinging her long arms around with
that fool stick, just because she lives in Minneapolis.' "[19]

Those eight weeks did end, but for the remainder of her life
Rosemond was reluctant to speak about the ordeal of that year. At the

end of May she must have felt like every child does when school is out. Leaving Toronto with huge hugs, kisses and tears, and love for her aunt and uncle, she returned to the world of the university, her true home. To Merle she wrote: "Tell Fuku [Fukiyama, a slight Japanese student] he'd better pick out which tree he's going to hang on to when I come rushing past, because I'm coming soon."[20]

If the fantasized bicycle trip became a reality, there is nothing to confirm it. At least part of that summer was spent taking Elizabethan drama and a German rapid-reading course. It was a summer she would recall later in a Christmas letter to Merle, in which she thanked him for the candy he had sent her: "It was like a piece of the old laboratory-feeds; saw me battering away at the ramshackle U of M Physics Dept typewriter underground & you doing Experiments for the love of God & science in the other corner. I guess mostly I was spouting Elizabethan Drama that summer."[21]

She was also spouting Milton, for, as she later wrote: "I first read Milton and Eliot through aloud in a laboratory, and the philosophy to which I was introduced in a scientific household filled with the arguing friends of three brothers in mechanical engineering, physics, and chemistry was not naturalistic positivism."[22] This close interchange between Rosemond and Merle would result in her almost scientific approach to literature—searching for truth in the text, not trying to impose her preconceived ideas on a poet's meanings. Merle, who was introduced to Milton by his sister, would often quote him in his speeches to scientific organizations in an effort to impose a moral tone on scientific research.

As fall approached, there were new upheavals in the Tuve family. Lew and Helen had moved into their own home the previous year, and with the arrival of their son, Robert, made Ida Tuve a grandmother. Merle, who had earned his M.A., was about to depart for Princeton University, where he would be an instructor in physics. At twenty-two, he was almost as tall as his father, but resembled his mother with his dark hair and eyes. He had an intensity of manner, tempered by compassion, that held a magnetic attraction for family and friends. His self-assurance, grounded in deep ethical convictions, made him the support on which the family leaned. Dick, a tall boy of eleven, with large blue eyes and an unruly mop of sandy hair that matched his temperament, was taking violin lessons from Theodore Finney, and in another year would be playing with the University Symphony Orchestra. His sister often enticed him to attend concerts of the Minneapolis Symphony with her, and dragged him along to the Art Institute, where she enjoyed endlessly the paintings, chests, and other art objects housed in the Jacobean Room.

To continue at the university, Rosemond needed another job. She later recalled: "I returned with joy [from Toronto] and (having become enamored of medieval literature) gave up the Christmas cards and addressographs to be student assistant to Friedrich Klaeber, who taught me to respect philology."[23] When she learned of the position with Klaeber, she taught herself to type overnight, undoubtedly on the "ramshackle typewriter" in the physics lab. At nineteen, she had matured in her year of teaching, and, with her exceptional college record, it is not surprising that a scholar of Klaeber's eminence would ask her to be his assistant. Her devotion to Klaeber was strong and lasting, despite the fact that he returned to Germany during the Second World War, and shared some of the German National Socialist political views.

With her correspondence course from Toronto and her two summer courses, Rosemond had enough credits so that by arranging a monumental schedule, she would need only one more year to earn her bachelor's degree. Ballads, romantic poets, modern drama, Middle English, Arthurian romances, Milton, history of the English language, advanced Chaucer, Faust (in German), and *Beowulf* completed the requirements for an English major and a German minor. She was elected to Lambda Alpha Psi for her achievements in the study of languages and literature.

In addition to her academic load, she sang in the Glee Club, swam for her gym requirement, and played Brünnhilde in a dramatic production, for which her mother sewed her costume. Participating in various student organizations such as Kappa Kappa Lamda, a religious society, and Kappa Rho, a literary group, she also served a second term on the Y.W.C.A. cabinet and was on the executive board of

Rosemond Tuve, center, as Ceres, the goddess of fertility, in a tableau during May Day festivities at the University of Minnesota. Reproduced from the the Archives of the Library of Congress.

the Lutheran Students' Association. She was active in the Cosmopolitan Club, an organization whose purpose was to promote international friendship and cooperation.

Dick remembered that his sister's ebullience, attractiveness, and warmth "made her a favorite in the class." She was chosen to be part of the annual May Day festivities, dancing around the Maypole and posing in a tableau dressed as Ceres, the fertility goddess, holding a large bunch of grapes. It was a prophetic image. Ceres is portrayed in allegorical portraits and myths as a sower of seeds, a liberal giver of Christ's "high good things."

Rosemond Tuve's first published work, "The Sixth Sense in Danish Ballad Poets," appeared in the 1923 winter issue of the *Minnesota Quarterly.* Written with a deftness and sureness beyond her twenty years, it reveals wit, imagination, and sober learning. We glimpse the style of her later writings in her use of homely images and colloquialisms. She reminds us again to read the poets, not the critics. "I feel a resentful sympathy for these ballad poets, deprived of their individuality by book-smothered scholars, not even allowed to *be,* or still less, to *have been.*" With obvious delight, assurance, and her own "sixth sense,"—humor—she identifies with the "childlike-mindedness, that delightful naiveté" of Danish ballad poets. "Usually the humor of the Danish ballads is not the more obvious, moving-picture humor—of situation—but rather that subtler sort that comes through a sensitive appreciation of human character."

It is to humor that she gives her allegiance. By declaring that "Emotional Restraint is the child of Sense-of-Humor," she understands how the Danish ballad authors escaped "one cardinal sin, the bane of all romantic and latter-day poets—sentimentalism." In an aside, she asserts: "I firmly believe that there should be a sense-of-humor entrance test to the University, with an especially devised, diabolically searching one for aspirants to the faculty. All individuals who lack one should be forever barred from higher education, for they are more dangerous than floating mines, and more depressing than the law of gravity."

Full of analogies, digressions, and parenthetical amplifiers, she shares the "roguish fun" and "penetrating insight into character" of the ballad authors. Although she recognizes that a "sense of the dramatic" was first developed by the ballad poets, she is struck by the lack of color in their poems. She notes: "We look in vain for any of the bizarre, meticulous use of colour to be found in later poets. It is not a fault; just a difference—the difference between a Strauss tone poem and a Mozart sonata." She concludes her essay with a warning: "The humor is there; look, laugh and be merry, for in this morrow there are no ballad poets, and the essence of wit is in custard pies and spilt milk."

In another essay, entitled "A Man With the Hoe (in Wordsworth, Burns & Crabbe)," she wrote: It would take more than Wordsworth to "convince me that the usual rustic walks 'in glory and in joy beside his plow.'" Farmers don't have a "dreamy imagination"—but "peasants" in daily contact with "Nature, must inevitably partake of some of the beauty of character and calm, temperate virtues which surrounded them." And as for Crabbe, she wrote, "My own immediate reaction is a desire to call up Crabbe (probably I should say call *down* Crabbe) and ask him how much he *did* for all his 'lonely, wretched old men', 'forsaken wives' and 'dejected widows', whether he exerted himself to change conditions or merely got a morbid thrill out of talking about them."

She ends her essay with another plea for the simplicity and restraint of the ballads: "Romanticists *did* give us a new conception and respect for humble life, perhaps they did give a humanitarian sympathy to the world without which there would now have been no orphanages, no public health movements, no community funds. And yet I find myself wishing that we might go back to the unsophisticated naiveté of an age that did not philosophize but took things for granted and enjoyed life. And there I am, crying up primeval simplicities like a veritable sentimentalist myself." Although critical of the Romantics, she wrote lyrically about them: "To pass from Burns to Wordsworth is like a sudden transition from a Scotch drinking song to—say Handel's Pastoral Symphony! Tranquil, chaste, almost austere, exquisitely peaceful—it gives me a Wordsworthian feeling just to think of it!"

Her professor Thomas Raysor had this comment on her paper: "This is a most interesting and stimulating paper. I *should* tell you to be more purely judicial, but your prejudice is too delightfully expressed. As for your treatment of Wordsworth, I allow it an 'A' because it has all sorts of imagination and reflection it it. But I hope that you will some day confess your sins in this paper."

Another professor's comment [possibly Kemp Malone] points out her complex style, which would become a continuing handicap in her critical writing. "Miss Tuve," he wrote, "you show through this paper the power of writing informally in the purest English. Then why all the colloquialisms and word-coining and parenthesis which you permit yourself? You love words, it seems; then why mistreat them so unscrupulously."

As the winter term was ending, Rosemond was suddenly thrown into turmoil by the possibilities of graduate school. She exchanged urgent communications with Merle. Through Klaeber's recommendation she had been invited to be a scholar in English at Bryn Mawr College. Professor Raysor told Rosemond that when Radcliffe asked him which of three women from Minnesota he would recommend, he chose Rosemond Tuve. On April 17, she sent a Western Union telegram to Merle: Will probably have choice between Bryn Mawr and Radcliffe. Are there any possibilities in your situation which might influence decision—humanly possible to be with you at either place? Must decide with professors help by about Monday.[24]

A letter to Merle, dated "Tues. eve. St. Mark's choir stalls," followed. In it she wrestled with herself over the relative merits of Bryn Mawr and Radcliffe:

> Dear Pill, Letter from Bryn Mawr today— scholarship there is O.K.—of course it means nothing but a point of departure & an excuse to go on as far as money goes—but that is what I meant it to be anyway. Bryn Mawr has Carleton Brown— (orig. of U of M) recog. authority—gives a med. drama seminar etc., which would probably confirm me as a medievalist. You see it rather means choosing my field. Radcliffe is opener—I should take more miscel. dope. Babbitt and Kittredge are there—B.M. offers certain advantages of atmospheric flavor etc. which are quite not at Minn. & rather not at R.[25]

At Bryn Mawr, the fact that the "grad. wing of the dormitories more cloistered" and the degree requirements stiffer influenced her decision. She suggested possibilities for Merle, which would bring them together, and let him know that her professors were also giving advice. It was Kemp Malone, then lecturer in English at the University of Minnesota, who favored Bryn Mawr.

Merle's wire in reply was of no help. "My situation too indefinite to count. Johns Hopkins possible but improbable."[26] He leaned toward Radcliffe. Then Rosemond, without the assurance of her brother being nearby and lending support, made a clean decision, without sentiment, standing firmly on her own intuition and judgment. She wired Merle on April 23: "Accepted Bryn Mawr. Hopkins intriguing. I will be your research."[27] And all the rest was given. Merle wired back on the 28th: "Johns Hopkins instructorship definite and I shall accept. If you were here now would celebrate together."[28] Through a letter of recommendation from Professor Zeleny, Merle, not yet twenty-three, would become an instructor in physics at Johns Hopkins and two years later complete work for his Ph.D. there. Launched on their differing, but shared, careers, brother and sister would have four more years of close companionship.

There were still two months left until graduation and another three before Rosemond would leave for Bryn Mawr. It was an emotionally turbulent time. Rosemond tried to help her mother when she could, but her courses were demanding and there was always the need to earn money. Next to these concerns, the formalities of her last weeks seemed almost irrelevant.

On Friday, May 16, 1924, the *Minnesota Daily* ran a front-page account of the Cap and Gown exercises that had taken place the day before. The seniors, after rehearsing "Our Commencement Pledge," traditionally sung on this day, had processed to the armory. Entering to the strains of Wagner's "Tannhäuser March," the Glee Club opened the program singing "Fly, Singing Bird, Fly." Announcement of the awards and prizes followed. A week later, Gregory Breit, a friend and colleague of Merle's, who may have been boarding at the Tuve home, wrote to Merle: "Your sister has been elected to Phi Bete. She is trying to do too much and cuts down on her sleep."[29]

Five weeks later Rosemond Tuve was awarded her B.A. degree,

cum laude, from the University of Minnesota. Her graduation picture did not appear in the yearbook, "The Gopher," until the following year, no doubt because originally she was expected to graduate with that class. The photograph has an aura of serene confidence, a frame for an intelligent, serious face.

A further honor was extended to Rosemond when Professor Thomas Raysor asked her to become a "reader" in nineteenth-century literature for the summer term. From him she learned to "temper the ideas I had got about Romantic poets from reading Babbitt."[30] (Irving Babbitt was an authority on literature of the Romantic period.) Then, "acting on the family principle," she borrowed a thousand dollars from "Uncle Lew," her mother's brother Lewis Augustus Larsen. Added to her summer's work, this would cushion her meager savings and enable her to give full time to her studies at Bryn Mawr. The journey into the unknown held more eager anticipation than anxiety. She had already come further than even she had dreamed; she would be a scholar in English, have the chance to go on; and, finally, she would again be close to Merle.

Rosemond Tuve at Bryn Mawr College, 1924.

3

BRYN MAWR COLLEGE captured instantly, and permanently, the imagination and loyalty of Rosemond Tuve. Tudor, gray stone structures, blanketed with ivy, patterned after an Oxford University college, thrust their towers through mists beside ageless oaks, symbolizing strength and permanence. In late September, during those autumn days when there is a hush over the earth that hangs suspended between the seasons, waiting patiently in expectation of changes to come, the mood is one of transcendence. Here, almost startled by the brilliant foliage, secure among the abundant green hedges that bound country lanes, she found seclusion, a cloistered, spiritual home.

Locating her room in the graduate wing of Denbigh Hall, she discovered it looked out on a memorial seat placed among towering oaks. "I sit on pillows in cloister & read," she wrote on a postcard home. "Dear Folks—This is certainly a lovely place to be—have my courses fixed—all profs delightful—glorious weather—summer clothes (go fine—quite O.K.)" were her first words home on a card picturing Denbigh Hall.

Casually mentioning that her courses were "fixed" was typical of her way of trivializing what was most meaningful—a seminar in medieval drama with Dr. Carleton Brown. She had chosen to come to Bryn Mawr not only for its high standards but because of the presence there of Dr. Brown, the eminent medievalist, as well. "You see it rather means choosing my field," she had written Merle, and "would probably confirm me as a medievalist."[1]

But this was not discussed in letters home. Of immediate concern were the "things unaccountably lost—gym shoes, bathing suit, (have had to borrow because am going in for swimming & hockey both).

Phila symphony Sat. nite & Ethel Barrymore Sat. P.M.—debauch after French exam Sat. which I suppose I'll flunk."[2] After getting her courses "fixed," Rosemond hurried to the Bryn Mawr railroad station to purchase a fifty-trip ticket on the Paoli local. Now, every Saturday, she would go alone to Philadelphia to hear a symphony and haunt museums and art galleries. Later she would write to Dick: "I saw a nice Rembrandt yesterday—in the Johnson collection on Broad Street."[3]

Freed from the necessity to earn money, from domestic duties and family obligations, Rosemond was afloat on a sea of new experiences. Life was an enormous buffet, and she feasted on everything. Any tensions she may have felt to conform socially seemed not to exist. She remained anchored in her own beliefs and lived them. Replying to a letter from her mother, she wrote, "That was Henry James on my table, not the Bible. I read it nite & morning tho."[4]

Her next card home was to Dick and pictured Pembroke Gate, "where all the step sings come. I have a Princeton blanket for my bed ... By the way I wonder if you'd pick out of the Mentors from (I *think* in the "Louvre" or "Nat. Gallery") the Titian "Man With a Glove" and the Sir John Haden etching out of "Etchers & Etchings" and also ask mother for my 2 little Mrs. Klaeber etchings. Walls pretty bare. Ask mama to send my gym shoes, can't play tennis or hockey—*awful*. Tell mother to make yellow taffeta dress 29 inches *from hips* (bodice ended there didn't it?) & lace 2 inches more—that's plenty long."[5]

The fall term at Bryn Mawr was one of self-discovery. Instead of living "in a scientific household filled with the arguing friends of three brothers,"[6] she was living in a women's dormitory and discovering her femininity. Every afternoon graduate students took turns, in pairs, setting up and serving tea for the rest of their hall. "I've become so used to tea every afternoon I would expire without it,"[7] she wrote her mother. One of the students with whom she frequently shared these social times recalls her "good looks and high spirits. She was tall and fair; she had a warm and infectious laugh." Another classmate remembers her as "in no way eccentric, rather as a happy, healthy young woman, glowing with life."

Another friend recalled this: "Rosemond was a stunning Nordic type, tall, strongly built, golden- haired with large blue eyes, rosy cheeks, and a friendly, deliberate manner. Her interests seemed to fit well with her background and fine physique. She was liked by us all. One amusing incident was occasioned by a Ph.D. candidate who gave Rosemond and me a test of nervous inertia, I think it was called. We were to write our full names as fast as possible and as slowly as possible. I struggled to write as slowly as I could and achieved ten minutes; Rosemond took a half hour! The speed test results were similarly different."

The fall term went quickly. On Sundays, when Merle could get away from Johns Hopkins to visit his sister, they both enjoyed a kind of life-sustaining intimacy. "We went walking a lot along Christopher Mews," Merle recalled, "up and down those lanes in the countryside, stone walls, hedges of mock orange, lilac, and honeysuckle. We rejoiced in the beauty all around us." It reminded him of Princeton: "Princeton was an eye-opener. The dining room, the great hall, Proctor Hall, was like a cathedral. The whole experience, the leisure attention to serious studies, is kind of pleasant. Princeton was a form of worship."

Thanksgiving was spent in Baltimore with Merle. At the suggestion of a friend, Lucia Murchison, whom they both knew, Merle had found a boardinghouse run by her aunt, Mrs. F. L. Coleman, on North Charles Street, near the university. When Bryn Mawr closed for Christmas, Rosemond sent her mother her plans: "Hope this gets you B4 you go to R [Ridgeway]—I am going to Bmore with Merle Sat. Merle and I are going to have lazy time. I'll live in dorm & make breakfast for him. Think its worth it don't you?" As a postscript she added, "Send us an OHenry from Grandmas!!! Both broke.!!"[8]

On Christmas night, filled with the joy of the season, wanting to share her contentment with her mother, and not a bit lonesome, she wrote Mrs. Tuve a long letter:

> We are sitting in front of Merle's fireplace with three books and three apples apiece; it is 7 o'clock & we're going to write Uncle Lew & Lew & Helen and feel virtuous ever after. We had dinner down at Mrs. Coleman's. I've stayed there instead of dormitory. That scheme went by the boards; had chicken & mince pie & all trimmings—just 4 girls there over

Xmas; danced & sang & ate candy afterwards. Merle & I went to Wildflower last nite—awfully good musical comedy—Edith Day—much snap. We had dinner at the "Chimney Corner" down cellar, open fire, candles only, dancing, few people; rats, cats & bats painted on all the walls. Went to Blisses to dinner Sunday—old Baltimore family, daughter B.M. '22; Prof. B. in Physics Dept.—will pay call tomorrow.[9]

On Monday, February 16, 1925, the day after a Valentine's party to honor Merle, who came up from Baltimore, Rosemond wrote to her mother:

We had much fun except I didn't get a chance to talk to Merle alone very much. I wish you'd say casually in your next letter that I wrote we had a very good time 'except that the other girls had more chance to visit than I did.' I was always going after tea, or something—it isn't a small job to give 2 parties—Just casually, please.[10]

And ten days later:

Incidentally—as you see I am in a reforming mood this AM—it being Lent—I was horrified to have Merle ask me which was the proper salad fork & also introduce Mr.Malone to Mrs. Coleman thus: Professor Malone, meet!! Mrs. Coleman—small matter only he says he is embarrassed so often by not having pd. attention to things & I wondered if Dick couldn't get them younger—all the things one does for girls & older women, & how to treat you out in company—& help you with guests.[11]

Although Merle's manners might need an "intensive course," the wisdom of his advice was quite acceptable. In mid-February she wrote him a long letter.

Dear Bug—
Prepare to ponder.
A woman (BM grad. & very nice to work for, Mary Isabel

knows her) was here to see about someone for councillor in Camp Miramichi, Merrill, on Chateaugay Lake, N.Y. Beautiful place, 72 girls, 19 councillors. . . . 9 weeks.

The pay is the obstacle. Get fare to & from New York City, a dress uniform to wear while there, board & room & $50. Would not clear the $50 tho because almost $25 other clothes expense, she said. . . .

Shall I try to get camp position?? Only 3 weeks to decide, & of course I have no claim on it. What do you think?. . .[12]

In late January, Rosemond had written her mother that Dr. Brown wanted her to apply for a fellowship in the English department. Carleton Brown was deeply impressed with his new student, whom he often likened to an Old Norse cup-bearer, or a "hostess in a mead hall." As in her portrayal of Ceres in the spring pageant at Minnesota, Rosemond is seen again as one who gives of her gifts with abandon. But to her mother, at least, she dismissed Dr. Brown's suggestion, saying she had told him "I must teach." She still owed Uncle Lew a thousand dollars.

But the seed had been planted and Dr. Brown persisted. He recognized her unusual qualities. In mid-April the English department simply offered her the resident fellowship for the 1925–26 year, with a stipend of $850. She seems to have put off making a decision until her dilemma became critical and there were only a few days left to decide. Merle, her trusted adviser came to her rescue. He traveled to Bryn Mawr to discuss her situation with Dr. Brown. Rosemond may have been reluctant to ask Uncle Lew for a delay in repaying her loan, or else the conference with Dr. Brown strengthened her position. Whatever the reason, Merle assumed responsibility for her decision, and, on May 23,1925, rather belatedly, wrote to their uncle asking permission for Rosemond to defer her debt. It was a letter of genuine caring for his sister, written with sensitivity and tact, explaining their dilemma:

"As you already know, in the middle of March Rosemond was awarded the M. Carey Thomas European Fellowship. This is considered the highest honor which she could receive. The recipients are chosen by the general faculty from the whole group of students (Bryn Mawr has 400 undergrads and 100 grads, approximately) and the day they are announced is one of the red letter days of the school year, as I learned from others than Rosemond . . . The stipend is unfortunately small ($500) but that is apparently the least part of it.

He continued: "There was no thought on Rosemond's part of trying to arrange to go abroad next year, of course, but as it was thrust upon her, so to speak, and as it cannot be deferred, there was nothing to do but to smile and accept. She and I planned as before that she should teach next year, and both of us kept our lines out for a place for her next year.

"The second week in April, however, another unexpected factor entered the situation. Dr. Brown, under whom Rosemond is doing most of her work, came to her and said that the Department (English) wanted her to be Resident Fellow at Bryn Mawr next year. This fellowship is a departmental one, and means that she was chosen for the (only) fellowship out of the English students there, together with between twenty and thirty applications from all the best colleges in the U.S., so again it must mean that she has done really distinctive work. I went up to confer with Dr. Brown about it, and he knows how Rosemond is situated, financially. His advice was unqualified. The fellowship, together with the $100. she earns at camp this summer will cover her next year's expenses, and he even mentioned the possibility of a loan from College funds if it was necessary to make payments on what she already owed. With such unmistakable conviction on the part of those who know her best as to what she should do, and advice carrying with it the outright gift of $850 the answer seemed clear enough to me."[13]

He assured his uncle that Rosemond was unwilling to make the decision without his approval, and as there was only a day or two to decide, Merle had come to her aid. Unable to talk with him first, he was writing this letter now. If his uncle had a serious reason for her not accepting, she could resign. The point was that neither he nor she wanted to appear arrogant in taking matters into their own hands.

He expressed his feelings further: "I have had doubts myself as to the wisdom of a girl taking a Ph.D., but after discussion with one of her Minnesota professors who is here at Hopkins [Kemp Malone] and with others who know her, I have been brought around to agree to it in her case anyway. The trouble with girl Ph.D.'s, rather I should say woman—Ph.D's, is that they lose all other valuable attributes and interests but the intellectual ones, and narrow ones at that, usually. But I have been assured by several who know her as well as by my own observation of her this year that Rosemond is going to remain normal despite the fact that she amounts to something in advanced study. The work she does is going to put her in a very restricted class, with opportunities for pleasant and profitable work and associates far beyond what would be open to her without it. She will be able to get a very good college position, with unpredictable opportunities ahead of her."

He continued: "As for her own attitude, her principle reason for going on is that she is doing what she loves to do, and it doesn't seem the *least* wise thing, anyway, with respect to the future, for her to keep on doing it! I firmly believe in marriage for a girl myself, as at *least* part of their life if not all of it, and I have sounded her out on this subject also. She believes likewise, and when she finds the right man at the right time, she won't be unwilling. I might also say that she won't miss the opportunity; if anything a brother is usually prejudiced in the opposite direction, but I have found Rosemond to be very attractive.[14]

He closed the letter with the hope that his uncle won't be displeased with what has come about. And, of course, he was not. Given the total support of her family and the overwhelming confidence of her professors, Rosemond passed another milestone. With renewed joy, she completed the final weeks of the academic year. On May 1 and May 2 she appeared as Samuel in *Pirates of Penzance* for two performances with the Bryn Mawr College Glee Club in Roberts Hall, at Haverford. With her height, strong alto voice, and dramatic expressiveness, she must have been a striking lieutenant.

On June 4, 1925, at the Bryn Mawr commencement closing its fortieth academic year, Rosemond Tuve was awarded her master's degree, the M. Carey Thomas European Fellowship, and the Department of English Resident Fellowship. Almost certainly, a proud Merle watched from the audience.

Although no letters exist from Rosemond's second year at Bryn Mawr, the pattern of her life remained the same. Freed from the necessity to earn money, with no apparent conflicts, she was on a firm course toward gaining her Ph.D., a goal she had hardly dared dream of.

Three outstanding scholars directed Rosemond's studies that year. A seminar in Middle English led by Carleton Brown headed the list, and she also attended Samuel C. Chew's "seminary" in English drama and a mediaeval French literature course with Winifred Sturdevant. A student in her French class later remarked that he had "never seen a young woman with such rapt enthusiasm." Yet her deepest interest focused on Dr. Brown's course, which reviewed again Arthurian romances and the development of medieval themes in later literature. It was Carleton Brown who suggested the subject for her thesis, "Seasons and Months, Studies in a Tradition of Middle English Poetry." It was the perfect vehicle for her consuming interest in sources, the history of ideas, art, and science. In her dissertation she is looking for the provenance of the stream of tradition that formed Chaucer's literary inheritance.

From Latin analogues such as Lucretius's Venus and Alanus's Natura, Virgil's *Georgics* and *Eclogues,* and Ovid's *Fasti,* through the Carolingian poets, she drew references to the seasons and months. She discussed at length the Carmina Burana, the Secreta Secretorum, and French lyric and courtly traditions. Her introduction outlines the plan of her work: "The different elements in the tradition are variously stressed and developed, . . . [and] relate themselves to literary tastes, habits, fashions, to new scientific interests and to the making of philosophical syntheses, to the history of art as well as to that of taste. To follow the development of the seasons-tradition is to see, from one particular point of view, some at least of what composes the history of thought."[15]

Her particular point of view is the importance in all these literary and artistic sources of spring. Spring is a "release from the 'crabbed' season; the resurrection of spring parallels a greater one; the eternal procession of seasons figures forth those four ages which shall end in a glorious last age, and the mutability that shall end in a great Sabaoths sight."[16]

Since her "shepherdess" days, when, seated on the prairie, Siouxie, the cow, grazing nearby, she first read Thomas à Kempis's *Imitation of Christ,* with nothing in sight but earth and sky extending to infinity, Rosemond had experienced an undefined sense of the unity of all life. She remembered "having a perception of something beyond what I understood, especially regarding union with something higher than one's petty self."[17] Now, in her study of the seasons and months, she discovered in various sculptures or literary portrayals a consciousness of profound implications rather than stated meaning. "These discussions or motifs may be concerned with the nature of the divine Cause, with the creation of the world in time and space and of all sensible phenomena, with the mind of man and its development; the basic concept of such cosmological discussions is often the 'unity' of God and his created manifestations . . ."[18] Later, these pictorial representations of seasons and months would become Christianized and appear as the four evangelists and the twelve apostles. It was the transmuting from one form to another that whetted her desire to search for the source of all archetypes in the mind of man, and in the mind of the Creator.

At twenty-two Rosemond had become a serious scholar, but she was also a "happy, healthy young woman glowing with life," looking forward to weekend dances at Johns Hopkins. It was a joyous outlet for the physical and emotional energy she was barely able to contain. Merle remembered, on his occasional visits from Baltimore, how it pleased Rosemond that "Bryn Mawr was such a stickler for high standards." They shared the belief that the whole experience, the uninterrupted attention to serious study, was "a form of worship." The search for truth lighted both their lives, and beauty was holy. Much later, Dick, for whom Merle was like a father, remarked, "You consorted with art, science, and music, and you awoke in her a lot of things just as you awoke in me the scientific side. You sparkplugged a lot of her verve toward . . ." At this point Merle interrupted with, "It may have been the other way around."

Rosemond's year passed, as a fellow student remarked, with "days of leisurely scholarship on a quiet campus and very happy relations with [her] professors." Yet despite Rosemond's conscientious, almost ascetic devotion to her work, she was not above a prank. Elizabeth Chapin, a graduate student and close friend that year, who later married Holden Furber, professor of history at the University of Pennsylvania, told her husband this story, which Dr. Furber later revealed: "Bryn Mawr has an old library in an enclosed courtyard, with aisles on each side, and a fountain in the middle. One warm Sunday morning, when it was usually closed, they managed to get inside the cloisters to read. Suddenly, it occurred to them, "why not take off our clothes and have a dip in the pool? So they did, and no one was the wiser."

Throughout the spring both Rosemond and Merle had "their lines out" for jobs for Rosemond for the summer and fall. As usual, Rosemond's extraordinary good luck held. She landed a position at the Bryn Mawr Summer School for Women Workers in Industry. The school, which first opened in the summer of 1921, was held for eight weeks on the Bryn Mawr campus. The retiring president of Bryn Mawr, Millicent Carey Thomas, whose name and that of Bryn Mawr are nearly synonymous, had a vision of the school as she rode her camel during a caravan trip in Morocco. Just after dismounting, while resting in a camp chair in the desert, "watching the sun set and the moon rise," ideas that previously had been incubating in her mind hatched as if in a vision. "I saw that out of the hideous world war might come as a glorious aftermath, international industrial justice and international peace."[19]

Hilda Worthington Smith, then dean of the college, left her post to become director of the summer school. The stated object of the school was "to offer young women of character and ability a fuller education, in order that they may widen their influence in the industrial world, help in the coming social reconstruction, and increase the happiness and usefulness of their lives."[20] Seven years later Hilda Smith would note that the school had begun a "unique development in education" that had already affected more than eight hundred women in this country. In addition, "College alumnae and teachers attributed to the school and their contacts with it fundamental changes in thinking which have reacted on their whole lives."[21]

Rosemond would spend the next three summers working at the school as "library tutor," never forgetting her enriching and satisfying contacts with her students. She later wrote that the experience had left her "forever (I hope) left of center, at least of where this country has taken to placing center."[22]

While Rosemond was at Bryn Mawr during the summer of 1926, Merle returned to Canton. Packing his mother and Dick into an old Buick, he brought them back to Washington to live. Ida had grown lonely so far from Merle and Rosemond, and with Lew teaching in Texas, it made sense to have the family together. Now Rosemond would no longer have to be anxious about "housing" herself in the summers and during other school vacations.

More important that summer, the "lines" put out by Merle and Rosemond had netted an even larger catch. Starting in the fall, Rosemond would be instructor in English at Goucher College, at a salary of $1,500. Goucher was at that time located just ten blocks from Johns Hopkins University. Rosemond found a room on 25th Street between the two institutions. Goucher had no campus. Its buildings were mainly dormitories scattered over several blocks amid Baltimore's typical brick houses, with their white front steps; grocery stores; drug stores; churches; and shoe repair shops. A community of graduate students filled the area, pursuing intellectual and artistic careers. Mary Parmenter, a friend during those years, recalled "running rapidly back and forth between the two institutions—sometimes the bus, ten cents to save time and shoe leather."

More than thirty years later Rosemond, in an introduction to a lecture at Goucher, would recall her two years there as an instructor:

"I did the first college teaching of my life at Goucher College, at the learned age of 22. We weren't the Beat Generation, we were the Liberated one. I taught a Freshman section, a Soph. Survey, a Chaucer course and an OE and Beowulf course. And I had time to go up to Hopkins every afternoon and read in Gilman till I was dizzy, not ALONE I might add. I still could find the exact red & yellow tree near the Art Museum under which I sat down to confront my first set of English themes, with the most extreme curiosity and pleasure. Might also say that at least 4 of the texts I shall mention tonight I first *read* up at Hopkins in between my Goucher classes—and for some odd reason they all kept finding their way into that Soph. Survey, or that Chaucer, or Freshman comp. I think this was because it never occurred to us to think we were living TWO lives, teaching and studying. We thought the whole gay affair came in One Piece."

She continued: "I will say that during the Liberated Generation, we were determined to escape from a lot of LIVING, or something that now goes under that name. WE scorned apartments. We didn't see any great lure in finding some place we could COOK in, or worry abt. curtains. We were entranct at being deliv'd from the Deadly Social Round our fr. that weren't in coll seemed to be squirrel caging ard.[around] in—We found us a 'Room' down there on 25th St., where one rack in the family bathroom was allocated to our towel, and we got us a Boarding-house, and then we lit out for where all our friends were, The Library. By Friends I meant both Living & Dead. We didn't make as much difference between these two categories as students do now. We even sometimes gave up an engagement w. a Boring Living ONE (either sex) to keep one w. a Bright Dead ONE. (In case you're wondering, about the Girls, in case we didn't marry it was because we didn't feel like it. Even girls, then, cd. choose wh. life they preferred. By choose 'which', I don't mean BETWEEN TWO, but Between Half a Dozen. We saw half a dozen lying out in front. So we picked what we enjoyed. As I say, we weren't the Beat Generation. We hadn't learned about Anxiety)."

According to Ruth Childs, who also taught English there in the mid-twenties, Goucher College had not yet reached the academic level of Bryn Mawr and other eastern women's colleges. Nevertheless "there were enough excellent students at Goucher to make for lively and interesting classroom discussions," she recalled. "The college had a more liberal policy toward admitting Jewish students than was customary in those days, and Goucher thus had a number of brainy Jewish girls. The daughters of some government officials in Washington were sent there, and some excellent students came from southern schools because their parents did not want them too far from home. Goucher also had many faculty members actively engaged in research in their various fields. In the English department, Ola Winslow, Florence Brinkley, and Rae Blanchard were fine scholars."

Miss Childs's memory of Rosemond is of "her striking good looks," but she saw little of her. "There were practically no department meetings, the English offices were not all in the same building, and the older members offered the younger ones no advice." If young scholars were given their heads as to teaching methods, and were free to pursue their own lives, it is not surprising that a nonconformist like Rosemond would create anxiety for her superiors.

Mary Parmenter, an assistant in the university's English department, who lived near Rosemond on Charles Street and also took classes at Hopkins, remembered vividly her "voice, her way of moving along, her laugh." It appeared to Mary that she just "enjoyed Hopkins, and worked for a living a while at Goucher." At twenty-two, "tall and long-legged," her mannerisms and colloquial expressions, her rigid standards of teaching, inherited from her father and spiced with her own dramatics, may well have "irritated" the English department. This was to be a continuing problem.

Mary Parmenter explained it more fully: "I don't think she was ever very 'popular' as a teacher [of freshmen or sophomores], though respected by the *best* students. If she wrote comments on their themes they usually couldn't read her writing or understand what she 'meant.' But if she talked to them, they liked that. She was, of course, very-good looking—tall, straight; her *blue* eyes, her curly, rough, *rich* (dark) *gold* hair, her high color. In her usual shabby rather tailored clothes (dark tweeds or something), she went striding along. If she ever tried to wear anything light or ruffly she looked ridiculous. (I used to mend a black dress of hers that looked fine on her).

"She and I never knew the same things, so we tried to instruct or inform each other in a spotty way. I think she told me about Plato and Aristotle, or what Elizabethans thought of them. She never really explained very much to anybody; she did make you want to *know*. She first 'taught' me about 'listening to symphony.' If we went 'downtown' on Charles St., and got off the bus at Peabody Library (at the Washington Monument Center) and *sat in back* part of stacks, on Friday afternoon, we could hear the orchestra *rehearsal* right through the *wall*, as we read. I think she told me that 'Freddy' had told her of that 'trick.'"

Freddy, or Frederick Hard, was a friend of Merle's whom Rosemond first knew in her Bryn Mawr days. He was an associate professor at Tulane, and was working on his Ph.D. at Johns Hopkins. Tall and reserved, an Episcopalian by adoption, he directed the Methodist church choir, loved Mozart, and played the violin. His Ph.D. thesis focused on Spenser's use of paintings and tapestries in the *Faerie Queene*. He and Rosemond were together often, and their mutual interests drew them into a close intellectual relationship that developed into something of a romance. Mary Parmenter said she "never thought either was much 'in love'—and if it ever came to having to decide to marry—or not—I am sure both backed off. *I* think the idea of being *married* to her, scared him to death." He was a "rather neat, mild man," perhaps a bit like her father, "*not* blistered or sunburned."

There was, of course, her continuing relationship with Merle. Her long letters from Toronto had revealed a comfortable and affectionate intimacy that would never change. In January of her first year at Goucher, in a letter to Merle, she revealed this fondness: "You are a *fine* boy—I was never quite so proud to know you—& have just tired out the landlady with a long recital of your ingenuous & Uncle-Lew-like characteristics. Certainly is too bad we are related in this awkward manner, I would be such a *whiz* of a damned unconventional wife."[23] It would be difficult for any ordinary man to compete with her brother.

"So far as *I* know she never 'had a lover,'" Mary Parmenter recalled. "She had *friendships* with both men and women who (to her) seemed 'interesting' or 'important' more as she would become for a time immersed in some book or *idea*, or 'area' of art or *thought*. So far as I know, it would have been vaguely embarrassing for her to 'have a beau.' I don't think she ever knew Goucher faculty or students— *not* interesting. She was a fond friend of Professor Kemp Malone." Dr. Malone, her former teacher and adviser from the University of Minnesota, was now professor of Icelandic studies at Johns Hopkins. Rosemond enrolled in his course in Chaucer during her first year of teaching at Goucher, and studied historical connections of Old English heroic poetry with him during her second year.

But it was Edwin Greenlaw, whom students like Fred Hard had followed from the University of North Carolina, whose interest in historical allegory in English literature became a guiding force in Rosemond's thinking. He was revered by his students for his commitment to learning, and remembered for frequently quoting Bacon's famous dictum that learning is "for the glory of the Creator and the relief of man's estate." His students never doubted that the life of the mind was a life devoted to divine purposes. Rosemond joined his seminar in Renaissance literature during her first year at Goucher and while pondering ever more deeply the recurrence of myths, romances, and historical allegory in the Renaissance and seventeenth century began moving forward in time from Chaucer to those later periods of literature.

Rosemond was invited to join the Journal Club, a group of professors and advanced students who met to read and discuss recent reviews and journal articles. Professor Greenlaw led the Journal Club and was undoubtedly the stimulus for her first article for the *Publications of the Modern Language Association of America,* which would appear in September 1929. Combining Malone's seminar in heroic poetry with her study of Spenser under Greenlaw, she developed an article entitled "The Red Crosse Knight and Mediaeval Demon Stories." With her usual assurance, wry wit, and eclectic references, she discusses traditional devil-commitment and supernatural-parent stories and romances. The pleasure she derives from her essay shines through the moral to which she is pointing: "for the Gentle Knight mortality is not a limitation and a curse, but a divinely-planned pre-requisite to an 'aspiration for the infinite.'"[24] It is through our mortality that we can aspire to divinity, to have a "sight of the New Jerusalem," to partake of the joys "never yet seen of Faeries sonne." But to have this sight we must be "assoiled" [absolved] of our pride, through struggle and repentance. These ideas had been recurring in her mind at different levels ever since she first wrote about not wanting to be a plaster saint.

In addition, her own developing ideas emerge as she summarizes the article with a revealing comment about Spenser's *Faerie Queene:*

"The stanzas which tell the story of the infant George are full of reminiscences of often-recurring romantic enfances—the shreds and patches gathered by an eclectic imagination and fused, as was Spenser's habit, into a new whole . . . It is only as we are aware of this unconsciously eclectic temper that such considerations as these have any importance in the study of a poet's 'sources.' For if by that may be implied only the conscious adaptation, into a consistent parallel, of material carefully scrutinized and deliberately selected,—only the making over of a *Rosalynde* into an *As you like it,*—if 'sources' may include that process only, then indeed we must admit this sacred river to be flung up momently from no source whatever. But there were caverns through which it ran, and though perhaps they are, to our sorrow, measureless to man, they are, after all, surely worth our remarking."[25]

In those caverns measureless to man lie the labyrinthine pathways of the unconscious, our links to the source of being. In recognizing that myths, like dreams, are part of the collective unconscious, she was ahead of her time.

By spring of 1928, her course work for her Ph.D. was completed, but she needed to go to England to finish the research for her dissertation. During the previous semester Rosemond had applied to the American Association of University Women, which administers fellowships, and was awarded the $1,000 PHI MU Fellowship for 1928. This, together with the Bryn Mawr European Fellowship, would provide funds for Rosemond to go to Somerville College, Oxford, to complete her work on her dissertation. For the summer, she would return eagerly to the Bryn Mawr Summer School for Women Workers in Industry. She wrote to Hilda Smith, director of the summer school:

Dear Miss Smith—I have been trying this week to think about whether I might in all conscience to at least make an attempt to get me a teaching job and make much moneys, but ah me, I can't stay away from either Bryn Mawr or the summer school, so I shall turn up in glee to throw books about with the old zest, a few days before every one arrives. When do we start this year? I declare I feel as related to that school as though I had been behind C.T. [President Carey Thomas] on the camel. I shall now live only for that day when we hand out the first glasses of tea and Lorna Doone's. I wish Baltimore were not 7.00 from New York. I should like to see you all.

My best to you—Rosemond[26]

4

Armed like the virgin goddess Athena, not with a spear and flashing gold armor inscribed with the Medusa's head, but with two fellowships, Rosemond Tuve sailed for England in late September.

She would later write: "I took out two years to pay my debts, teaching at Goucher and going to Johns Hopkins; then adding an A.A.U.W. fellowship went into residence at Somerville College, Oxford. There I swam among the Bodleian manuscripts—a sort of imrama for anyone working as I was on medieval subjects."[1]

Her diary for October 1, 1928, the first of many she would keep while abroad, begins, "Monday—landed Plymouth, moonlight." Not until the eleventh of October did she take the "bus to Oxford," and on the twelfth wrote, *Somerville, Oxford*—mostly lost luggage & Walton Street." Saturday October 13: "Matriculated in mediaeval Latin by the Vice Chancellor, in the Divinity School. Interview with Miss Darbishire [Helen Darbishire, Principal of Somerville College]." Sunday, October 14: "Evensong at Christ Church with Peg [Stevens]." Monday, October 15: "Introduced to the Bodleian by K. Constable [later Kathleen Tillotson]. First mss." Tuesday, October 16: "first lectures—Tolkien, Nichol-Smith, Simpson." She also tried out for the Bach Choir in New College. Her rich alto voice and her familiarity with the Bach B-Minor Mass, which they were singing that fall, ensured her a place in the group. Now she was safely transplanted.

Rachel Floyd Salter, with whom she established a lifelong friendship, recalls that her first impression of Rosemond when she appeared at Somerville was her "zest for living. Always afterward, when I would hear her unmistakable voice on the phone saying 'Hey Ra,' I knew she had arrived in England." During a ten-day trip they took together up the Rhine, Rachel never forgot hearing Rosemond chatting with two homesick soldiers, and "how easily she could talk with anyone of any age or background."

On Wednesday, October 17, she "bought bicycle £2" and rode over Magdalen Bridge. Acquiring a bicycle would transform her life. Now she could ride about to "see the sun come out" or "take a turn about Merton Street in the late twilight." These solitary excursions gave her a chance to fill up with the beauty around her and often included a pause to read: "Rode out to Kensington, up the hill & read Blake under a hedge, the sun coming through the mist early afternoon."

Thursday, October 25: "Bicycled about early. Long and morose day chiefly in bed." At times these excursions alleviated a "blue mood." Her separation from a full and rich life in Baltimore may have contributed to her feeling "morose."

A letter from Merle, dated October 10, indicates how completely she had shut out her past life. He wrote: "Mother told me yesterday that she had not heard yet whether you arrived in England, but I will trust your Norwegian constitution to survive the North Atlantic without serious damage. I sure wish Win [Winifred Whitman, whom Merle had married the previous year] and I were there to stay with you. The work goes on as fretfully as usual, always trying to get something done, never seeming to. Don't do the same, you take the year off for philosophical contemplation."[2]

Rosemond knew instinctively how to handle the bad times, times perhaps of loneliness or homesickness. An entry in her diary during some of England's cold, damp days records: "home at 4 with cakes to cheer me up. Tea and Nicholas Nickleby," or, "to bed with chocolates, apples and Trollope." These forms of nourishment were as necessary as her solitary excursions. She wrote: "off to Iffley, down past the King's Arms to lie on the grass by the locks & read Gray's *Journal in the Lakes* home by the tow path after twilight," or, "off in a high wind, & damp, out past Kensington to the wood road, sat on a great stump & read Shelley's *Hellas.*" Another day she rode "out beyond Old Marston, by a stile, looking over the fields, the sun coming through a blue & grey sky like the Last Judgement."

November 9: "Bodley. Court, 'had up' w. Peg & fined 10 bob. went to Magdalen Cloisters for consolation—worked hard at Bodley for conscience." There is no indication as to why she was in court, but we may assume she could have been riding her bicycle in a restricted area, or perhaps recklessly? It is difficult to imagine anything more serious. Later that month she wrote: "Lost in the tube, cried all the way down." But her mood swings were always wide and seldom lasted long. On November 27, 1928, her twenty-fifth birthday, she wrote that she was feeling "very high." On Sunday, December 2, she recorded: "Mary read me *Emma*." Mary Grenfell, later Waldegrave, was a close friend of that year. Four years later she invited Rosemond to stay with her while she worked at the British Museum. Mary later observed this about her friend: "If for some reason depressed and sad, something beautiful: a natural scene, a building or picture, or a passage in one of her best-loved authors was brought to her attention, it lifted her out of a sad mood at once."

She was invited to spend Christmas in London with one Oxford friend, then went on to Paris with another. Limitless energy and curiosity drew her toward every experience. With awe she would enter the Bibliothèque Nationale, and with reverence the Louvre, Notre-Dame, or St. Chappelle. She visited Chartres and Vézélay, to wonder at the beauty and to study the carved figures on the tympanum and facings, and the stained-glass windows, as she had done since early childhood in Canton and at St. Marks. She would be able to amplify her thesis with her appreciation and understanding of what she observed. In future years she would return again and again to "sit and stare," always finding allegorical figures that worked their way into her thinking and writing.

In early February 1929, Rosemond received a cryptic letter from Edwin Greenlaw.

"Dear Rosemond," he wrote. "I enjoyed your breathless letter very much and wish all my students had your vigor and enthusiasm. There are many things to be done on Elizabethan philology, but historical, which will contribute to this history of learning, and linguistic. M. Ericson wants to come back here next year to work on Spenser's language; I'd like you to come back and work on the historical side, which would be quite definitely history of ideas. To that end, I hope you *won't* get a job elsewhere. You remember your promise to get your degree and then come over in my field. Of course I'll keep you in mind, and if a job so good you oughtn't to turn it down should appear I'll get it for you if possible. Get your degree & apply for a Johnston— it's only $1500 but there's honor in it.

"It was good of you to send me a card from Herrick's old church. We spent a happy day with the old vicar there, an ardent devotee of archery, who showed us trophies he had won and Herrick memorabilia with equal gusto. Write to me again." It was signed "Cordially yours, Edwin Greenlaw."

One of Rosemond's memories of that year at Oxford, later confessed to a student, Ann Mendelsson-Iger, was "how lovely C. S. Lewis had been to her, when she was this timid American, not sure whether she belonged there. He was charming, encouraging and gentlemanly." On the other hand, "J .R. R. Tolkien was so "harsh and sarcastic and unpleasant that he intimidated her for life."

Yet doubt about her worth never seemed to diminish her confidence in her intellectual abilities. Writing in the March 9, 1929, issue of *Fritallery*, the "Magazine of the Oxford Women's Colleges," she boldly reviewed an orchestral concert. The voice was her own, her knowledge of music sure, and her allusions from life and literature typically added spice and color:

"The most important number, was the Beethoven first symphony. The cool gratefulness of the simple statement of the main theme that one has been accustomed to rely on, in the first movement, had this time got rather mixed up in the warm and over cheerful bustle of the rest; the second movement was in too slow a tempo, as was the Scherzo, where, as in a slowed-up film, suspense of pursuit was quite lost, uncompensated by the satisfaction that comes of arriving at end-rhymes simultaneously with the author.

"Mr. Arthur Schnabel's playing of the last Beethoven sonata made one realize to what extent execution can be creation, in the controlled strength of the great theme of the second movement, and the curious, concentrated excitement of its development, like the play and interplay of white light on many-faceted surfaces, and connected in perhaps the same way with that conviction of transcendence which makes metaphors of light the mystic's common idiom of expression."[3]

Sentimentality scorned but imagination awakened, she writes of the "catch in the breath as a note is almost not there and suddenly comes through softly, from silence. It is a Corregio-like softness almost, and this is a generation with a wearisome taste for astringents."[4] A final criticism brings to mind her South Dakota childhood as well as, no doubt, her trip to Paris during the holidays. "The Bach *Chaconne*, . . . made one want to hear the first half done austerely, like scales played in early morning upon a frosty air, with no attempt at an 'interpretation', no Baedeker double starring of the beauties."[5]

During the spring recess Rosemond rode her bicycle farther afield. Her diary for March 19 records: "Shottery in the grey morning mist just lifting from the trees, then *Stratford*—the churchyard green & mossy, ugly windows, old registers, tombs of the family, & S's [Shakespeare's] bust smirking—old streets of almhouses quite lovely, but birthplace infested with *1,000's* of guides telling you what Elizabethan script is, had to eat cake and tea by Smithfield Lane going to Warwick."

Riding on, she reached Tintern Abbey where she saw "the mist like smoke with the hills through its mullions." Back in Oxford, as the days began to lengthen, she was up "at 5:30, cup of tea and off to Magdalen—just in time for the Amens, away up the High in the early light, with all the world in a circle." Not only did she attend Sunday services, often twice, but she frequently went to Evensong to hear the boys choir sing a Palestrina mass or a Byrd motet as well. Although she remained a Lutheran all her life, she was drawn increasingly to the liturgy of the Church of England. In addition, she would search out Norman churches in England and Celtic remains in Ireland. To her they were holy places.

Despite her adventures, a prodigious amount of work was accomplished during the spring term. In addition to the B.Litt. course requirements, Rosemond devoted hours in the Bodleian to working on her thesis. Miss Dorothy Everett, of Lady Margaret Hall, criticized for her the final chapter. She also completed the research and writing for what would eventually become her fifth publication, "A Mediaeval

Commonplace in Spenser's Cosmology," which appeared in *Studies in Philology* in January 1933. Greenlaw's influence is obvious in this work, for a footnote in the article states that "the present article attempts only to note a few of the possible 'sources for Spenser's ideas' which Dr. Greenlaw says 'have not yet been systematically studied.'"[6]

Rosemond's hours of intense research and writing were always relieved by a variety of activities. During the final weeks of May she began writing "Horae" (in Greek religion the Horae are the goddesses of the seasons—hence, orderliness). On June 7 she "stayed home and read for once—tea, and gave my lecture har! at P. Simpson's class." On June 18, she was "off in a canoe with Tee—in, late, at 11.25, meeting the bursar, but forgiven (even without a shilling)." This is her first reference to the mysterious "T" who appears from time to time in her diaries.

When the Somerville term ended, she had completed "the B.Litt. courses and viva, but being unable to complete my residence [for financial reasons] returned to teach three years at Vassar, finish the Bryn Mawr Ph.D., and teach three more summers at the Bryn Mawr School for Women Workers in Industry."[7] Before sailing home in time "to hand out those glasses of tea and Lorna Doone's," she returned to France to study again the facades of Vézélay and Chartres, then on to Italy to see the Sistine Chapel and San Clemente in Rome and the cathedral at Modena. Her year abroad had established her as a serious scholar; she had expanded both intellectually and emotionally; and she had made valuable connections.

One adventure was reported by Mary Parmenter, her Goucher friend: "When Rosemond was on a train in Italy, third class, as always, she was sharing bread, cheese and onions with farm workers who were engaged in the onion harvest. She decided to join them and help harvest onions, to earn some money with which to proceed somewhere else."

When Rosemond received an appointment as instructor in English at Vassar, beginning in the fall of 1929, she must have felt like little Jack Horner pulling out a plum. Nothing seems to have come of Edwin Greenlaw's efforts to find Rosemond a place at Hopkins.

Instead, she would be teaching critical writing, the English novel, and Shakespeare at a prestigious eastern college, and be close enough to Bryn Mawr to complete work for her Ph.D. One of her students at Vassar remembers her vividly: "She was tall and fair and beautiful. She rode her bicycle recklessly, her hair flying in the wind, while she ate an ice-cream cone. The bicycle basket was filled with books and the papers flew too."

In January 1930, she wrote to Hilda Smith about returning to the Bryn Mawr Summer School for Women Workers in Industry:

> Helen Lockwood told the Faculty Club about Workers' Education last night so well and so valiantly that I am all agog about knowing and doing some more, although she also certainly made one realize the difficulties and the importance of the implications. However,—does it still seem possible that there will be an English instructorship open? I should like awfully much to be considered for it if there were, and if that's impossible, perhaps for the library or some Odd Job—I do hope there's a possibility of the English opening, though.
>
> It's a great job to come in and catch on to a whole new world (with its courses !!) at Vassar, but it's a nice, pleasant, stimulating place to be; good students and lots of lectures and music and Clara Marburg a grand girl to live with.[8]

During her first spring at Vassar she wrote to Mary Grenfell, now married to Geoffrey Waldegrave:

> The spring is very lovely in up-New-York when it does finally come. I am sitting on a blanket by a stream, with the pussy-willows & red beech trees & little cypresses & sycamores all coming out in twenty different colors all around me, & the mountains very blue & clear away off as far as the Catskills, to the west. This is lovely country; but it is too bright & clear & sunny, & seems alien to me somehow. By now you have got very used to the little house & all, so I aim to make you start writing again, & tell me just what each room looks like one by one & what you do on Mondays,

Tuesdays, Wednesdays, holy days & Fridays & what not. I am
happy on each of those & indeed all; this is a very content-full
life. . . .

O dear Mary, I would give anything if your great husband
ever had anything to transact with the Big Business of New
York, & I could see your curly hair again, you goose. Write me
a letter. I know you're happy. Don't leave him for too long at
a time; I got un-engaged the summer after Somerville from
too long an absence! Plumb went out of my head & never
came back.

Undoubtedly there was tacit agreement between Rosemond and
Fred Hard. Despite their similar intellectual interests, the differences
in their personalities and the fact that he was a Southerner, which her
mother disliked, made the gulf between them too great. Although
Rosemond sometimes fantasized about marriage, wondering what
she might have missed, it was far from the top of her agenda. In a letter to Mary Waldegrave some time later, she wrote, "I told you didn't
I that I got disengaged; & idyls which I have now somehow don't affect
me permanently—I finished off one last night." It seems certain that
she is referring to Frederick Hard.

In the following spring of 1931, she wrote again to Mary
Waldegrave:

A lovely hesitant spring day. But this country has the
tiredest springs you ever did see. I hate the coldness & the
eternal wind & the air always thin & sharp. As you remember
I am a great one for mugginess—of air, mind or imagery. This
is not the quality which made me love your letter; you are still
the clearest serenity that ever walked with perfect directness
out of a college to get married. I do dote upon the story of
you & Geoffrey going out to tea in Oxford & deciding to just
never do the next week's lectures. I'm sure it has something to
do with the clarity of nature which makes you read Jane
Austen better than anyone that ever lived—do you remember
sitting on my floor reading *Emma* to me?

It's odd to think you're not quite as old yet as I was then! & here is the infant accomplished & all. I must be allowed to come & see her, & you, & the house, & Geoffrey (whom I remember as a kind of margin to your raspberry colored evening dress at the Hyde Park Hotel ball!), when I come. It may be next year—if I can get myself a small grant, as seems probable, I shall come over & work—chiefly in Paris I believe. If one could only get a job—at one of the innumerable foreign schools for spoiled American children, even!—but it seems rather doubtful.

On weekends Rosemond could escape to Bryn Mawr to finish work on her Ph.D., stopping off in New York on her way back to visit art galleries and museums. In October 1931, she went to Bryn Mawr to take the orals for her degree. Rose Jeffries Peebles, then chairman of the English department at Vassar, later wrote about Rosemond's performance: "People there thought her doctor's examination brilliant. By some mischance her examiners left out philology on her exam. [When] called back after the usual pause to discuss the results, they asked her if she would prefer to take the exam then or later. She said, 'now' and they were all astounded at the power she showed. When questioned she asked if she might go to the board, [where she] demonstrated the whole thing admirably."[9]

In the spring of 1932 Rosemond suffered a severe blow to her pride when she learned that she would not be asked to return to Vassar. Two years later, Miss Peebles outlined her feelings and those of her department in a letter of recommendation to the English Department of Connecticut College:

"It is difficult to give what would seem to me a fair account of the impression she made. At the end of her first year everyone, it seemed to me, thought her unusually delightful, charming, and of great promise as a teacher. She had been sent to us with the most remarkable letters from all people who had earlier come into contact with her at Bryn Mawr, Goucher, The [Johns] Hopkins. During her second year there was some criticism of her carelessness in posted notices and of the cursoriness of comments made on students' themes. At the end of the third year it was thought that she had not yet grown up entirely, or developed her powers as a teacher, and so she was not asked to return. . . . I at the end opposed her departure. To me her unusually rich experience—born in Dakota, educated with great difficulty by a pioneer family determined to educate all its children, her successful conclusion in three years of her work at Minnesota, her brilliant record at Bryn Mawr, her English experience, her success in the Bryn Mawr Summer School for [Women] Workers, made her seem to me a very good person for a college like Vassar to get hold of. She had done so many different things and had been enriched by them all. It is true she did not seem to me to have digested all this experience which she had lived very vividly, nor to have grown up in one sense, but, as I said at the time to the Department, I was willing to bet on her future . . . . I thought, and still think, that when she comes into full maturity she would be a very rich person indeed . . . .

"I do not think she had digested, as fully as one might expect, her Bryn Mawr and Oxford experiences. She had little notions that seemed to some fantastic but to me amusing as to how life ought to be conducted. I thought she might be living a little according to some ideal design . . . I may be wrong but I think in a few more years she would be a very valuable person indeed."[10]

What was least amusing to some of the senior faculty women, peering through the windows of Williams House, was the sight of this great, gangling girl riding by on her bicycle, wandering absentmindedly along the pavement, blissfully savoring an enormous ice-cream cone. Yet her students remember her with enthusiasm: "She was an excellent teacher and made learning fun." Another student, finding her a "total delight," added that, "she was however different from the usual eastern college teacher—a difference which enchanted many of us. Her method of teaching was to talk to herself about the material we were studying and to let us listen. She was a scholar thoroughly entranced by her work and eager to share her joy with us." But there were others: "Rosemond Tuve was my composition teacher during my freshman year at Vassar (1929–30). She was a rosy-cheeked, curly-haired buxom young lady who tore around the campus on a bicycle. I remember that we had a weekly composition. If our theme was late or unsatisfactory, we had to write an extra one. One week I had four to do! I am sure she had a glass through which I saw only darkly." This young woman later taught English composition herself.

Being let go from Vassar, however, had a positive result. It released Rosemond, as she had yearned, to return to England and Paris. She had been awarded her Ph.D. in May 1932, and was required to have her thesis published. When she learned that it would be less expensive in Paris, she had one more excuse to go abroad.

At Vassar, Rosemond had formed a friendship with another young English instructor, Eleanor Terry Lincoln. Beyond the two women's shared interest in literature and art, their personalities complemented each other's. Rosemond was highly emotional and tended to impulsive behavior. Eleanor was consistently even-tempered, gifted with innate good judgment and emotional maturity. For the remainder of her life Rosemond would write her friend, chronicling her adventures abroad or sharing concerns. In 1934 Eleanor Lincoln joined the English department at Smith College, in Northampton, Massachusetts, so their proximity enabled them to share occasional visits and, eventually, five trips abroad. The first of Rosemond's letters to Eleanor is from Paris, September 14, 1932:

> Dear Eleanor, you great hatpin
> *how* do you bear life without Ivor? [name given to Rosemond's bicycle, which seems to have been stored at the railway station while she was in England.] I went with Elizabeth [possibly Elizabeth Chapin] to her handsome mediaeval town *Provins*, on Sunday, & got on a bicycle for the first time since I took mine over that one hour early in the heat. Oh lovely sensation! Even on cobblestones, & with 1? views per minute so that anything more than a walk is too fast. You see Eliz. is reading the cartularies of, or writing studies of the mediaeval fairs of, or something incomprehensible, of Provins. So I got my information by the square inch, very grand & archeological, but everything too swift in both time & space—the single Sunday we stayed there being scarcely

sufficient for appreciating the beauties, & the bicycle, i.e. the only possible Feet-Saver, being an unworthy way of telescoping a mediaeval walled town. Isn't it dreadful; first you can't get here at all, & then you have all the same old monkey works of food drink & sleep to arrange for. Not that any of those would be given up by me, the Original Glutton, speaking from the lovely background of a steak-Chateaubriand, an epinards-a-la-crême, & a Cointreau.

Shall I start in again, more orderly-like? I've been in Paris three weeks (3), almost. After an entirely satisfying discovery of Germany—(which is utterly charming & really *has* the painted gables & the fabulous beer & the *gemütlichkeit* & the carved & painted ceilings)—and two weeks walking (?) in the Tyrol, staying in little scraps of villages composed of nothing but 1 inn & the sound of the icy water coming down from the Aadensee or the Nordensee or the Whateversee, *and* two weeks roasting in Rome in the shadow of St. Peter's, visiting Renée at the American Academy (chiefly mint juleps with occasional lucid discussions of the Works of Art decorating the studio being occupied at the moment).

STOP don't tell W.S. [Wylie Sypher, a colleague at Vassar] or anybody else not even Aunt Amy [Amy Reed, a large, comfortable woman, a mother figure for Rosemond, whom she knew as a professor of English at Vassar] 1) that you couldn't read this letter or 2) that it was all in 1 sentence. I'm relaxing, on you. It gives a more continuous impression of my summer, which is rapidly becoming geographically & ethnically mixed in my mind. STOP

Rosemond varied her language, using several voices. She had a formal voice for addressing students and for professional occasions; she had a "gentle, soft, musical" voice when speaking with friends; and she had an idiomatic, slangy voice used in letters for fun and with close friends. She continued:

I am now negotiating hard on the blessed thesis, which is giving me its first proofs in a week & a half. Chiefly though

I'm working in the Bibliothèque Nationale, that is, *after* going out at 7:30 & breakfasting on croissants & café, on the quai, & then off to a church or a view or whatnot, and arriving lazily about ten fifteen. And *before* leaving at 4 P.M. stop to stroll around the galleries, or look at the windows of the Ste. Chapelle, or take another look at the Cézanne *Cardplayers* in the Louvre, or merely to sit stolidly in the Luxembourg reading François Mauriac, my new Passion (following Duhamel's Salavin books, which I think I was exploding about when we knew each other [if so]). There have been some good shows here. A Manet [above the line, in case the writing isn't clear, she inserts: MANET: I *hate* Monet] exhibition which was *miraculous,* great guns what pictures! Have you seen the *Olympia,* the courtesan with a lovely mouth & very aware eyes (P.S.; virginal idea of a courtesan, nicht wahr?) lying with a necklace on, on a dark green bed. And several of the portraits of Berthe Morisot, charming & poetic & all the rest; & still-lifes almost to make you believe there are others besides Van Gogh & Cézanne who saw motionless things living. (*Quelle phrase gonflée*). I am getting very much attached to Utrillo. And we're going down the rue de la Boëtie tomorrow to see some more Derains. *Quelle pleine des richesses.*

My pen—as you see. So I'll stop. I can't get the transatlantic attitude about letters, darling; reconcile yourself to these sudden outbursts of inconsequentiality. I'm writing in bed; excuse everything, if you please. If not, at least—your love, as mine to you.

Mrs. Feitelbaum

Not only did Rosemond's friends, both in London and Oxford, welcome her back, but also some sort of reputation must have preceded her. On October 22, after a visit to Cambridge, she wrote in her diary: "Straight to the Fitzwilliam. Sidney C. Cockerell over it with me: esp. the new Cortauld Galleries: (everything beautiful) *Vincent of Beauvois.*" Sidney Cockerell, who was knighted in 1934, was a prominent bibliophile, director of the Fitzwilliam Museum at Cambridge,

and a founder of the Courtauld Galleries. He was also an avid collector of medieval prints. What is astonishing is the way Rosemond was
accepted by as eminent a person as Cockerell and the many distinguished scholars she would come to know.

By November Rosemond had found a room at 7 Tariton Street in
London and almost immediately wrote to Mary Waldegrave. "It's
me—Here in London thank God. I am in an enormous inflation—
(Entirely spiritual, I might add—I am over to publish my thesis, &
you know the last-minute ways of printers.)"

Mary responded with an invitation to spend a weekend at her
home in Shamley Green. Rosemond wrote in her diary: "Thurs
evening on the train—the house & the garden, the drawing room
beams & fire, & talk, & white wine & God knows what all. Geoff's
funny family childhood (ever so effete)."

On Sunday she took time to write a letter to Merle, including
Winifred, his wife. Unfortunately, there are no letters or diaries in
which Rosemond mentions events leading up to Merle's marriage on
October 27, 1927, or the wedding itself. Rosemond's feelings would
have been mixed, but she keeps them hidden. Winifred Whitman was
the niece of the Reverend and Mrs. Rasmussen, the Tuves' former
minister, and his wife, in Canton. Merle and Winifred first met when
they were students together at the University of Minnesota. Winifred
Whitman became one of the early women psychiatrists in this country and practiced under her maiden name.

[1932]   Nov. 13 ?, or Sunday at any rate
Dearest Merle & Win: I am having a long weekend (i.e.
Thursday to Wednesday!!) in the most heavenly spot you can
imagine. . . .

I have been welcomed by my Oxford friends with the
most *surprising* & gratifying warmth & activity, & indeed this
is very much to the point, because not only do they have
houses & husbands & babies in the country, like this one, but
also one has just written a novel . . . & another is just getting
a volume of damned good poems published—Joy Scovell, her

name is; read them if you see them. . . . So I have to work hard at the B.M. & read like a toper & correct proof like a solemn owl & pretend to take myself seriously.[11]

The morning following her visit to the Waldegraves', Rosemond wrote this poignant letter:

Dear Mary and Geoffrey—
   You would probably be entertained if you saw me today, though I assure you it is not too rambunctiously entertaining. I am *moping* about, *mes enfants;* I am almost surprised at myself; I did think that one thing at least I could do—walk from world to world with out wishing it were the last or the next one. But indeed this time I am Caught. I got up cursing my city view. And was too cross to take a tub in my definitely non-nursery bathroom—not a single miniature shirt to avoid knocking off the line. . . . I sound—Depressed, don't I? Adam & Eve leaving the G. of E. & even worse, being Eve alone. Hélas, what is the good of a professional-so-called Existence? Plumb unnatural I call it. You are you know altogether the most delectable household. I did love it all.

On New Year's Day 1933, she began the first of two diaries that record her life for the next two years—years of joy, filling up with the beauties of nature or illuminations in early manuscripts. On January 1, 1933, she wrote: "New Year's; Sunday. My package from home full of peanuts & coffee perk & divinity & black walnuts & cookies came N. Year's Eve, so the day was full of Canton, & cracking walnuts on the cistern, & popping of corn, & Dick [probably her brother] in his blue military suit. OEW [Ola E. Winslow, scholar and former colleague of Rosemond's at Goucher] & I walked down Chelsea Embankment, over Chelsea Bridge, et. al. & had dinner at Slater's Picc'y. [Piccadilly] After proof all A.M."

On January 5, after correcting the proof of her thesis, "Seasons and Months," she dined with "Aery Faery Lilian (Winstanley i.e.)" at 3 Granville Place. Winstanley was an established Spenserian scholar, and generous in her acceptance of Rosemond.

Many of Rosemond's friends from her Somerville year pursued literary and artistic interests. This helps to explain the expanding web of artists and scholars with whom Rosemond socialized. One person led to another, until she seemed to have a whole circle of valuable and stimulating acquaintances. Her own attractiveness, vivaciousness, and serious interest in scholarship led inevitably to these various and numerous introductions.

Rosemond's article "Spenser and Mediaeval Mazers: with a Note on Jason in Ivory," on which she was working at this time, didn't appear until April 1937, in *Studies in Philology*. In it, she continues her search for Spenser's sources, for his "imaginative use of suggestions from other than literary materials," particularly his use of what he observed on medieval English mazers—hardwood drinking bowls. She admits that this is "only a small instance of Spenser's way of com-bining for his own purposes many things from many places. But it is nevertheless significant of a certain habit of mind and of a particular texture of imagination."[12] With these remarks she reveals her own close identification with Spenser. In conclusion she asserts that "one reason for his extraordinary clarity of descriptive technique may lie in this combination of literary and visual 'sources'—a combination which I think could be pointed out far oftener if we knew as much about his artistic interests—or took as much cognizance of them—as we do his literary 'sources.'"[13]

At the end of January, Rosemond spent a weekend with the Cockerells and found time before tea on Sunday to write to Eleanor Lincoln:

[Sunday, January 29, 1933]

My dear Eleanor,

. . . I wish you were here to take a book & a packet of digestives & an old coat & go off on a bicycle with Rachel & me (Bath friend, teaches officer dorters at the Royal School— poisonous "gord school") from Shrewsbury via Ludlow to Dolgelby & about Wales as far as possible. (Possible on 4/6 per night.) We intend to start about April 6th—for one week anyhow. Thereafter I shall return to the B.M. And *how,* do you think? By living on the edge of Surrey next to Sussex & being taken with Mary's husband Geoffrey in the car to Guildford mornings, & met there evenings.

Mary was also up when I was, but by now has quitted Oxford & borne a handsome black-eyed daughter. And the cottage is a plenty fine one, pale red brick, & black half tim-bering, oak beams in my room & my library & our drawing room, & a heavenly garden, & nothing for miles except green field & trees and a cottage or two, & the village of Shamley Green in bicycling distance when I want to go to town early.

So that's how my life is. I dote on it. How do you like yours?

On February 16 she wrote in her diary: "Found suddenly at the end of a Gower *Conf. Am.* [John Gower, *Confessio Amatis*] in Bodley that had belonged to 'Anne Russell'—2 Latin couplets—*Spenserus!!* Perhaps really he. Very exciting, (if the pale lamenting yg. man in the library doesn't think so—! sniffed when I asked him. Pooh.)"

Rosemond's exciting discovery of "Spenserus," written in what she believed was Spenser's own hand, would result in the most painstaking research, and, in the last essay she would ever write, the courage to commit to paper her tentative and imaginative arguments for the validity of this signature.

The rhythm of Rosemond's days had a quieting effect that offset the urgency of a seemingly frantic existence. Her walks in Christ Church meadow, her visits to museums and to the various churches around Oxford, both to worship and hear the music; and her atten-dance at lectures combined to form one Gestalt. In biting cold, with snow "right in my teeth, & wickedly cold, & wind like a Gothic novel"; or splashing through flooded roads, with rain spitting in her face, she was never deterred from her daily excursions on her cherished bicy-cle. Although her focus and her energy were given to her research and writing, there was always time to socialize. Through Dorothy Everett she was introduced to the renowned crystallographer Polly Porter; she formed an abiding friendship with the eminent scholar Percy

Simpson; and continued her connections with the Cockerell family. Her days were filled with the joy of discovery in libraries or the beauty of the natural world. She lived in a continual state of exaltation. Years later she would write from Oxford to a former student: "It is the early ones (musicians) that simply rapt me out of this world into another, and I often cannot quite come back." She was referring to the prevalence of Palestrina, Byrd, and Bach at the evensong services.

The poignancy of Rosemond's diary entries at the end of March reveal the transcendent feelings that she often experienced while she was at Oxford and indeed during other times in her life. On March 30 she tells us she sat on a bench beyond the river, in Christ Church meadow, just "staring" until supper. Two days later she sat for an hour in the antechapel at New College. But in the next few days her mood changed as she finally packs to go to Shamley Green and to work at the British Museum:

"April 4: finished packing, great drying of teapots et. al. Off to see the Sheldonian, gown in fist. Also St. Mary's which I can never learn is ugly, & All Saints, *rather* nice but why not woodwork like Trinity? Then the meadow for the last time—in a lovely green & pinkness under an exquisite sky. Off on 12.25, met by Geoffrey at Guildford—bike into the Bean & all. *Home:* lovely country! Unpacked, put on me yaller dress, Sally & 'Papa' (Lord Waldegrave—being the Original Saint) & Lady W. (like Geoff) & Mary & Geoff—tea outside. Dinner, quiet, moon, pear tree, bliss, etcetera!"

At the top of the page for April 5 Rosemond wrote these words: "for 2 months: *au sain de* the Viscountess Chewton being Poor Mary—Lord's Hill Shamley Green, Surrey."

Rosemond soon fell into a routine of days in London at the British Museum and evenings with the Waldegraves. Despite her intense involvement in the daily life of the family, however, Rosemond was true to her promise not to be underfoot. She maintained her own daily rhythms, which she knew would sustain her. Only the settings changed. "April 7: Waited up till they came in (from Somerset), full of the new house & "Hugh McMurtrie" & "Aunt Mary" & other Mendip news."

This is the first mention of the Waldegraves' plans to move to

Chewton Mendip. The idea of any change was surely unsettling to Rosemond after having just established a new routine. Her "home" with the Waldegraves was *"un paradis terestre—que je les aime!"* But the reality was the necessity of finding a job. Often, in her dairies, she discusses this over lunch with friends and speaks of writing a "job letter," and, of course, the Waldegraves knew of her concerns.

At the beginning of May she set off with Rachel Salter, whom she had known at Somerville, on a bicycle tour. Rachel recalled this trip many years later: "It was always fun to travel with Ros, because her own enjoyment was so apparent & infectious that she made me more aware. She seemed to sharpen all my senses. "I remember too how I gradually came to understand & respect her deep religious faith. She didn't preach at me, but I clearly recall one incident. I must have said something—I don't know what—that sounded snobbish or insular. Ros's answer was 'Don't forget that God so loved *the World,* not only the people you were at Oxford with.' It was a rebuke I've never forgotten."

The tone of Rosemond's diary seems to shift after leaving Rachel in Llangollen on May 5. The two young women had traveled through the west of England and just into Wales, and now, while Rosemond's mood became more meditative, she also rode her bicycle recklessly down the mountainous hills. She was free to have a total interchange with the natural world around her. Her imagination fired more intensely. Her sensitivity to beauty in music and nature lifted her to another realm of being.

The next day she was back at the Waldegraves': "Home for tea, & talk, & Sally, & both, & dinner, & coffee machines, & civilization, & shampoo, & tulips out, & forgetmenots & my darling family—just Lady Waldegrave & the Earl & Re & Sally at home. Lovely time. *Amen.*"

"Re" is Geoffrey Waldegrave's sister, Lady Irene, with whom Rosemond developed a close friendship. They exchanged letters until the end of Re's life.

Despite her week's vacation, Rosemond was so intent on seeing both Geoffrey and Mary that she gave up another day of work. Her fondness for Geoffrey was being noticed. There are hints in her diary about receiving suspicious looks, and, later, a friend hinted of her "crush" on this attractive and intelligent Englishman.

As the diaries reveal, Rosemond had been talking with friends and writing letters in search of job possibilities, but without luck. She had booked passage to return home in September, unaware of how fate would again intervene in her destiny.

Twice in her diaries for May, Rosemond wrote about finding it difficult to work. There could be many reasons for this. Foremost, no doubt, was her affection for and involvement with the Waldegrave family, in particular, Geoffrey. Also, Rosemond liked to have plans in place well in advance, and as her efforts to find a job had borne no fruit, this could have contributed to her anxiety and interfered with her work habits. Then, there were the many friends with whom she was tempted to socialize, constantly attending concerts and visiting museums. After the intensity of years of studying and teaching, it is understandable that she would relax her strict work ethic and seek time to absorb the bounty of this time in England. It was a stimulating and satisfying life, but her conscience nagged.

Lew and Helen arrived in England at the end of May and Rosemond showed them around London, including a show of Epsteins at Leicester Gallery. Rosemond recorded in her diary their "*tremendous* effect of vitality." At the Tate she has a "great argument, Lew saying that the representational idea & the expressionist idea do *not* displace each other necessarily, but can alternate like the seasons."

Rosemond's diaries, filled as they are with the beauty and joy of each day, seldom reveal feelings or thoughts about her future, even though plans were always brewing. She hoped to return to teaching. Conversations in the Waldegraves' drawing room, and with friends, often turned to a discussion of her future. Her two months at Lords Hill were ending, but Geoffrey and Mary had again shown their generosity. There was a very primitive cottage at the back of their estate, which they offered to to Rosemond for six shillings per week. And so, at the top of the page for May 31, is written: "*P.S.* I AM TO COME BACK TO LORDS HILL! ! ! *Alleluia* ! ! !

On June 3, Rosemond met Lew and Helen in Oxford to spend a few days with them there before going on to Paris together. From there, Rosemond would continue on to Germany by herself. In Paris, despite a great deal of sight-seeing with Lew and Helen, Rosemond managed to inquire about a job at the American University and to correct proofs of her thesis, which she was still struggling to get published. On June 9, she noted: "To Josephine Baker's follies at *Casino de Paris*—good machine act, black & silver, excellent jazz-band & Josephine, (like Matisse) *Clever.*"

Only a fragment of the letter Rosemond wrote to Mary on June 11 remains, but it reveals once again her longing, as Eleanor expressed it, for a revelation of the divine. Her sensitivity to beauty took her out of herself, leading her to truth, to the world of being, to an almost mystical experience.

> The Luxembourg seems to be between us and everything, so that we walk across it in a continuous stream, thus relating art life and nature. I went to Chartres early Saturday and sat all day in the cathedral. It is a hardly bearable kind of loveliness, I think; the way one is almost physically drunk with the color is a sort of relief. I don't think we are made so we can mix Dante-an exaltations with our ordinary existence any more.

During the next few days she inquired four more times about jobs, and each time noted succinctly "n.g." or "no job, of course." Her diary reports "Monday, June 19: to see M. Desclos, in re assistante job. Very complimentary. Tuesday, June 20: left Paris: Gare de l'Est, 7.15! (i.e. métro at 6.40!!) To Saarbrüchen—where it was suddenly no longer France."

Rosemond's journey took her on to Speyer and Worms (which she underlines to express her horror of real worms), then to Mainz, where she visited, almost in a state of elation, every castle and church she could find. "Crossed to *Rüdesheim:* some Rüdesheimer wine—*frisch und gut!* & home to a humpfsteak & karotten. (damned expensive)" On her return trip through Frankfurt, Mainz, and finally Paris, there were more stopovers to look at yet another garden, *kirche, or schloss.* While staying again with Augusta on her return to Paris, she wrote to Merle:

(35 rue de Fleurus, Paris),

a post card would	but only for 4 days more
answer this.	actually, I live still in
	England—i.e. care of the
	Viscountess Chewton
	Shamley Green, Surrey

Dear Merle—

Hey hey, *What* would you do if, just in case, there should happen to turn out to be a place as "assistante" (correcting papers & having conversation classes) in English, in a French *provincial* secondary school or *école normale,* & they offered it to you (if you were I of course)? There is no salary, only board & room (& the food's *not* good!) There are only short vacations, & the schools are usually stuck in little French cities. It's not certain that there'll be one—they belong actually to 3 Harvard graduate students; but M. Desclos, of the Exchange Board for France, said he'd not heard from them yet, & would write me in about 3 weeks. I must say I should be up a tree, if offered it. One learns French,—but that's hardly my stage (I mean: so vague & unnecessary a Good, at the moment, for me).—I can live here with comfort on the little I know, & I read it like English *almost.* Purely marking time. Otherwise it would be, I should think—long hours, *cold,* bad food, no money, no real courses of your own, no interesting other person, almost certainly all women. Still, it would be food & a roof, of a kind, & it may be that I won't have either otherwise.

I have written every university I could think of, & college, & registered with 2 good bureaus, & BMC, written all my profs etc.etc., said I would accept a school job, etc. But *no returns whatever.* I have at least booked passage home on 10 Sept., arriving 18th Sept., N.Y.C., S.S. *Dresden,* N.G. Lloyd. The people I talk it over with think I would be sufficiently quickly on deck, with that date. I am very sceptical about getting anything by being *present*—I have good enough friends so that they would really give me a job if they knew of any— & after all I have got good degrees, & have published lots—of a sort—& the thesis looks very handsome as a book.

It came yesterday, & looks fine. I have not got the bill for author's corrections, & am terrified. Printing alone was $250—supposed to be $225, & in francs that's a tremendous difference, so that I have been so *sunk* I have nearly perished of depressions. However I suppose 25.[francs] isn't such a terrific lot. Oh dear. The thesis is so long—250 pages I guess, or so. But nicely done, & a fiendish piece of printing to set up.

I just came back from a week in Germany, but it's too expensive, with the £ so low—besides, in England, I live terribly cheaply because my friends don't make anything on me, poor things. I have got them tons of presents in Paris, to try & help make up for it. They say they more than break even— & after all things are cheap. E.g. my sleeping-room (across the back garden) is only 6 shillings per week (in a cottage— because the house is full of relatives—perfect darlings)—I hope Mother's told you about my charming arrangements. I live with about 2 pages of Burke's *Peerage* countesses and earls all up & down the passages. It is entertaining.

I met a Vassar girl in Germany, & we lived together in Marburg, a lovely university town in Hessen—she says your fame is all over U.S., so I swoll up wit pride & joy. You are a Fine One. Always were.

Excuse the business letter—will you, dear Merle? I think more & more the French *assistante* is about as poisonous a stunt as is imaginable, but I think I must ask someone, besides Mig Couser (Irish friend) says I am to live at least 2 months in Bryn Mawr with her, & teach her Spenser. I will do it, because she is the kind you accept from without embarrassment, & I'll do something for her, next.

I can live a little while with Helen & Lew & teach H & the children French—but probably not long—'Ows for teaching you-all Magyar? The rest of the time I'll simply have to borrow something somehow, & sponge on Mother—(at least to the extent of working together on no funds, & still eating & sleeping. Usual Tuve stunt).

Dear Merle (& dear Win, whom I've not included because this is obviously not a *letter,* but a nuisance), God keep you employed! Lord, it's dreadful. Though I don't think much about it.

Would you tell Mother you've had a letter? I've written her one about Germany, but shall keep it till I'm ready to send the postcards in it. Love to you—& forgive the boring correspondence—Rosemond[14]

Five days later, she boarded "the boat from Dieppe, at 12.15, moonlight, considerable sleep." On July 6, she landed at Newhaven, and was back at Lords Hill by 11. "Tried on Sally's new clothes, sat on the lawn & read the *Times* & Spenser." After staying in the country for a few days, "just to feel like home," Rosemond's life resumed its special rhythm. Tea with Aunt Amy, to the Tate to see "the Degas *colours!!* again, the little Manet *Café,* the Cézannes."

.Meanwhile, Merle's reply to her long letter seeking help was swift. On July 25 she wrote to thank him:

Darling Merle, You always come to & help me out of my difficulties. I hope you never come to mind my asking you advice, because I plainly see I shall do it all my life.
Bless you. R[15]

Rosemond's hope of staying in England looked bleak. Her savings were dwindling. She had booked passage for America on September 10, from Galway—one more opportunity to see Ireland. But with no prospects of a job at home, she was open to any chance to stay in England. The charm of the Waldegrave household and her schoolgirl crush on Geoffrey, not to mention the lure of the British Museum and the Bodleian, were strong deterrents to going home. On July 22, without any comment, she recorded in her diary that she "worked on Walpole & Alain Chartier." Two days later, on Monday the twenty-fourth, she wrote, "Quiet day. Walpole & Alain Chartier 'Q' sort of work in the B.M." The reason for her sudden interest in Walpole was a letter from Wilmarth Sheldon Lewis, a "born collector" from Farmington, Connecticut, to Geoffrey Waldegrave.

Two years earlier, in 1931, following the death of Geoffrey's uncle, the 9th Earl Waldegrave, Lewis had gotten wind that considerable manuscripts, pictures, and other relics that had belonged to Horace Walpole were in Waldegrave hands. They had survived the 1842 dispersal sale at Strawberry Hill, and were now housed in the Priory at Chewton Mendip. Strawberry Hill was a museum of sorts, created by Horace Walpole and left to his niece, Maria Wentworth, while she was still married to James 2nd Earl Waldegrave and before her marriage to the Duke of Gloucester.

Wilmarth Lewis sailed to London, where he stayed, as always, at Brown's Hotel, and from there drove in a "hired Daimler" to the Priory in Chewton Mendip. Mary Waldegrave recalled that his "snake-charmer's sense, by then highly developed, had informed him that inside those crenellated walls and Victorian mullion windows there lurked much important Walpoliana. He was courteously met, but firmly shown off by Mary, the widow of the 9th Earl Waldegrave, now a very old lady." "Lefty," as Lewis was known, "took a swift look round and evidently decided he had better wait."

He waited until 1933, when he wrote to Geoffrey: "During the last month I have let myself in for a life sentence, nothing less than a new edition of H. Walpole's entire correspondence—letters to him as well as from him. As this is much too big a job for one person I have taken it to Yale and got their cooperation . . . . All this is leading up to the request that you let me have photostats made of your H.W. MSS. I particularly want the letters but should like the Memoirs too . . ."

When Geoffrey's uncle, the 9th Earl Waldegrave, died in 1930, the Priory and other family holdings in Chewton Mendip passed into Geoffrey's hands. Geoffrey's cousin, the 10th Earl, and his father, the 11th Earl, were excluded from the property to save death duties. Therefore, it was at this critical time, when the family was preparing to move to Oddgest, near the Priory, and Geoffrey was taking on the management of an inherited estate, that Lewis's letter arrived. Lewis was anxious to photostat the letters. But the prospect of two men in the Priory, one clicking cameras, the other turning the estimated twenty-four hundred pages of letters, was unacceptable. Geoffrey, with Rosemond in excited agreement, would permit the Walpole letters to be transcribed, but only if Rosemond was employed to do the work. Lewis did not like the idea, but could see that Geoffrey was obstinate about photography and agreed to this as second best.

On August 3 Rosemond wrote that she spent an "excited A.M. doing Waldegrave Walpoliana —at which I am startled & respectful!" The next day she and Geoffrey composed a letter to Lewis requesting that Rosemond be hired to transcribe the Walpole–Mann [Sir Horace Mann, 1701–1786, British envoy at the court of Tuscany] letters. Rosemond wrote in her diary: "Geoffrey wrote the letter to W. S. Lewis in the evening, *re* the Walpole job—a stunning letter, me hanging over the sofa-back and helping sentence by sentence. *(if* W.S.L. knew, *quoi?)* Darling Geoffrey."

Then: "Tuesday [August 15]: *Chewton Mendip.* Off after tea & biscuits, at 7.30, in the Morris major. Hog's Back, lovely morning sky . . . the long lovely stretch over Salisbury Plain, with one pale coral house, & a lovely lovely sky with rafts of light & drifts of green & paleness. *Stonehenge.*"

Mary Waldegrave recalled one such trip over Salisbury Plain. "Ros was, I think, very highly strung and easily upset emotionally by widely diverse stimulants. I remember once when we came over the road in Willshire which gives a first, rather dramatic view of Stonehenge, Ros was quite overcome and had to be restored by taking some of the several pills she always carried with her in quantities— and a similar alarm once took place on seeing a very minute caterpillar in a dish of raspberries!"

Rosemond's diary continues: "Wednesday, August 16: Brown's Hotel—Geoff 1st—I walked around Bond St., & into the Redfern Gallery. . . . Then to Lewis's drawing room—big exciting talk—from the H More letter to the books, the Cole marginalia; he takes me on!! Geoffrey darts me triumphs.

"Friday, August 18: Saw Mr. Lewis in the B.M.—all settled: $1500 & travelling & photostat etc. expenses, when I close up the collections!! The Chute portfolio excited him. Zip! Cancel passage, write Mother ... Somerset & London next year!! When I got home Re met me w. a letter from Hilda Bennett—she'd found in the gun room bureau 5 letters from "Maria" to H W & "lots"! from Eliz Laura to HW.

And so the fateful decision was made that Rosemond would rent a room in a farmhouse near the Priory and begin her work for Lewis in October.

Much later, in an article in *The Book Collector,* Mary Waldegrave recalled this venture. For brevity, she refers to herself as M.H.W.: "At Somerville M.H.W. [Mary] had made friends with an interesting and rather overwhelming American then reading a B.Litt. A very large lady, much fly-away untidy hair, curious clothes, an incessant smoker and a good deal of a hypochondriac. But a true scholar, her speciality being Spenser–Milton studies, but the width and depth and detail of her knowledge in almost every field was shaming to lesser types, and her subsequent very distinguished career proved that she was of the first water scholastically."

She went on: "When she left Oxford she longed to stay further in England, but had to earn a living somehow. When this 'transcription' idea was mooted at Chewton, the plan was formed that this lady should be lodged near the Priory and that Lefty should employ her to transcribe the Mann letters. He didn't much like the idea, but could see that we were, for the moment anyway, obstinate about photography and agreed to this as second best. It was supposed to take the lady about one year, and installments of her work were to be sent to Farmington as completed. Unfortunately it soon became plain that correct transcription was totally beyond her powers, and that she had an uncanny knack of making typescript illegible."

The article continues: "Just as this was becoming painfully evident she took a fall from her bicycle and was brought to our house with a fractured skull. Recovery was slow and convalescence long. Lefty was incensed by the whole thing. The scholastic lady was not his type in any way, and inaccuracies and illegibilities had no place in the team working for the Yale Edition; his remarks were sarcastic and the whole matter came to a rather distressing end. By 1935 Lefty had forgiven us and wrote from Brown's Hotel in July 1935 where he had arrived on another Walpole reconnaissance:

"'I left our librarian in the Yale library happily returned to her old love Edmund Spenser. When I came to try and decipher those piles of strangely typed tissue paper I found it was all but hopeless. Heaven alone knows, I fear, what they are all about. Enormous industry, good-will and confusion . . . what a woman!'"[16]

And finally, Rosemond's diary for October 9 has one line: "Began work!"

Rosemond often wrote in her diary several days after the events she recorded, and her diary is blank from December 3 until December 9. Then, in her nurse's handwriting the events of that day and the fall from her bike are recorded: "Evidently fell off my bike about 7 p.m. opposite church—seem to have been taken to P.S. [post office] by Rectory garden boy & propped in chair! Whence rescued by Geoff & Re. Remember nothing except Dr. Charles trying to get patella reflex out of me. Quantities of H W Bottles & not being allowed to blow my nose." Three days later Dr. De Widgery, a specialist, is called in, and on December 20, Rosemond is "shattered" when "Widge" tells her it will be six months before she is able to go back to work. But, she notes, "considering the weakness of the intellectual work involved expect it will shrink."

A letter to Eleanor Lincoln started on April 11, 1934, and mailed on May 12 relates her adventures for the next four months:

Chewton Priory, near Bath—
A thing *will* get dirty if you
carry it around from 11 April
until 12 May, finishing its sentences!

Dear Eleanor—

That was a great stunt I did just before Christmas—knocked a stone wall to pieces, & fractured my wretched skull, & forced my poor Waldegraves out of enough of their bedrooms to house me & my nurse in an already full house, and there I lay like a great Lumpe, everybody expecting me to have a meningitis or a paralysis or lose one eye any minute. But I didn't; I recovered like anything, & was read Horace Walpole to with great charity by the entire family, and then went ineffective, is how that ought to end. Because look at the date it is now! I suddenly got an even *more* tremendous conscience than I had had, about work, & the last month have worked every working hour. Except those like between early-tea-&-bath, which I had consecrated to the *Nation,* & one hour's bicycling to any near village-with-a-church, or up-on-the-Mendips to see the gorse-coming-out-of-the-red-earth.

She continued:

You know the tight feeling, of before an exam or something, when you feel that life must be reduced to 1) work 2) food & 3) exercise. I usually get rid of the tension with a week's hard slavery, but this time I feel so very much the hot breath of time's chariot on my heels (should have said cooling my heels, shouldn't I) that I get as wound up as a permanent gramaphone. I shall chuck that time-saving notion though, because it ain't my nature & only causes me to make an interior psychological novel out of the minutiae of daily existence—the world's easiest transmutation, in a country house, where there are so few exterior events except those you spin out of yourself. I now perceive why Henry James went Jamesian. I only wonder why Jane Austen didn't go Joyce, long before the astronomical clocks were set for it. Probably this seems obscure? It's not really. It's an observation on The Village in English Literature; & translated, means—that if I didn't take a weekend in Bath & Bristol occasionally, I should concoct so many novels out of why X said Z to Y in a Q-ish tone at the tea table, that I shouldn't be able to *see* Walpole.... How I do go on!

She went on:

But these are the make up of my social existence, my professional one consists of digging out the Waldegrave-Walpole letters from boxes & tin-uniform-cases, & leather-dispatch-bags, & editing them for the new Yale edition; & of doing the text of the letters to Mann, which sit here in the "Walpole cupboard", in a charming state of confusion with family archives, charters & accounts & manorial-court-rolls from Richard II up to the land-enclosure-act, & a few oddments such as a

Johnson letter, a Maria Edgeworth one, lots of Hannah More stuff, & some 30 boxes of unedited early xviii century diplomatic correspondence belonging to the Waldegrave who was ambassador to France then. I shan't embark on a narrative of how I went to Vienna to "rest" after the accident, & ran into martial law & barbed-wire-barricades.

What are you doing next year??? Isn't it fun studying again? I miss teaching though—after two years, & want to get back to it. Also I'm perishing to sneak up on the Second American Revolution; *what's* it really like, living in it? Do write me some social-economic comments! (The only social-economy I know now is British Farming & Estate Management.) What's this about Boswell? Are you going to Write On Him? Or on something else? Do tell me, if there's a thesis blowing about your handsome head. Oh dear I've not seen a picture since March. Except a lot of Romneys & Gainsboroughs etc. here in the house, that is.

But *do* write & tell me about 1) new poetry 2) the great American novel 3) your PhD plans 4) where you'll be in September when I expect to come home—I *hope* with a job. Are you having one? Meanwhile love to you & for God's sake don't reveal to anyone the illegibility & inconsequentiality of this letter. My love to you, you lovely old goose. R.

Rosemond made no mention in her letter to Eleanor of her plans for a job next fall. Perhaps she felt that they were too tentative to discuss. In her diary on Sunday, March 19, she casually mentions a letter she had written to Dr. Carleton Brown: "Sun & clouds, March wind magnifique, but cold—walked around garden, in to bkfst. with Mary. Wrote Dr. Brown—to Church—lovely hill & field & a white-gray tower."

The reason for writing Dr. Brown, her former mentor at Bryn Mawr, is revealed in a letter written to Dr. Edwin Wells on March 27, 1934. Dr. Wells was then chairman of the English department at Connecticut College in New London:

Dr. Carleton Brown, under whom I worked at Bryn

Mawr, has written me that you may possibly have an opening
in your department for the coming year. . . . I want very much
to re-enter the teaching field. If you are interested, would you
be willing to ask the Bryn Mawr Bureau of Recommendations
to send you the letters (from heads of departments, professors, etc.) and other information which they have on file concerning me? I do not ask them to send it you directly because
I should not like having you bombarded with these materials
without your consent. I must unfortunately stay on here in
England where my MSS. are, until September, which means
that except for the possibility of there being someone (now or
later) working at the British Museum who might see me for
you, there is no way of accomplishing a personal interview. I
can of course give you other references than those on file at
Bryn Mawr, if you wish.

I should be very happy to hear from you. I know only
from Dr. Brown that you will probably have a position to fill,
and I am anxious to teach again.[17]

A flurry of transatlantic letters followed. To Wilmarth Lewis's
credit, he withheld any personal irritation with Rosemond and on
April 29 wrote from Brown's Hotel to Dr. Wells:

"Professor Carleton Brown has written me a letter, which has
only just reached me here in London, about the possibility of Miss
Rosemond Tuve going to you next year. I have just cabled you,
'Recommend Rosemond Tuve highly, Writing.'"

"I can understand your not wishing to accept anyone unless you
have seen them personally, but I think you would make no mistake in
taking her . . . (I think she has used judgment & intelligence, great
modesty & enthusiasm.) She is uncommonly anxious to please & conscientious and would make, I feel sure, a very 'easy' member of your
faculty.

Her work for me would normally have ended about the middle of
August. She lost two & a half months by an accident, from which she
seems entirely recovered, but I can arrange for her to make this up
next summer, & would do anything within reason to facilitate her

going to you. For your own information, I am paying her $1500. for a year's work."

What he mercifully did not say was that Rosemond lacked the patience for accurate transcription, and in the end infuriated him. Later, to the Waldegraves, he referred to her sarcastically as the "only person I ever knew who could type illegibly."

Stevens College in Missouri was also interested in Rosemond. Again Rose Jeffries Peebles, Rosemond's former department head at Vassar, supported her:

"Her positive assets are that she has the keenest desire for knowledge in its full and broad sense. She is insatiable in research; she finds the opening up exciting. Moreover, she has what so many people who set out to teach English literature are not provided with—a genuine liking for literature. Her room was always supplied with new poetry, not because she thought it was her duty to keep up with trends, but because of her sheer delight in reading.

"She is in addition interested in art and music. I went to some exhibitions in London with her and was always interested in her account of what she saw in New York. Many of her students got a zest for poetry and art from contact with her. She has courage and persistence. Part of her failure to meet the ideal of teaching here, I think, was due to the fact that she did not accept it altogether.

"I hope all this will enable you to get my sense of this rich and various and as yet not wholly developed personality. I may be wrong but I think in a few more years she will be a very valuable person indeed."[18]

In another letter, to Marian P. Whitney, formerly chairman of the German department at Vassar and now a member of the board of trustees at Connecticut College, Miss Peebles gave the same high praise, if a bit more cautionary:

"It has occurred to me that perhaps you might be interested in taking a chance with Rosemond. Your demand for spirit and verve and delight in living turned my mind to her. . . . She has all these qualities and makes use of them. When I was in England last year I met some of the friends she had met during her year of study at Oxford. I was surprised to see how they have taken her in, what a strong connection there was, and I liked the people. She is now, as you may have heard, with one of these friends near Bath. . . . One more thing about her here: the students liked her. They went to her apartment and took her out to talk about modern poetry, etc."

Here Miss Peebles faltered: "I do not mean to say in all this that there is not a little risk. I don't know whether she will ever make a great teacher. While here she had not entirely broken away from a stricter method of Minnesota to the less formal at Vassar; but I suspect she learned a great deal while here about adapting her work to individual students. She certainly practiced such adaptation in her work at the Bryn Mawr Summer School. I saw her too, I may add, with a young Russian who had been at the Bryn Mawr Summer School, and she made me think of Miss Wylie so simple was her contact with this knitter of sweaters, who was a most interesting girl. Under Rosemond's hand she told us all about her family's flight from Russia. . . . I am giving you all these examples of human contact to show that I believe she really makes them up and down the social scale with no difference that I can see."[19]

On May 6, Katharine Blunt, then president of Connecticut College, wrote to Rosemond offering her the position of instructor in English, at a salary of $2,000, with the chance for early promotion. There was further correspondence until May 15, when Miss Blunt received a telegram from Rosemond containing a single word: "Accepted." Then on June 4, a final letter was posted from England: "I am delighted that you decided to let me come unseen, & shall do my best to prevent its redounding in an unfortunate way upon the friends who have taken responsibility for me!"[20]

There were still three months left for Rosemond to try to finish her work for Lewis. Her days were spent editing the Mann letters, or other Walpole correspondence, always relieved by a bicycle ride.

As August approached Rosemond's life became more frantic and emotionally charged. When the Waldegrave family went away for a few days she was left alone: "morose, wep' over the photograf album." She spent a final weekend with Jan Watson at her parents' home near the North Sea, followed by two final days in London with Rachel. "Too much to do. Selfridge's ice cream then *Lady Strachie: et* mon Dieu! In a hat, & black crooked mouth, & burst of friendly rigamarole." After a long conversation about her Walpole connections, but no pictures or other memorablia, Lady Strachie merely "presented" her "with creme de menthe, after tea on checked cloth from *pub* teapot! Then dinner with Miss Peebles!" On her second day in London she "worked like hell" at the British Museum, and had lunch with Mary Parmenter, who had come to London at Rosemond's urging. After a final dinner at Bertorelli's, they went to see *Man of Aran*. Rosemond erupted at the end of this page of her diary with "oh *Ireland,* thank God! still to come!"

On August 15 she made a final visit to the Tate: "my lovely 2 Cezanne's . . . the delicious Manet café." The next day she "Worked too damn hard—merry bkfst—even made Geoff laugh—at 10 A.M.! I packed & sorted—got into a muz over the wretched tea basket forgotten on the slab. I went to evensong —with Ld. W. & grand'mère & Gay—a nervous, *ill* man with a piercing quivering voice rent your spirits." Her final day with the Waldegraves was too busy for her to give way to sentimentality. She "finished packing. Geoff came in and insisted on giving me the 2 Hokusai's—a 'permanent loan'. Mary in after lunch just to be nice. Sally darling, walked about & looked at the heavenly tower in the sun—oh *dear.* Last walk up the Folly. All of both families to tea—Geoff buzzed around w. luggage tags, & he & Re took me to Stapleton Road—& bought me cigs. & magazines & papers & all as should be. So goodbye."

Rosemond left England on an Irish boat to Cork, then to Glengariff, "—*mountains!* in flowers, lovelier & lovelier, dramatic blues & bright white cottages. Arr. 3.15, walked & sat by bay, looked at Island, had tea, walked thru glen, towards Kenmore—*lovely* place. To Bantry: *golly* the mts.—magnificent color—sunset after I got there, melting the harbour into colour—strange empty 2 streets up a hill. *Harbour View,* McCarthy's 4/ b.b. & tea & fire 6d—*comfort!* hot water! read & wrote a card. Bed."

At eight in the morning she returned to Cork to meet Mig Couser and say final good-byes to Helen Roe and her mother. "Saw sunset from Bala, & supper at Enda's Hotel." The next morning she was "off on tender at 9.—boarded Milwaukee in Galway Bay, & off to America."

With a flourish of wavy marks on the last page, she ended her diary. To read of her final hours in Ireland, it is clear that her emotions were overflowing. Everything she did, and her manner of expressing it, exposed the inner workings of her mind. The strange hypnotic effect of the diaries is hard to leave. There is an ebb and flow to her life, a rhythm that enfolds us. Her evocation of beauty mesmerizes and transports us to her world of transcendence. Each day is woven into a consistent pattern, which gives her the freedom to express herself in both work and play. Her extraordinary intellect and intense work habits alternate, like yin and yang, with recklessly riding her bicycle while immersed in the beauty of nature. Each heightens the awareness of the other, and she seems to reach another level of consciousness.

~ 5 ~

W HEN ROSEMOND TUVE arrived in New London, Connecticut, in September 1934, she was two months short of her thirty-first birthday, and precisely at the midpoint of her life. All of her early years had been preparation, intellectually and emotionally, for the second half of her life. Except for the hiatus of the previous year, when the sentimentality she scorned had diluted her judgment, and she had succumbed to her love for England and her infatuation with Geoffrey Waldegrave, her life had been focused. Now she had found a home, a haven after peripatetic years, a space to grow and flourish.

To be hired sight unseen was surely an academic first, and she more than vindicated her supporters. Despite the fact that she remained controversial in her struggle for recognition by the college, Miss Peebles's predictions proved prophetic. Her twenty-nine years at Connecticut College, the same number of years her father had been associated with Augustana College, witnessed her rise to become the "foremost Renaissance scholar of her time" and a teacher of "extraordinary powers." Never forgetting what her ancestors had taught her, that "each man's mind and spirit was the measure of his excellence," her life would read like an allegory of this knowledge.

After first finding an apartment, she was greeted as she was returning home from buying a teapot by one of her new colleagues in the English Department, Catherine Oakes. Several days later, she wrote to Geoffrey and Mary:

> Dear old Samson and Delilah, I have just romped through my first two lectures, & that is always to give one a charming sense of exhilaration. Which even when falsely acquired does

great good to those as has it. . . . This is a *very* beautiful place. The ocean is excessively ocean, none of your mere second-hand glimpses by way of seeing an occasional mast, or a wharf with bales professedly going to far places & no visible opportunity, but fifteen minutes to ride to the open sea, from where I live. I'm in the town itself, about 20 minutes fast walking, up-hill, to college; this arrangement makes for a Robust Private Life as cf. living "just off campus" & being restrained from inelegance or indiscretion by the imminent eyes of your students and colleagues. Of which the latter are far more likely to pay attention to your inelegancies & talk over your indiscretions.

As to the College, there it sits on a range of hills with the so-called Thames rolling along beside it, three quarters of a mile wide, very noble moving sight, with just enough craft going up it to look well, and a bridge that heaves up and lets them pass, and not an industry in sight—only another range of hills across the river with fruit and maize farms climbing up it, and white clapboarded houses set in elm trees & pricked out in a pattern of white fences.

This is what I see out of my lecture room & office windows, and whenever one crosses over to the library or walks up from home to college one sees the open sea with the river emptying into it, all sun & blue clouds by day & lighthouses and foghorns by night. I am gibbering in an attempt to grasp the alphabetical rearrangement of America; it's a FERA or a PDQ everywhere you turn. No one says anything but good of Roosevelt, despite the way he keeps saying how no one shall starve in America this winter & everyone knows that the answer to that is like hell they won't. But the talk is all anti-employer, not anti-NRA, so far as I've yet picked it up. Mostly I am plumb ignorant as yet, I've been too busy catching me a place to live and being fed lobsters & clam chowder by such other members of the faculty as think that alas they can't simply call & have it done with but had better Ask You to Something.

I have got me a funny little apartment & anglice-flat, full
as I told you it would be of compact and ingenious devices;
but alas for incinerators and having the telephone-operator
downstairs wake you, as I suspected New London has only
one proper apartment-house & all but the 7-room apts. had
been taken by the wretched Navy-&-its-wives-&-child-&-
dog, which seems to winter in New London apropos of a sub-
marine-base up the river and a Coast Guard Academy down
it. So I was distracted for a while but am now reconciled to
the lack of an elevator & finding the milk & the N.Y. *Times* in
the dumb-waiter upon arising, by the fact that have gone
modern & had a carpenter fill my sitting room with cream
colored shelves, and great box-like couch-ends with shelves
on the inside for cigarettes & on the outside for books, so that
I've a great giant of a square, formal, linen-covered, cream
colored, horizontal monster of a couch, under my two pictures hung against a shantung-curtain, and a great rustcol-
ored box-armchair, and nothing else much. And what with
having to dispose of everything non-horizontal in the other
rooms, I rattle around from century to century whenever I
open a door; but at least I can do my sitting in the calm and
spacious repose of the twentieth. Sic.

New York is unimaginably lovely; I kept falling out of
buses with amazements. DO come to Newfoundland. And if
you do, I want to take your the first walk up Fifth Avenue....
Does Jinny begin to creep? [Mary had given birth to her second daughter.] Bless you all. R

Rosemond was teaching two sections of freshman composition,
and a seminar for upperclassmen devoted to Renaissance and seventeenth-century literature. One remarkable fact about her years at
Connecticut College is that she never gave up teaching the freshmen.
It gave her special pleasure. Almost twenty years later she would write
to her brothers: "Our Freshmen are all around and I meet my own in
a day or so; it is a very endearing stage, and one of the most valuable
moments of the 4 yrs."[1]

Connecticut College, whose first graduating class was in 1919, was still in its infancy. This might excuse an unfortunate dramatic performance that occurred shortly after Rosemond's arrival. In celebration of the initiation of the amphitheater in the Arboretum, with the lake in the background, Milton's masque, *Comus,* was produced with period dancing by the students. Years later Catherine Oakes, who had invited Rosemond to join her, recalled the performance:

"It was probably fitting that a scholar of the seventeenth century and a lover of John Milton's poetry should arrive at CC just as the college was planning to celebrate the 300th anniversary of the Ludlow presentation of COMUS. It was unfortunate, however, that she came too late to offer suggestions and/or advice concerning the festivity which took the form, (I shudder as I think of it) of an evening performance of the masque, in the Arboretum. At that early period of the college history few students had read more of Milton than the minor poems, and no faculty member was an authority in directing and presenting this special work. Vividly I remember the lamentable failure, dimly viewed through a September fog rising from the lake and thoroughly chilling the spirits of actors and audience."

She went on: "Rosemond Tuve, sharing my steamer rug, was courteously silent throughout, though I cannot forget a sharp "Oh!" of disbelief? anguish? despair? when a rabble appeared clad in (of all garb!) ALICE IN WONDERLAND costumes which apparently someone had decided "would do" for the nonce. Comus himself was followed on stage by several stray dogs who pursued their own activities as the masque continued. That this same actor did not know his lines and had frequent recourse to flashlight and palmed script was only a further instance of anachronism during that unhappy evening."

"R.T. never referred to it again as far as I know; and I am glad that I could not read her thoughts."

Of course this was written in retrospect. Catherine Oakes was not only seeking to befriend Rosemond, but she also respected her scholarly credentials; however, Rosemond's "inelegancies" and "indiscretions" hardly blended with Catherine's formalities and reserve and they were never close friends.

As soon as she was able, Rosemond was off to visit Eleanor

Lincoln, who had left Vassar to accept a teaching position at Smith College, in Northampton, Massachusetts. Her tenure there would last for thirty-four years. From the following letter it appears that Eleanor had moved some of her friend's belongings from Vassar, or perhaps from the railroad station in Poughkeepsie, to the railroad station in Northampton.

Dearest Eleanor,   [December 1934?]

Well I had the *grandest* time. I loved Every Minute, as they say, Of It. And I thought it so *stupendously* gracious of you to put my things in hock for me. There they were, & not a whimper (or even a Bang—I've just been re reading T.S.E. [T. S. Eliot] from the R.R. Co.

Busy as hell, aren't you? Where do you go Christmas? I leave Friday for Baltimore And Pts. South. Will you be at Swarthmore? DO BE. Because I'll see you there if you are. WON'T I? Or will you throw me down for your Big Bostoners? I am agog over worker's evening classes & want to teach some again. Went to Providence Saturday to a conference, & came back A-Gog. I am one of your prime Agoggers I guess. Susceptible.

Do you know the *Waste Land* is harder than ever? Let's read it again next time we meet, hey. And see if life has taught us to understand. Since the last time.

This is just a note to say I think you are a Grand One, just as before. And that I was never treated nobler. And that I heard a Bach Chaconne & the Bruch concerto through your efforts & kindness. And that I owe you about 50¢ or something.

And love
        from
            Rozzy

say. If I should go early to New Haven, say 2nd to 5th Jan.—where could a girl sleep cheap? Could you suggest anything? Post card here will follow.

Because Eleanor Lincoln often traveled from Northampton to

New Haven, where she was pursuing her Ph.D. in eighteenth-century literature at Yale and working on her thesis on James Boswell, Rosemond assumed she might know of places to stay in New Haven. Like Rosemond, Eleanor later shifted her field of concentration to seventeenth-century literature, giving the two friends another valuable connection.

Despite her obvious delight in her new position and the pleasure she found in the beauty around her, in March Rosemond wrote to Katharine Blunt, the president of the college, that she would be leaving. She now had a combined total of six years as an instructor (two years at Goucher and three at Vassar) and felt she deserved the promotion to assistant professor that had been suggested in her contract. It was not granted. When the chairman of the Trustees Committee on Education wrote to her, urging her to stay, she acquiesced. Although she received a two-hundred dollar increase over her starting salary, it was not the reward she was seeking. It would come the following year. This was just the beginning of her struggle for recognition of her value to the college.

By June, her spirits rebounded, and she was planning to spend part of the summer in New Haven, working in the Yale Library (where Wilmarth Lewis last saw his "librarian") in order to complete her contract with Lewis and continue her own research. Before leaving she wrote to Eleanor.

[June 1935]

Dearest Eleanor—I expect you've gone home to Fergus Falls. But I shall write you a note to Smith anyhow, now that the great Fair & Market is over, & we've packed off the all-set-to-be-married young ladies with their B.A's, & set ourselves to the serious work of the summer. We commenced yesterday, in a tent, having no auditorium as yet, & in good God what a wind. And had the ass't. sec'y of the Treasury being a lady, to speak to us, & she talked unionization of the bituminous coal industry, & I sat & hugged my Bryn-Mawr-Summer-School pink tendencies & watched some of the parents & trustees go gray.

Rosemond's first semester of her second year at Connecticut College had been crowded with a seemingly infinite variety of activities, as her next letter to Eleanor describes.

Dear Eleanor—   1/24/36

The silence is I admit that of a Pig. On the other hand, I have felt at times, that of a Robot. It's on account of how I've just worked like *hell* this year. The extra course is just one too much, added to all the others as before; yet it's been so much fun (the Spenser to Milton one I mean particularly) that I wouldn't have not had it for anything. But it has chopped off all my extra curricular activities such as letters & Serving Tea to Friends, & riding about viewing country. To a great extent, anyhow. Shall probably catch up *sometime*. I try stoutly to refuse giving up some non-utilitarian reading at least, though I'm so behind on me labor news that I feel like a member of the Liberty League. Also try to have one 3 hour session per week on what they call My Own Work—now almost indistinguishable from my advanced-course work, so that it's a naughty shame that I can't get to more of it—from the teaching point of view. But nevertheless, a good life.

Full of beans on acct. of a modern-dance symposium last night, just a few of the girls & a person teaching here who's worked with Martha Graham, Weidman & Humphreys. Came away busting with new notions about The Arts, & you know those are my pet notions. Also doing Oratorio Society this year, & just sang Haydn's *Creation.* Also a discussion group on labor unions with industrial girls from downtown & students here, which sets me off. Especially when doing the Modern Drammer with my Freshmen, & converting (yet *trying* not to Endoctrinate!) a bunch of little conservatives to some *semi*-openmindedness at least.

Hey Eleanor. I do want to see you. I'm in a larger, nicer apartment, room for you And Friend. . . . I should dote upon a conversation—especially, do you like Eliot's play about Becket? How do you feel about Winterset? Etcetera. Drop me a card if there's a chance of seeing you & try to MAKE one if you can see your way to it (*and* would like it; I *should*).

Love to you—Ros

When Rosemond had considered leaving Connecticut College in the spring of 1935, she was flirting with the idea of going to Duke University. It is probable that several friends there influenced her decision to spend two weeks at Duke in the summer of 1936. A letter to Eleanor describes her experience:

[July 22, 1936]   Mrs. Wm Quynn
                          Box 261 College Station
                          Durham, N.C.
                          Thursday Wednesday
                          [Thursday was crossed out]

Dear Eleanor,

. . . So now I've come down to Duke to foregather and work for a fortnight and indeed it's a fine place for the former, but there aren't any books in the library except maybe the complete works of Scott and DeQuincey. I'm going to let the book-work go and do some organizing and writing. The house is full of interesting people: Dorothy & Bill Quynn are Mediaeval history & French, and full of wits. And Merritt Hughes from California (Spenser & Virgil: a good scholar, & quite brilliant to talk to) is here with his Scotch wife, & they are exceeding great fun. So we have fine conversation, & the whole house buzzes with combined & separate activities. How is Bozzy? Bless the boy.

Rosemond also wrote from Duke to Mary Waldegrave, but only a fragment of the letter remains:

Conversation on the Highest Plane Possible; when not Spinoza substitute Francis Bacon. Very finest life and I get some whacks in at writing in the mornings. Everybody is very gay & amusing.

I'm still having a good time at Connecticut, & the world

goes prosperously, little brother married to Non Descript Nice Girl, alas; Merle more spectacular than ever & bursting out unexpectedly on whole pages of the N.Y. Times.

At the end of the summer, Rosemond wrote Eleanor that she was "finishing up 1st drafts of 2 practiclly-writ artikels of indifferent value." It is likely that the two articles are "Spring in Chaucer and before Him" and "Spenser and Mediaeval Mazers." The first of these essays was written to correct an article by J. F. Hankin, in which he attributed Chaucer's source for his description of spring to Virgil. Rosemond's thesis and first book, *Seasons and Months,* had elaborated in depth on the myriad sources from classical and romance literature and medieval illuminated manuscripts for Chaucer's images of spring. She contends that the "Prologue as well as Chaucer's other references to the season, spring from a complicated tradition of seasons-description in Latin, French, and Middle English, and from no single 'source.'"[2] She concludes her article with a variation on a theme that would course through many essays: "And, as always when a great poet makes use of what has gone before him instead of 'inventing,' the result is as different from what had gone before as spring from winter. His sources and models were innumerable; what he makes of them is new and his own."[3]

In "Spenser and Mediaeval Mazers" she wrote again to correct an assertion in an article by C. H. Herford as to *what* mazer Spenser had in mind when he wrote the August eclogue of the *Shepheardes Calender.* Spenser's sources, she argues, are not only from classical descriptions such as Virgil's, but also from actual English mazer bowls he undoubtedly saw. Rosemond, as we know, had spent hours in the Victoria and Albert Museum studying these bowls. It is an example, she continues, of how "Spenser's imaginative use of suggestions from other than literary materials, and the process by which Spenser anglicized his poetic material," led to his own imagery.[4]

Also in 1936, the article she had finished on a trip to Ireland just before she started work on Walpole for Lefty Lewis was published in *Studies in Philology,* under the title, "Spenser's Readings: The De Claris Mulieribus." She establishes her thesis from the notes, readings, and illustrations she has so painstakingly studied, as noted in her diaries, continually searching for evidence of what Spenser read and how he used his learning. She writes, "This article will deal with a small but fairly simple and clear example of the relationship between Spenser and Boccaccio: with what traces there are of Spenser's having read the *De claris mulieribus*, with the question of which form (and in fact which edition) he read it in. . . .It has importance not as a study of Spenser's borrowings, but as an attempt to see what part was played by mediaeval tradition of this kind in building a background for Spenser's almost symbolic use of certain story-figures and motifs."[5] Myth and symbol, and how they were used to point to truths that were otherwise unsayable, were her abiding interest. This explains her fascination with figures in stained- glass windows and illuminated manuscripts.

Rosemond remained deeply concerned with the plight of workers and their education. This interest led to her early involvement with the Industrial Committee of the New London Y.W.C.A. The following year, on Monday, March 8, 1937, her picture appeared in the New London newspaper *The Day*, with the caption that she was attending the Southern New England Industrial Conference under the auspices of the Y.W.C.A. She was now chairman of the local group. In a letter to Eleanor in October 1936 she writes briefly of her activities. Only the second page exists.

> cf. literature is a Y. W. Industrial Committee I'm chairman of—
>
> I'm waggling about now wondering how Advanced a propaganda play I dare read in the next discussion group— esp. since a Navy man's wife is on my Committee. I don't want no traffic with the Defense League. Do you belong to the Teacher's Union? I'd a rip roaring good time talking with Helen Lockwood at U.C. [University of Connecticut], had had the TU in mind for here but too dangerous to start, & discover even the daring UC people only bold enough to belong as Members At Large.

In May 1937, she wrote again to Mary Waldegrave:

> Connecticut College, as ever was Spring
> and such a spring as you can't imagine
> Acct. you creep up on yours; we burst
> out of ice into flowers

Dearest Mary,

I hope the coronation isn't hitting Somerset [the coronation on May 12 of George VI]. I shouldn't be writing a letter, I should be writing a lecture on the scrap between the Ancients & Moderns & what a Bad Idea the xvii. century had when they had the Idea of Progress. But yesterday the usual weekend bicycle-trip fever caught me & I lope off on my bicycle with two books & a nightgown, & it was such an English cloudy-misty-blue day, & I ambled through such pastoral green landskips, that I could have believed I was in Somerset again, if only a parish church or so had hove in view. So I had to write you. I don't ordinarily miss the p. churches, because the sea keeps dipping in & being very handsome & incredible, and also chiefly because do you know what has happened, I have become so *amused* at the peculiar kind of gingerbread they thought was nice for houses around here, & the way it takes the seaside sunlight, being brilliantly white and wildly ingenious in pattern, that I have gone practically Baroque. Isn't that a downfall. I even take the gothic Revival, the New England form of which galloped off into ornament of the most recklessly abandoned nature, with roars of laughter. I dote upon this section of the country. All the bad things are amusing, & the good ones very lovely. I love living where I seldom see anything I can't either laugh at or think is handsome.

Dear me, what a girl for digressions. Perhaps when I arrive at that state of financial maturity which means a car instead of a bicycle I'll learn to keep to the Point, Get Somewhere, Write Sensibly, and otherwise & similarly Fit into our Generation. Mary must all your young poets write weak communistic jingles like Mr. W.H. Auden's to fit into their generation. I've tried handsomely to skip along after Stephen Spender & es. [especially] (just out of respect to Joy Scovill, who you remember was in love with him—did you go with us to what I thought a perfectly 1890 ish Aesthetic Tea at Univ. black short jackets & the curtains drawn & candles, in broad daylight? I'd been in England 3 weeks, I remember, & said to myself "The English are very Immature") But I can't find myself moved by Auden & Spender, I really can't And you've gone & let V. Woolf get a little fuzzy too, I think.

I have lep out of my i. tower into Workers' Education in a big way—that's not so big except that I'm in a high state of exhilaration with having just succeeded in sending off two textile workers to a workers' school, and getting one of our undergrads accepted as an assistant . . . For the which she will come back at least a Socialist, & that will mean her life will be full of Conflictks for her father is a Republic Steel big-boy. So that's good for her. But me I am wore down with making speeches & managing benefit concerts, & am going to retire into academic leisure till college is over. Query what & where is academic leisure. American Colleges have lost touch with the sheltered life. Maybe I will skip over this summer. Time I tended to Spenser a little, & sat quietly in the British Museum and thought a few thoughts. . . . If I come I'll probably sail about 19th June, & stay in France & England for some six weeks . . .

The trip to England hinted at in her letter to Mary is confirmed in this letter to Eleanor:

[5/37]   Home

Dearest Eleanor,   Sunday

I'm really alarmed at how my ideas about how much work I ought to do have changed the last two years. I am perfectly reckless about Soshul Engagements. You know I never would agree to more than two hrs. at a time; I've got so I go off in Cars and Dont Come Back. This is how it is when you

realize that your mind is not so elastic as it was and you got
to rest the poor thing some. I could never do work just for the
Perfessional Reasons, and damned if I am going to start; so if
I feel Unable to Cope, I just dont cope.

Have really had too much teaching these years; am going
to rest myself in England. That's prob. just brag; when I smell
the Bodleian I shant be able to resist sitting in it just as long
hours as ever. I sail 19 June, Europa.

In July she wrote to Eleanor from the Waldegraves':

> 46, Courtfield Gardens S.W. 5
> London—July 10
>
> Dearest Eleanor,
>
> only I'm not really in London at all, am out in
> Somerset and we've just got back from what Geoffrey termed
> an Estate Tour, the great point of which was to determine
> whether or not reforesting 450 acres of Geoff's old bracken-y
> waste landon the new Gov't. scheme which leases it for half a
> crown an acre for 250 years (aren't it a sweetly reliable & sta-
> ble notion of society?) would Destroy the View, & Alter the
> Character of the Mendips! . . .
>
> I go back to London tonight, where I've a flat with Hope
> French, a Geneva-Paris etc. etc. friend of Elizabeth Chapin's,
> who is also here in London. It's all very warming the way peo-
> ple take one back with such open arms—I seem to have seen
> half the people I played with in Oxford, am doing weekends
> with some and Paris with one, and altogether a delectable
> summer, and only too full of Amenities, from the work point
> of view. Never mind, am 33 already, girl got to see her friends,
> can't fill All Life with what's in the British Museum, can do
> some of that when 34, I've no doubt. That's how I'm getting.
> Lax. Aint it awful. But I had to go see Penshurst, who would-
> n't? Had to go visit with my yearls and countesses, werry edu-
> cational, wot the hell. Have to go to Dorset, don't I? sure do,
> Hardy. Write a girl a p.c., Eleanor dear, why not? I sail home
> 20th August—oh dear me. But I shall look forward to a great

gabble with you in the fall—best summer luck, & my best to anyone I know there, & my love to you, angel, don't melt, I 'm wearing 3 thicknesses of wool [Here she draws her trademark smiley face.]

  Ros

Apparently, Rosemond reentered the confined world of Connecticut College with ease, and made good on a promise she had made earlier to bring Jan Watson, a good friend from Somerville College, and Eleanor, together. In November, she writes:

> [November 1937] Wednesday [crossed out]
>   Tuesday
>   Well who cares anyhow.

Dearest Eleanor,

  Buzzing as usual. Just came back from Eating a Simple Steak with Pres. Blunt, that's what it is to have a tiny college, that great big simple unaffected girl Eliz. Grier just invited the President to dinner same as if she was any other pair of old shoes, & we sat up & et steak fresh from her kitchen & talked & laughed & laughed, & it rested the poor old President considerable.

  She's a *nice* woman Eleanor, next time you come you'd ought to meet her. Jan stayed till last Thursday, so I'm just catching my breath. I did get woeful behind, but yet I'd not have had her shorten it, I dote on the girl. I was disappointed we didn't get more chance all 3 to foregather, you two didn't really see each other, but nevertheless enough so that when you go to England you must get into Jan's motor car & see the coast of Dorset, or be took to Norfolk to sail, & such. She having made large statements, entirely concurrent with my own ideas on subject, of how you were *What* a Nice One. I did want you to Know each other & thus another international friendship. And then there weren't enough space & time. Next time we get our breakfast when hungry, other girls or no other girls.

  It's pretty weather, teaching is noble, & I am full of Beans.

That weekend too damn short, lots more to talk of, needs leisure. . . . Dutch in very fine fettle right now because I'm being good to her because she's got a temperature every afternoon & I hope to God it's not T.B. from the eye. She's going to the doctor. If it is, good God I . . . [The remainder of the letter is missing.]

E. Alverna "Dutch" Burdick began her long career at Connecticut College in 1926 as a member of the Physical Education Department, teaching anatomy, kinesiology, and hygiene. In 1930 she was appointed dean of students, and in 1948 was promoted to dean, a position she held until her retirement in 1958. She was a woman of unusual presence and compassion, with great wit and wisdom. Her warmth and understanding enabled her to become a "mother figure" for many students, and undoubtedly for Rosemond as well. She and Rosemond complemented and learned from each other. While Dutch "deaned" Rosemond, her insatiable desire to learn and understand poetry was a mutual trade-off. They often read and discussed poetry together.

After spending the previous summer in England, Rosemond stayed put for a year. She was, no doubt, completing work on an article entitled "Ancients, Moderns, and Saxons," which was published the following year in the *Journal of English Literary History.* Another article, "Spenser and Some Pictorial Conventions: with Particular Reference to Illuminated Manuscripts," appeared in *Studies in Philology* in April 1940.

Fortunately, she was able to get away for a month, with her mother to the same cottage on Rogers Lake that she had borrowed the year before from Dutch. Dutch and her mother joined them.

This letter followed the hurricane of September 21, 1938.

> Still on Williams St.
> with trees lying all about
>
> Tues night
>
> Dearest Eleanor,
>   Are you Safe I take it you must be since the papers say Smith is. We are. I mean this coll. and all yr. Acquaintance.

I haven't had the heart to ask or inform with all the war
news seeming worse than hurricanes, till God bless Mussolini
as of yesterday, but of course who knows as of tomorrow.
(Prob. as of today, but of course we have no radios; I write
you by candlelight; NL has been in darkness since a wk. yesterday, naturally.) Very natural, considering that the wires lol-
lop across and around Wms. St. and its fallen poles and great
trees lying on the ground and on the roofs of houses. We
havent bothered much with trees that just obstruct houses or
roofs or walks, for the first days it was Noble when you could
get down 2 sts. with a car.

I was at Beatrice's, we didn't know it was so bad, and that
the power plant chimney at college fell, windows blew in and
roofs off, etc. but all hurting no one!!!! till we came out of hid-
ing about 6, to learn this, and that NL was on fire. I couldn't
stop for food, but rushed for home to avoid wires and trees,
before dark. Clambering and retracing. To discover, after 2
hours at home, and the wind still blowing the fire toward me,
and it so light you could read by the window, that I didnt wish
to stay there one bit; so I packed one suitcase of duds and best
books, instructed it to be saved, and beat it for college, about
1 1/2 hours walk with my hat tied on with a string, and slept
at Dutch's. Already a couple of stranded families in her com-
mons room on cheers. Weel we didn't burn, and here we are.

In the spring of 1939, Rosemond was still an assistant professor.
Her salary had increased by only four hundred dollars during the five
years she had served the college. She wrote to Eleanor:

[March 1939]   Sunday
hello beauty,
So you are worrying abt. tenure and prom. too; with us
it's that we are all ashamed to death ever since fac. meeting
last mon. that we teach in a college that has gone and put in a
scheme to work in cahoots with a Htfd. [Hartford] dept.
store, and 6 wks out of their vacs the 10 Students involved will

go up there and sell ribbons. We feel it is a Scheme of that damn Chase Going Woodhouse, wch. I got no respect for (once at Smith, ever hear anythin of her???), wch. is a Promoter pure and simple. Well that subject is too big except by word of mth., Miss Blunt is in a towering bad humour acct. we weren't very nice about it. Also because a few got together and wish to have Winnie Smith (!!!—written to, believe it or not, by yrs. truly, acct we are Friends [at the Bryn Mawr Summer School], by request of the Faculty discussion committee!!) down here to discuss what is the Teachers Union please and why.

Before leaving for England that summer Rosemond wrote to the president about a different living arrangement for the coming year. She was anxious to be closer to campus, where a new boxlike apartment building, housing four units, had just been constructed. It would come to be known as Independence Hall.

Saturday 13 May [1939]

Dear Miss Blunt,

I am much disturbed about the present status of the apartment situation.

I would like to ask you whether or not the selection of Dr. Smyser for the third apartment has been definitively settled. Though Miss Dilley took her action without my knowledge, neither of us feels happy about the arrangement. We feel equal as candidates on grounds of 1) extreme anxiety to make a change and 2) need to do so, in order a) to be near campus b) to have more fruitful contact with students c) to make up for extra expenditure by means of what a woman can do in a kitchen. We both feel that the last three reasons are more cogent in our cases than they are for a man, have understood the anxiety to be rather less in the other case than in our own, and you are acquainted with the preferences of the other apartment holders.

I am therefore being bold enough to ask you whether there is any possibility of a reconsideration of Dr. Smyser's appointment to the third apartment. I hope it's not a shocking thing of me to do.

    Yours sincerely,

    Rosemond Tuve[6]

President Blunt's reply was immediate and terse: "My dear Miss Tuve," she wrote. "Miss Dilley has withdrawn her application for one of the apartments in the new building so that one is assigned to you without drawing lots. Very sincerely yours, Katharine Blunt President"[7]

Rosemond sailed happily for England where she visited her friend, Jan Watson. In the middle of the summer she wrote again to Eleanor.

Sat, 29 July [1939]   21, Strand on the Green

                           Chiswick W. 4

                           London

and I guess *that's* a good place to be, *sitting* in Janny's sitting room (Functionalism) from the which the Thames is exactly 5 feet from the front gate—tidal, of course & sometimes it's more, but not when I come home early to tea from the Museum on a Saturday. . . .

I've been in London only a couple of days—Oxford for a week & a half, as lovely & wet and full of gardens as ever, the usual bats of work in Bodley with hasty frequent runs down all those steps to go to the *Camera* john in the rain after one has DeniedNature all but too long. The bicycle trip in Britany only 3 weeks past seems like the Middle Ages, & fully as romantic & picturesque, & just more fun while living in it than the MA [Middle Ages] could have been. In other words, I'm full of Fine Stories & lovely sights, & wish to hell you were here, & look forward to making you green with envy I hope to the end *that* you will one day be a co-bicycler some-equally-beautiful—where.

Dutch is back at CC. August 1st—She's had a Horse for the month of July & is in great form. Go see each other, why don't you? If I were *either* of you, I couldn't Keep Away, you're both such Nice Girls. This is a lovely country & I cannot bear that it should be thinking a war is to blow it up soon. I will preserve all serious remarks till I see you, though. . . .

and love to ya,
from Ros

Rosemond Tuve, circa 1941. Courtesy Connecticut College Archives.

6

ROSEMOND WOULD NEVER LOSE HER INTEREST in workers in industry. If the time she had for actively serving their causes diminished, she could inspire students to carry on the work. In January 1940, in a letter to the Board of the Industrial Group of the Y.W.C.A, she resigned, with regrets, from her position as chairman. But ending her active involvement with labor never quieted her gnawing conscience about their problems. Later, she defended this stance:

"But it can be very annoying when the intellectual, the scholar and artist, has this seemingly irresponsible attitude toward getting the work of the world done. You call her up to serve on a rummage-sale committee. 'Oh, I haven't got time.' This is part of the price. If society wants to see farther than its own nose, it has to value and support those who "haven't got time" to do what looks like their duty, because they are hell-bent on finding out what exactly Abraham Fleming said about Virgil's Eclogues in his translation of the mid 1500's.

"Because although a great deal is made of old Nero fiddling while Rome burned," she continued, "it is essential that someone fiddles while cities burn. I grant you that if Nero were responsible for the fire and for not curbing it, I see some evil in his violin, but by and large unless we dedicate ourselves to the principle that somebody has to keep on with the violin instead of waiting till the fires are out, we won't have any cities worth saving. 'Life,' naked and unqualified, isn't valuable. What life? Beetles have life."[1]

Rosemond had been patient up until now, but finally started fretting over her lack of recognition by the college. After nine years of teaching as an assistant professor, two years at Goucher, three at

Vassar, and now six at Connecticut, she felt, and rightly so, that she deserved a promotion. She had made inquiries at, or received an offer from, Lawrence University, for an opening in its English department. On April 2, 1940, she wrote to President Blunt.

Dear Miss Blunt,

You were right in saying that promotion to the associate professorship is an operative point. But I do not wish to force your hand in any way. I have re-studied the letter and it seems to me I have given you as honestly as possible its purport, as well as my own feelings about staying here. If those feelings conflict with what I ought to do professionally, I will do what I ought to do, nevertheless. But after all I haven't the offer in cold black and white, and if you prefer I will proceed to make absolutely sure that it will reach that stage. It is true, however, that if I follow it up I intend to proceed fairly toward the other institution, and if they meet me I shall accept it.

I thought it right to go to you before making such a move. But I came only to get some clear notion of my professional value here, not to bring pressure.[2]

The President's reply was less than satisfactory. On April 5, 1940, she wrote: "I sincerely hope you will stay with us. I am glad to tell you that I think there is a strong probability of your promotion to an associate professorship next year or the year after.

"It does not seem to me suitable to make any further statement than this at present."[3]

Rosemond waited a week before responding.

Dear President Blunt,

I write in connection with our recent conversations and in answer to your letter. I have decided to stay on at Connecticut, and am happy to be able justifiably to decide on remaining.

I have exchanged letters again with Dr. Bethurum, [Dorothy Bethurum, who came to Connecticut College in 1940 as chairman of the English department, was then professor of English at Lawrence University] and although the rank could probably have been raised superior to my present one here, she tells me that President Barrows [president of Lawrence University] could not appoint another full professor in a top-heavy department without seeming to discredit the work of others already there, hence the chairmanship will be held by a present member of the staff. I have decided that earlier attainment to associate professorship is not sufficient to make me leave a college I am attached to and a department in whose coming development I am deeply and hopefully interested.[4]

Nevertheless, Rosemond never got over a nagging disappointment that Connecticut College failed to value her in proportion to her devotion to the college and her continual efforts to raise its standards. It was not financial gain that she sought, but rather some acknowledgment of her intellectual worth. It wasn't until 1942, eight years after her arrival, that she was promoted to associate professor, with a salary of three thousand dollars.

In a letter to Eleanor in May, she had put behind her this unsettling problem, no doubt having thoroughly discussed it during her recent visit.

[May, 1940]   already Thursday my god.
Dearest Eleanor,

I have got the radio on talking German to hear their version when they start saying it in English. I am trying to Reconcile Thought and Feeling. For the life of me I cannot distinguish between them; it's funny to listen to the B.B.C. with a perfectly ordinary vicar such as I know so many of so well, telling what you do when you're one of the Home Defense and sit on a hill in a van all night to watch the coast line. It's so much like the fires being lit for Boney, and indeed so much like how I know almost everyone there is thinking and feeling, that I can sit here and watch my Thought bolster up my Feeling and both of them getting awfully English. I shall take all the measures I can—but do you feel very neutral?? In spite of thinking that there's probably something phoney behind the socalled defection of Belgium. Weel, I dont know what I'm writing all this for, acct. in a couple minutes I shall be all extrovert, what with a old student that went into Workers' Education coming back to converse again with the fountain of Crusadism. Ha, that was the funniest you ever taxed me with. I want to say that due to your unsympathetic one might almost say stern attitude, my poison ivy has SPRUNG FORTH into ardent activity, and I am having a warm time. I just hope you catched it offen the dish towel. Oh dear I guess I never did no work. You were very Kind and Easy on me this visit. Maybe that's why I came back so inspired with the Yeats conversation that since Sun. night I have gone into two separate eclipses and not only sat for 8 hours at the typewriter thinking painful thots on subject of Mr. Brooks [she is referring to Cleanth Brooks's book *Modern Poetry and the Tradition*, for which she was writing a review for the *Modern Language Quarterly*] and his various notions & how they apply to My Junk, but also have engulfed the Ramus part of Mr. Perry Miller's book with similar typewriter session, and large ezpansion of Idears. I think that an excellent book, I found it exciting to the nth degree, tho I swam about among disjunctive syllogisms till I was dizzy. Only read that portion so far. Mebbe he gets Dull and Mouldy later. It was more or less the dinner-companion-campus-speaker side of him you and Jean were slating, no??

Well I liked that weekend almost even better than the other one. You are a hostess of vast versatility, my pearl. Golly I wish there were some more time; I am full of notions, half-cooked, which I wd. like to submit to your stern appraisal. Do read the rest of old Brooks, wont you. . . .

with love from
Britomart

Britomart was one of Spenser's central characters in the *Faerie Queene*. She was a powerful woman who jousted and triumphed over an array of challenging knights. Britomart, who represents chastity, most often appears in knight's armor carrying a magical spear. When she casts off her battle gear, she is revealed as a handsome woman with flowing, golden hair, a picture of the ideal heroine. Spenser modeled Britomart on the mythological Athena, and here Rosemond has identified with these two legendary types.

In November she wrote to Eleanor again.

> dear eleanor
> Hey we had a wonderful convoc. series, I mean symposium. My own idea and I am sold on it. None of your haphazard speeches, but 2 in a doubleheader and makem cooperate. The whole campus buzzed, Tillich of Union and Wolfers of Yale, on The Future of Europe, and one talked it in every class, and I feel positively cheered on the student's capacity to see the Point. . . .
> I must stop—11 pm and i've 2 classes to get ready for yet and 3 more letters. love to you beauty COME AGAIN AS SOON AS POSSIBLE. If you go to NH [New Haven] to investigate Burton, stop by and sleep here instead of elsewhere. I wish you'd come down and assist (in the Fr. sense) Tues. 8 PM Lewis Mumford and Wed. 4 P.M. Niebuhr—in concert & sidekicks by choice—on Can Contemp. culture preserve democracy. Consider it. It would be worth seeing. Dec 3 and 4.
> > with love from
> > the Fat One

[In her own hand, she wrote sideways in the corner, "Didst get galoshes? I sent them the day after you wrote of their existence." Then, in another corner, "meant to insure yr. galoshes & didn't get to take them *myself*—so . . . . . hope they got there safely. Insure that Inwaluable Shoit. *yellow.* My fav. color." Here she drew a smiley face.

It is difficult to understand from her constant exuberance the amount of serious scholarship to which Rosemond gave long evenings and weekend hours. Increasingly she was becoming noticed in the field of Renaissance studies, and was asked to contribute to scholarly journals. In April 1940 one of the articles she had been working on in England, "Spenser and Some Pictorial Conventions: with Particular Reference to Illuminated Manuscripts," was published in *Studies in Philology*. Her review of Cleanth Brooks's *Modern Poetry and the Tradition* appeared in *Modern Language Quarterly* in 1941. Meanwhile, she was struggling with an article on Ramus and metaphysical poets, which she read at an MLA meeting in 1940, but now it needed revision in order to satisfy the publisher. Her élan vital continually bubbled over into teaching, college committees, and cultural concerns.

In the following letter to Eleanor she wrote of the New England Renaissance Conference in which she was intensely involved. Founded in 1940 by Leicester Bradner, of Brown University, it had no organization, no membership, no dues. Each year, in order to divide the work, a different college would sponsor the meeting.

[February 7, 1941]
you lovely thing,
well so that's over. I mean exams. Nothing else is. I got TERRIBLE things on my mind. . . .
Now this letter is especially about the Renaiss. conference which this spring is HERE. You remember I had such a noble time at Brown I didn't talk about anything else for a while? All the 35 or 40 felt the same, so doubtless they'll all come again, and we got the Yale gang by the neck, and Brown is coming in droves from scientists to philosophers and all between. And a noble program arranged tho some of course may fall thru as all programs do in the asking. You'll get a paper presently, but meanwhile save May 2–3. Leicester Bradner came by and we planned noble things: the most astounding a session on primitivism and related ideas in arts and in thought with LOVEJOY AND PANOFSKY. Well I hope they will—they will be intrigued by the idea of a symposium together I think. Then one on music, with either Smith or Lang from NY. And one on Latin drama wit Tucker B [Brooke] and Leicester and the continent—Spanish esp. with Gillet from BMC. Then a

stunner—defining the baroque, with Hitchcock the mod.arch.man and Castrow and Peyre for literary disciplines.

Now my plot is that you come and meet Helen McMaster here. I'm writing her. You see she kindly writ after my MLA paper on imagery ["Imagery and Logic: Ramus and Metaphysical Poetics."] (which went beyond all measure noble. I nearly died of Compliments) asking me if I'd a publisher. And so we corresponded some. [Helen McMaster had written Rosemond: "I think that you have got something very special; in fact, revolutionary in the repercussions that it should have on criticism of contemporary poetry."] And it would be a perfect idea, and now you save May 2–3 (Fri.aft. and Sat. til mid-afternoon), and if you both come, sleep in my beds. You MUST OF COURSE COME ANYHOW, it would be Professional Suicide not to, so there. If we have trouble housing some of the Famous Spikkers, I may put you in the Dean's bed which she would like inordinate, and give up my flat to someone.

But you write H MCM and hold yourself out for a carrot. Because, dear mandrake, you simply must, it's going to be exciting.

All the Best People.

love to you beautiful, I got to go to bed.

r

And then you stay on after, and we'll talk about everybody and ride the horses.

Although a prophet without honor in her own bailiwick, colleagues from other, more prestigious institutions applauded her speech at the Renaissance Conference. Her good friend, Merritt Y. Hughes, of the University of Wisconsin, wrote: "What I have had time to read of this key to your scripture makes me keenly aware that your general thesis anent Metaphysical imagery is going to make me furious with jealousy."

In the spring of 1941 Connecticut College held an auction to raise money for the war effort. Both faculty and students were asked to contribute a favorite possession to the sale. Halfway through the event a woman in a flowing cape (one student recalls that she was dressed in a Victorian beach outfit), riding an antiquated bicycle, swooped down the carpeted aisle of Palmer Auditorium. Somehow she managed to get the bicycle on the stage, and rode in circles while the auctioneer took bids. The bicycle was Rosemond Tuve's donation to the auction. Her appearance is the sort of "batty" (as one colleague described her), uninhibited performance that had become Miss Tuve's trademark.

In a more serious vein she wrote to Eleanor:

> June '41   3141 Adams Mill Road
>   Washington   Sat. night
> Dearest Eleanor
> be nice for you to have cross-word puzzle for your lonely
> evenings [here she drew a smiley face] but do not intend to
> write cross words. On contrary, loving gratefulness for card to
> tell me property not lost. I was plunged
> > into
> > > Despair
>
> at idea of tinkering further with artikel. Do not believe I shall
> be able to understand their desires & comply—. . .
> Well hell I do hope I am able to understand what they
> want & do it, but it may be I should have sent to a critical
> review since I down writing what *must* be addressed to cer-
> tain groups of critics. I do get low thinking about it acct. do
> have to make tracks & work hard on other 3 things soon as it's
> July 1.

The article to which she refers, "Imagery and Logic: Ramus and Metaphysical Poetics," which received such praise at the meeting of the Modern Language Association, was now being prepared for publication in the *Journal of the History of Ideas*. Arthur O. Lovejoy, chairman of the editorial board, critiqued her paper stating that her "principal theses are manifestly not only original and interesting but of considerable importance, if successfully established."[5] But he also found "serious points of difficulty in the paper," which he enumerated at length in the language of a logician. For Rosemond there was "truth in a metaphor as in a proposition." This article became the basis for her second book, *Elizabethan and Metaphysical Imagery,* which a colleague described as "the only one that really matters" in the field.

Rosemond's letter to Eleanor continues:

> . . . I do hope you will help explain to me what is wanted on that blasted essay—for I feel sure I cannot do it—if the whole front end is to have a substitution which will seem Fine Proof to the scholars who do not write on these matters & miss fire [sic] with the critics who do, alas. And I shan't know how to do it.

Shortly after her paper was published, Douglas Bush, of Harvard, wrote to Rosemond that "it is reassuring to have someone really saying things about a difficult subject." And later Hallett Smith, of Williams: "Anybody who can show the unity of Elizabethan criticism and poetic practise is producing a revelation—and a revolution."

Rosemond was also making an indelible impression on her students. Under the heading "Candids," two students wrote a profile of their complex teacher that appeared in the February 25, 1942, issue of the "Connecticut College News." Introducing her as the "the lively lady with the unruly auburn hair, the penetrating blue eyes, and the deep, hearty laughter," they launched into a description of her apartment as "furnished in modern simplicity. On the walls are modern etchings, several sketches by a young Indian artist, and two Oriental prints by Hokusai [the gift from Geoffrey Waldegrave]. The article continues:

"In one corner of the room are books on early and modern drama, on American art and photography, on medieval literature and philosophy. The limits and boundaries of Miss Tuve's interests follow no narrowly defined course, yet all hinge ultimately on her one interest, to know, and if possible to understand the world we live in.

"In temperament and personality Miss Tuve seems thoroughly as unpredictable and many sided as in her interests. Slightly bohemian, eccentric, and astonishing in her ways at times, she is at other times equally serious, intense, and purposeful. To her students she is known for her remarkable abilities as a teacher, for her riotous and rambunctious sense of humor, and, last but not least, for her inimitable prowess astride the bicycle. Those who know Miss Tuve outside the classroom, know her as a quiet, understanding person with a genuine interest in student activities and a keen, penetrating mind. She spends a great deal of her time in study, often working steadily for six hours on end, and is now absorbed in the editing of a sixteenth century philosophic poem [Palingenius's "Zodiake of Life"] and in a study of imagery in Renaissance and modern poetry.

"In teaching Miss Tuve follows, as far as her students can see, at least three suppositions: first, that her work as a professor proves most fruitful when she too is a student; second, that advanced students learn best when obliged to do their own thinking, with the minimum of actual direction from the teacher; and third, that if the teacher bangs the door when she enters the classroom, her students will immediately wake up. It is superfluous to add that Miss Tuve finds it unnecessary to bang the door when she leaves."

Rosemond's deep concern for the intellectual development of her students included educating them about social issues, sometimes creating conflicts with the administration and faculty. In November 1942, she wrote the following:

Dear President Blunt:

I left Saturday morning feeling that we would not have been so at odds if I had stated more clearly what principles I feel are involved.

I sympathize very strongly with the ideals of free learning which we symbolized in our November 17th assembly, and I am anxious to stand by those ideals when students feel the need to go outside their normal experience for pertinent information on a problem. It is not a question of being for or against labor, but of believing in the democratic process.

Unless they are doing something wrong, or educationally unsupportable, I particularly hesitate to interfere with students' decisions through their chosen committees, at a time when the democratic process is under fire. I feel it my duty to encourage them to find out about the modern world—and not only academically—and to take seriously their responsibility of knowing more about questions upon which people are divided.

I do not believe we are in basic disagreement about this.

Yours faithfully,

Rosemond Tuve[6]

Hope Castiglione, a student of Rosemond's, recalled an event which may have prompted this letter: "Having first met Miss Tuve in the humanities (English class), I soon after became associated with her social science interest by joining the Student Industrial Group (SIG), a student organization of which she was the sponsor. This was the only 'liberal' group, the only group concerned about social issues, on the campus at the time. I remember that in my freshman year we (SIG) did a survey of racial attitudes of the students which landed us literally on the living room carpet in the President's house." [This survey was done prior to the arrival of the Hampton Singers, a recognized chorus of black students from Hampton College, for a concert on campus. The question asked of the students was whether they would have any objection to the choir staying at the Mohegan Hotel in downtown New London. Of those polled, 88 percent answered yes, because their parents and boyfriends often stayed there.]

"The maids [mostly black] who cleaned the dormitories had seen in the college paper our article summarizing the results of our survey. They were, not surprisingly, alarmed, and carried copies downtown to the Black community. A committee of Black clergymen had called on Katharine Blunt to express their concern, and we in turn were called on by her to explain what the hell was going on. The ultimate result of this brouhaha was some joint meetings of the club members and members of the Black community—for that time a really remarkable bridge between the two groups.

"The SIG was very much interested in the labor movement, in the unions and workers in New London and the surrounding areas. I remember going with Miss Tuve and some club members to a union meeting—a meeting of workers employed at a silk mill in Groton (I think), and of visiting on another occasion in the home of one of the workers (probably the president of the local). I remember being impressed by Miss Tuve's sitting in the living room discussing politics with the men while I helped the women prepare refreshments in the kitchen. I have a feeling that SIG was established as a result of Miss Tuve's connection with the Bryn Mawr Summer School. Each year one Connecticut College student would be an undergraduate assistant at the school."

Castiglione's memory of a particular class remained vivid: "I sat in a front seat. She towered over us. Somehow in the course of class discussion the girl sitting next to me made a very disparaging remark about Italians. All hell broke loose. Fire, smoke, volcanic ash spewed forth from the enraged giant. How could she (the student) denigrate a people who were among the greatest contributors to world culture in the history of man! Etc, etc. I have often wondered whether the nerve assaulted by the student was the one labeled 'Renaissance Scholar' or the one labeled 'Justice and Humanity.' "

By this time Rosemond Tuve had attracted the attention of the Committee on Renaissance Studies of the American Council of Learned Societies. They honored her by asking her to write "A Critical Survey of Scholarship in the Field of English Literature of the Renaissance," which appeared in *Studies in Philology* in April 1943. Leicester Bradner proclaimed this effort a "masterpiece."

The survey covered all fields of study in the Renaissance. On one subject she makes this rather tart comment: "The study of the history of ideas does seem certainly the pursuit of wisdom; yet though one cannot but take fire at the excitement of the chase and the beauty of the quarry, there is a little of the hunting of the unicorn about it, and great fewness of virgins in the company."[7]

The unicorn, a symbol for pride, can be tamed only by the virgin, who represents humility. It might be inferred from Rosemond's tone that she claimed for herself the role of chaste virgin who struggled to achieve true humility in her own life. She also seemed to imply that there is little humility among scholars. [In this connection it should be noted that Tuve often invited her class, when they were studying Milton's *Comus,* to meet at her house to read it aloud. Miss Tuve invariably took the part of the virgin.]

Near the end of this long survey, she reveals some of her own unwavering critical doctrines: "Scholars of literature feel compelled to study not only a man's works, but what he read, his education, the arts, religion, and political ideas of his day; and not only the great writers but the minor and even the ephemeral ones. Preliminary research of the utmost importance, before we can generalize on 'intellectual climate', is investigation of the reading actually done in the period."[8]

Stressing her own focus, she argues that "scholarship in the Renaissance field has suffered because students have been insufficiently aware of the relation of their aims to that ultimate question of poetics."[9] She taught her own students that they should be humble before the texts, before their own inadequacies. The poem will tell you everything you need to know, not the critic. To find truth in the poem is like "journeying to Canterbury."

"But," she continues, "if discussion of the matter could be brought out of the domain of controversy and be used rather to instrument the clarification of legitimately differing aims, scholarship in the field would be better served than it has been by the attacks and defenses which have so far characterized the discussion. For meanwhile it is also true that, in the very heat of the quarrel, a remarkable unanimity of response has characterized the reception of good criticism by whatever approach. It may be far from a merely weak relativism to argue that the approaches of "pure" critic, literary historian, scholarly investigator, are all valid for users with differing predilections so long as they are used by conscious choice and with the integrity which results from being more interested in journeying to Canterbury than in elucidating the deceptions of the other pilgrims, much as this adds to the comedy."[10]

Rosemond's letters often revealed her concern with the war in Europe and the events in Germany. Her background made her keenly sensitive to the needs of immigrants. In July 1943, Rosemond journeyed to Black Mountain College, a summer school founded by a group of Quakers in Black Mountain, North Carolina. She had volunteered to teach English to displaced intellectuals who fled Hitler's Germany. Artists, writers, and scholars from many fields gathered at the college to work and share ideas.

> Black Mountain College,
> Bl.Mt. Nth.C. Saturday, 10th or
> > so July
>
> Dearest Eleanor,
>
> I use this scrap of paper [the letter is written on three cut-up pieces of paper] not only because I am living in an economy of scarcity, but because it will give on the reverse side an amusing example of my present pursuits. [On the back of one piece she wrote: "That Miss Tuve scythed the paths thus for every Thursday is the 30th myth." This was the exercise given to her students for practice in saying the sounds of s and th.]
>
> The sentence is one I have just been teaching to Sigmund Freud's Son a Sensitive Sivil engineer, resuntly domisiled in the united Zdates. I took on a volunteer 6 weeks tutoring in the Quaker Seminar for refugee scholars, its end being so to prepare academic or professional persons in English that they can get away with holding some post. Even if, as in the case of my Vienna judge who is one of my pupils, said job is that of glorified errand boy in the institution for Difficult Boys in Litchfield Conn.! The air zizzles with th's, such as in rizzim (the preferred pronunciation of the former leader of the Prague Opera House, for example).
>
> It at least furnishes a mountain of stories and future conversation. More from the place where we are guests, see above, than from the Seminar itself. BM is more respectable academically than you might think, I consider; at least their determined attempt to hold the 4 humanistic disciplines at

the center of all specialized education of any sort is a pleasing relief, after a year's pushing from our administrative end to shunt gals into anything that wd. prepare them rapidly for technological posts.

This place is completely beautiful—rimmed around by mountains, and a fine lake for swimming. I do hope we see each other SOMEtime, and I can tell you some of the loot from both sides of this quaint 6 weeks—

Much love to you—here comes my judge for his lesson—
Love from Rozzy

Rosemond also wrote to Merle.

Dear Merle and Win,

This is an extraordinary place altogether. In many ways it seems to me to go beyond what orthodox colleges can do with students, but in others the educational policy as it turns out in practice is enough to stand your hair on your head. HOW, e.g., start a boy off right in physics and chemistry with a few hours in an old bath-house containing almost no apparatus? even if the one who teaches it is supposed to be (I dare Merle knows if it's correct) one of the Largest Living Authorities on Magnesium—Hansgirg is his name. He's shored up, after having been in Kaiser's yards, awaiting release from the status of Enemy Alein or something such. But if Tryg [Trygve, Merle's son] shows any signs of musical talent—you ought to look into this place. I never saw such a music faculty in my life. We have Beethoven sonatas played as if for Carnegie Hall, at the turn of a wrist, and I am taking a theory course the like of which I never saw before anywhere.

The real purpose of this epistol is to enclose the append-ed. I teach Freud's son—name Oliver, profession construc-tion engineer, psychological state Jitters. They are our latest arrivals, in US, and haven't got used to having more food turn up regularly, and no one on their trail. I like him awfully, her less—but she is feeling more the effects of a long flight night and day through the Pyrenees. Of my three private pupils, he is the most intellectually alive (though I've a Vienna judge of the most endearing half-humorous humility combined with magnificence of manner; I just helped him finish arrangements for a job as a kind of glorified errand-boy up in the Conn. "Junior Republic" for difficult boys.) Freud says he has lost touch with this man as per enclosed; he had worked with him on one of his jobs, and knows he is in this country and would like to get his address. He must be in Merle's Roster, no? Perhaps Freud too should be, sooner or later. He is at the moment down in Williamsburg; we sent him off to interview for a job he was recommended for, teaching at Wm and Mary—Army Specl.Tr. Program, physics and chem. He is doing some teaching here at the college proper, statics, physics, and Phys. Geography. He is rather amusing about his father, neither partisan nor critical.

We live quite at one with the rest of the college community and work camp—I meant to offer to hoe corn with the students, but schedule has been too tight; besides some Intonation group lessons and private lessons and tenses-drilling I suddenly had to get in shape a weekly linguistics lecture, and there are some difficulties about teaching non-philologists the historical development of English in a way which can be immediately practically enlightening.

I have to get ready to help a Russian on the gerund—she's a translator, and in general very good, but the gerund is as hard for them as *th*. So good luck to you all, and if you can tell me where is Dr. Marcus, Freud would appreciate it greatly.

love from

R[11]

During the war years, owing to shortages of food, members of the faculty who requested one were assigned a plot of land across from the campus, near the river, where they might grow their own vegetables. Rosemond took up gardening with great gusto, becoming a familiar figure riding her bicycle along Mohegan Avenue, her rake and hoe dangerously balanced in front of her, a large straw hat shading her face from the sun. She often wrote of her joy in gardening to Eleanor.

Sat p m [November 1943].

Dear Eleanor,
I am enjoying 1st weekend without engagements every minute, in weeks. Not that I am not due over at Hardy Wickwar's (new polit. man, Briton, their baby was born from our apt—they borrowed Dilley's in a pinch, having borrowed mine during the Black Mtain era), to take care of the baby while they go to a dept. party. And not that I just didn't get back from long-overdue burning of my corn stalks down at my garden, prior to manuring which College furnishes us, at a Fee. Only bought veg. twice since June. Even this time, I returned with radishes, broccoli, carrots and beets, and fetched up a tomato from my storeroom on the way. . . .
I cant get anything onto this sheet about new Pres. and so on.

Rosemond was referring to Dorothy Schaffter, who was inaugurated on October 28, 1943, as president of the college. Rosemond either was being discrete or didn't have room on the page to express her feelings about the new president. Schaffter turned out to be extremely unpopular and resigned in the spring of 1945. Rosemond felt Schaffter had been responsible for pushing girls into "anything that would prepare them rapidly for technological posts."

In 1940 a few members of the college faculty who enjoyed singing joined to form the Palestrina Group, vowing to sing only sacred polyphonic music of the sixteenth and seventeenth centuries. For Rosemond anything later than Bach was "way too late." Under the direction of Dr. Paul Laubenstein, professor of religion and college chaplain, the group, which also included students, met weekly in the basement of Mary Harkness Chapel. Although they sang chiefly for their own pleasure, eventually they achieved enough skill and confidence to give an occasional concert. A colleague of Rosemond's remembered this incident: "When Dorothy Bethurum was having difficulty singing her part in the 'Et incarnatus est' section of Palestrina's 'Missa Brevis' a discussion arose as to why she was having this trouble. Ros chimed in, 'She can't sing it because she *don't* believe it.'"

During the forties and fifties, Rosemond kept an engagement calendar. By writing in the columns that were designated for morning, afternoon, and evening she could record three years on one page. Almost the only notations in the calendar are the books she read—five or six in a week. There was an astonishing variety, from Jane Austen to Henry James, whom she reread many times. On the same page might be a story by Charlotte Yonge and a philosophical work by A. N. Whitehead. The extent of her reading reached from St. Augustine to Conrad and from Hawthorne to Jung and Freud. Any social engagements, department meetings, or other interruptions to her daily regimen were excluded.

In the summer of 1945 Dorothy Bethurum invited Robert Penn Warren, whom she had known in her Vanderbilt days, to give a seminar at Connecticut College. Years later Warren recalled the long talks that he and Rosemond had "every day or two, most about poems and critical theory. She was truly learned but, unlike some learned people I know, had not lost the inner perception of poetry. So what she had to say, in that combination, was always exciting to me. [There was] a constant growth of mind and feeling that came to me during those weeks, and a real affection for her as a person. She had no meanness in her—tough-minded but kind—Rosemond was a real presence for me, and I'd read her work just to try to renew something she had given me. That's about it. So little—but so much, and permanently much. She was for me a sort of wonderfully productive and happy accident, and I've had profit from it over many years now."

Three years elapsed in which no letters to Eleanor Lincoln appeared. Although they most certainly kept up their visits, Rosemond was chiefly occupied with work on her book *Elizabethan and Metaphysical Imagery,* and stayed close to home. But her voice emerged in the September 30, 1945, publication of the "Connecticut College Bulletin":

"I have had the usual kind of cooperation of other departments in attempts to make the students see connections between the literature they read and other aspects of civilized life (of the Music Department, in lending printed scores and records which I play for various classes at my house when teaching poems set to music; of Dr. Bouvier, in attending and criticizing two students' attempts to dramatize excerpts from plays read in the Drama course; of the Art Department, in helping my students find materials in their library and collection, when I have been teaching freshmen to see literature as intimately connected with other arts and aesthetics generally). I find this kind of emphasis to be an eye-opener to younger students especially, and (like most people, I imagine) commonly have students working on all manner of "inter-departmental" subjects, from the stained glass of the chapel and its mediaeval prototypes, to the social reforms of More, or the music composed by the poet Campion. The greatest single asset in enlivening earlier eras to students has been their opportunity to see classical and Renaissance plays in actual production.

"One's discoveries when attempting to relate students' work to their life in the modern world are far from uniformly happy. When I assign the weekly reading of one of the "liberal'" critical periodicals and ask the students after a month to write a 'modern' chapter of *Gulliver's Travels*, I find them woefully ignorant of what goes on in their own society. When, in studying Elizabethan critical treatises, I ask them to apply the ideas to a modern rather than a Renaissance poet, I find them far from well read in their own contemporaries."

In the spring of 1946, Rosemond wrote a long letter to Merle. Merle had been instrumental in the development of the proximity fuse that was used to bring down V-1 buzz bombs over England during the war, checking the German advances at the Battle of the Bulge. In 1946 he received the Presidential Medal of Merit, and was made a Commander of the Order of the British Empire for his work. It had been almost forty years since he had experimented with reconstituted batteries, electrical coils, and wireless telegraphy in Canton. His extraordinary energy and dedication to science equaled his sister's commitment to literature and teaching.

Saturday afternoon [spring 1946]
Dear Merle,

I see how Mr. Bowman [the president of the University of
Minnesota] says in his Pres's report that you are a Ph.D. from
Hopkins and made a Fuze. Also I see by the Mpls. Journal
with a picture, how you are the Big Chief now. [Merle had just
been made director of the Department of Terrestrial
Magnetism at the Carnegie Institute.] This clipping was sent
on to mother by some friends of mine whom she met here
last summer. They took quite a shine to her, and since the
husband happens to be one of the three or so possibly most
likely-to-last poets writing in America and also a novelist of
parts and distinction, you see you are making inroads in the
field of the Humanities.

She is referring here to Robert Penn Warren and his wife, Selina,
who had thought to send a newspaper clipping to Ida Tuve. The letter
continues:

The field of the Humanities is in my bad books right now
acct. we have a plethora of meetings trying by the mouse-in-
a-maze method to see whether we could possibly give the
young ladies a better education in that area than we now do.
I don't hold so much with these "General" or "Common Core
of Knowledge" courses as some do, and think the Harvard
Plan has its immaturities. Everybody thinks these Over-all
Surveys are just fine in all fields they don't know much about,
which rouses my suspicion. Even I query the virtues of teaching "Science" instead of A science—I don't believe students
get the realization of what scientific method and conscience
are through being told about it but by hearing others praise
it. The same goes for the great writers of the world, somehow;
ain't no way to get rich quick, gotta read 'em and be struck,
laid low, catch in the throat and tear in the eye. But we did
have one bang-up series, whole college in attendance—
Jordan of Radcliffe for the soc. sciences, Wald the Harvard
bio-chemist for the sciences, and Howard Lowry pres. of

Wooster for the humanities, with discussions every few
minits. H.L. wound up so impressively that the students
clapped four minutes by the auditorium clock.[12]

The series to which she refers was presented in early April as part
of Freshman-Sophomore week. Dr. Wilbur Jordan, of Radcliffe, initiated the lectures with this explanation for the need for three areas of
learning: "All knowledge is as a whole so vast that, for convenience, it
must be divided into three parts, the humanities, the natural sciences,
and the social sciences."

Later that spring, Merle stopped by to see his sister. Shortly after
he left, Rosemond wrote a letter to congratulate him on yet another
honor.

Dear Merle,

Eating dinner peacefully in a downtown dive the other
night when one of the few Enemies I have on the faculty
stepped up to the table (we're Veiled enemies—see under
Moslem) and said have you got a brother called Merle I saw
how he was decorated they put the three important ones first
in the N.Y.Times notice and all the other seven came along in
another paragraph. So I said Thank you yes I have Oh he's
decorated all the time. All my brothers are. [Merle had
received the Presidential Medal of Merit.]

Despite which Dutch and I looked in all the Timeses I
haven't been able to read on account of painters in the house,
and cut out the clipping for Mother, and I now write to congratulate you. What, again? Yp, again.

You wouldn't know my place. I just had it painted yellow.
With all that blond wood and Indian paintings and one oil
painting of a magnolia over the fireplace it looks like something outen the Museum of Modern Art. Grey in the hall; ever
so subtle.

I am rolling around on ninepins acct. you have doubtless
heard that Dick and Rik and Max [her brother, his son, and
Dick's wife, Maxine] and I start for San Francisco next Wed.
morning. . . .

If I don't scoot down and get the rest of my carrots and limas in I'll have nothing to eat in August, and God knows I won't have nothing to buy store-food with.   so with love from

Rosemond[13]

Rik Tuve never forgot that trip across the country when he was eight years old. "You can imagine what that was like," he told me. "A traveling companion I was constantly with and she had such an enjoyment of life, it kind of pervaded the whole atmosphere. She was fascinating. She would just get so excited about—'oh look, over there.' She loved the Midwest. It was unbelievable."

One of Rosemond's students in the early forties recalled her surprise at seeing her teacher in her hometown of Bryn Mawr. While driving near the college one fall weekend she saw "a figure sitting on a curb, long legs outstretched. It was Miss Tuve. I didn't stop, since at first sight it didn't hit me that I had seen her, but I asked her later what she had come down for. 'Just to see the leaves,' she replied."

It was not just Rosemond's brilliance, but also an ineffable quality of personality, that drew increased attention. She was sought after as a speaker, and was being sought by a number of colleges for positions on their faculties. Rosemond was still only an associate professor and remained, apparently, a dubious asset to Connecticut College. Her relationship with colleagues at Duke University, always solid, had now reached the point where an appointment was a possibility. On April 20, 1946, she receives a letter from Newman I. White, chairman of the department of English at Duke, offering her a position at the university. He wrote:

"We are in the midst of appointments here, and we are considering one or two appointments of women. . . . [But] there is considerable uncertainty as to what the dean will approve after our recommendations are made. I have had a committee, of which Allan Gilbert is chairman, studying the Woman's College angle of the problem, and this committee would very much like for us to be able to add you to our English staff here. . . . Meanwhile, I wonder if you could tell me, off the record, just how you feel about it.

"I would like to be able to recommend you for an assistant professorship at a salary of about $4,000."

Rosemond answered the letter on April 25, 1946:

> I imagine Allan Gilbert told you something of the way I am situated up here. My chairman had already recommended me for promotion to full professorship this year; this was not done for reasons I myself thought sensible enough—that is, if they were the reasons. Even an assistant professorship at a university, especially at a salary $500. higher than I shall receive next year, would not be entirely unattractive if I were going to drag along here as associate professor; on the other hand, if there were every likelihood that I would be made full professor next year (my sixth as associate), then the difference would really be too great.
>
> I know that you had had some thought of the barest possibility of an associate-professorship appointment. But in any case, with a dean who would make you put up a fight for a woman in any event, I was not going to evince an interest that would make you go to bat with the dean for the best conditions possible—only to discover that the Powers up here would make this job too good for me to leave. Hence I had to see the President, and tell her just exactly the situation, in order to see, if I could, just what I would be weighing against what.
>
> First she was away a day and a half, and then she had to think. I was really in a quandary, because I should like to work under you, I should enjoy the rest of your department, and I like universities. I tried to be as honest as I could all 'round; I was really stumped to know how to answer you. As things turn out, I guess it would not be very sensible for me to leave here. Evidently I am almost certain to be promoted to full professorship next year, although I am not telling this in the streets of Gath . . . Women have such a hard time getting to top rank in this profession . . .

She closed her letter with a warm and complimentary recommendation of Josephine Bennett for the position. Later, Allan Gilbert wrote these reminiscences of Rosemond: "As chairman of an MLA group, I was so fortunate as to be able to put on a program the paper which developed into *Imagery*. Merritt Hughes, after hearing it, spoke of it as "Copernican." On my retirement at Duke, in 1957, I secured the approval of the department of English for her appointment as my successor. The appointment was blocked by a stupid dean, who said that men wouldn't come to her for direction. I knew that they would."

The day after mailing her letter to Newman White, Rosemond wrote to President Blunt:

> I forgot to tell you that two publishers have written and asked to see the MS. of my second book [*Elizabethan and Metaphysical Imagery*] as soon as I can send it. But it is a big book (as is the one already placed, *Palingenius's Zodiake of Life*); that's a $5.00 book but the publisher says orders are already coming in). The second one is really finished, but since it will be expensive to do, I may face some difficulties of revisions—and I also forgot to say that a place with a university press hence has a little pull upon a person in circumstances like mine.
>
> One of the people at Duke had read the second book, which he calls "Copernican" and I rather suspect that they would not be unwilling to have me publish it as of their department and not this one. But its size will nevertheless put some difficulties in the way of speedy publication.
>
> I also meant to say that 2–3 months ago I would have been much *more* willing to leave here because of the possibility of our losing one of the best department heads there is in the profession [Dorothy Bethurum]! I'm not the only one that feels this way, here or elsewhere. Ours really *is* a good department to work in.[14]

Dorothy Bethurum came to the college in 1940 as chairman of the English department and remained until 1962. It is not known what circumstances may have caused her to consider leaving. She and Rosemond enjoyed long careers together at the college; after

Rosemond's death, Bethurum spoke of how much she had genuinely loved and admired Rosemond.

When Dorothy Schaffter resigned as president of Connecticut College in the spring of 1945, Katharine Blunt was prevailed upon to return as acting president for one more year. Following President Blunt's retirement in June 1946, Rosemary Park became acting president, having served in the administration as dean of freshmen since 1940. In the fall of 1947 she was inaugurated as the fifth president of Connecticut College. Since coming to Connecticut from Wheaton in 1935, as instructor in German, President Park had developed a close friendship with Rosemond. A graduate of Radcliffe, she received her Ph.D. from the University of Köln. Over the next fifteen years of Miss Park's tenure, Rosemond would make many valuable suggestions concerning the educational policies of Connecticut College, assistance that was offset by her continual and ever-increasing requests for leave. Edward Cranz, a colleague, remembered her as "a mind and a spirit loosely attached to where she was."

In April 1947, when Rosemond finally received an appointment as full professor, she wrote to President Park.

Dear President Park,

I perceive that I have delayed in my acceptance of the appointment you offered me in your letter of 14th March, to which I was to give an answer by 15th April. I write on the assumption that the offer still holds good, and that procrastination does not shrink a new Professor into an Associate again.

I had put off answering because I have one question (and because I had a certain distaste for looking my new salary in the mouth, if you catch my figure): what is my position with respect to tenure? Your letter speaks of a three-year term. This is my second 3-year re-appointment to a position of or above Associate Professorship; it must be my fifth in the College, which has thus had a fairly respectable opportunity to see how I would turn out. I have not actually struggled with all the possible interpretations of the sheet-of-rules, but it would be my impression that I had fulfilled the requirements usually imposed, unless the College—-regarding the case as highly problematical—is anxious to press every possible interpretation to avoid commitment to the dangerous attitude of permanent willingness in my direction.

I do not wish to be an exception to the system, which I am aware is automatic. I have not troubled to make inquiries beyond what I happen to know, but since I realize that tenure was granted some time since in one very comparable case (after much shorter service), and since, with the vicissitudes of human affairs, we have all found that it is possible to regret not being more business-like, I should be glad to have my position clarified. If not contrary to the rules (in letter, as it certainly would not be in spirit), I should be happy if you would be willing to indicate, by the granting of tenure, that the College no longer sees grave risk in regarding my appointment as permanent, D.v.; or if you would speak to me regarding the extreme hesitancy shown in extending the probationary period from 13 to 16 years. It somehow seems odd that the rules should work to make the Leah-period extend through all four ranks and well into the Rachel-situation.[15]

The reluctance of Connecticut College to grant Rosemond tenure is inexplicable. Perhaps her eccentric personality prevented the administration from rewarding her performance as a teacher and scholar. She was described by a colleague as having a "towering intellect," yet reverting at times to "childish" behavior. Finally, on April 21, 1947, after examining the number of her appointments and consulting with the "Advisory Committee," Miss Park wrote to Rosemond telling her that her "new rank carries with it permanent tenure."

Also in April 1947, *Elizabethan and Metaphysical Imagery* was finally published, as of Connecticut College, to resounding acclaim. Thomas Roche, later a devoted colleague of Rosemond's, remarked wryly: "With the publication of *Elizabethan and Metaphysical Imagery*, she had to be taken into account. Before that she was just

Miss Shambles." Now she was a scholar of distinction. Two years later, in her annual "Report of the President," Rosemary Park wrote:

"It is a matter of special pride to record here the award to Professor Rosemond Tuve of the Rosemary Crawshay prize, through the British Academy, for her book, *Elizabethan and Metaphysical Imagery: Renaissance Poetic and Twentieth-Century Critics,* published by the University of Chicago Press. This prize has been awarded in the past to only one other American woman. The college is indeed proud but by no means surprised at this recognition of Miss Tuve's ability."[16]

Rosemond dedicated *Elizabethan and Metaphysical Imagery* "To the First Scholar and to the First Lover of Books that I Knew: A.G.T. and I.M.L.T. [Anthony Gulbrand Tuve and Ida Marie Larsen Tuve]." It was a proud and moving acknowledgment of her heritage. In more than four hundred pages the book is an attempt to show that modern criticism is too narrow to fit the criteria for Elizabethan and metaphysical poetry. It is a "revolutionary" study of the use of images by poets of the period against the background of rhetorical practices.

Once again the scientific—using principles of rhetoric and logic—is joined to the poetic— sensuousness, imagery, and aesthetics. And, as always, she stresses the moral, or didactic, aim of poetry. "Images have efficacy to move a reader's affections, to quite properly affect his judgments; they move him to feel intensely, to will, to act, to understand, to believe, to change his mind."[17] For, we are told, "the nature of the imagery and the intention of a poem are indissolubly connected." It is the particulars of the imagery that reveal the "blinding light of significances." Or, poets of the period selected "images with known significances, like those of myth," that "will best indicate the intended universal."

What she stresses throughout the book is that seventeenth-century poets used the three criteria of poetry—logic, rhetoric, poetic—to reveal the transcendent. The methods overlap because all three disciplines contribute to the communication of truth from one human mind to another. "Poetry's share in the common aim of establishing an active relation between the whole man and the living truth is accepted not with rebellion but with enthusiasm, is considered not as a restriction upon poetry but an enhancement of its dignity."[18] Her

interweaving of imagery with logic and rhetoric is like the sophisticated counterpoint of the music of the era.

Early in 1947 Rosemond had been invited to participate in a symposium titled "The Teaching of Literature." F.R. Leavis, Mark Van
Doren, Austin Warren, and René Welleck also contributed.
Rosemond's address, entitled "More Battle Than Books," published in
the *Sewanee Review* is a passionate and powerful declaration of what
every educator today would do well to read and consider. Packed with
facts and ideas, as well as criticisms and imaginative solutions, it is a
stunning critique of the problems that undermine the teaching of literature. "Literature," she asserts, "as an aesthetic experience for students seems to have shrunk in the last hundred years," because "at
each stage of the educational process the push of the crowd against
the gates has weakened the standards . . . . 27,000 M.A.'s were given in
1940; of these 9,500 were in Education, 900 in English; a moment's
thought will produce conclusions anent the teaching of literature."[19]

In stressing the importance of learning to read "mature literature,
by oneself," literature that will "shake the reader by the roots," she
argues that those "books mean most if they [readers] are able to contemplate and embrace certain 'absolute' values; these range from pure
loveliness of sound to newly understood great ideas." Literature is
"experience grasped *through form;* and the first essential if we would
read literature is to be quiet and listen to the very words the man
uttered." For "the miracle of literature is identification, living the very
life of another mind."[20]

From her own experience Rosemond knew that "teaching is one
continual fight to keep students from parroting the teacher's synthesis, or substituting our critical judgments for their own aesthetic
responses, and all the other dozen apings they try—to avoid the hard,
hard task of making the relations themselves. A synthesis, like an aesthetic experience, is something one has by oneself." And then she gets
to the core of her values: "I owe my chance to learn what they [my
teachers] could not tell me, or did not believe, to their reticence and
disinterested passion; thank heaven their allegiance was to their

authors and to learning, and not to my welfare, for this is the condition of freedom."[21]

She goes on: "I return, at my close, to the unhappiest point of all. Insofar as we are a business civilization, our values are opposed to the values inherent in aesthetic experience. Literature aesthetically considered has no cash equivalent, no advertising status; it does not Get One Anywhere. There is a distribution problem for literature as for all commodities which fill human needs; but this particular need itself is flat nonsense to a society organized for and around material profits. The postulate of literature is that life is something else entirely."

And finally, the "teaching of literature" would best be served if we fought the "forces that are out and out against the love and understanding of literature. These forces are not weak; nor few."[22]

In November 1947, Merle, perhaps in response to Rosemond's speech, wrote to his sister about his plan to organize a hundred seminars, to be led by outstanding educators. He, too, had been troubled by the descent of education into technical and "how-to" concerns, and was eager to restore the primacy of the humanities, of which science was a key component. In response to Merle's proposals, Rosemond consulted with her closest friends at Connecticut College and wrote a long reply, which ended:

> Dutch said, and we agreed, that the essential in all this (touching both selection of people and specific plans) is a belief that values *have* power, as cf. the mere manipulation either of things or people. Those who believe more in manipulat'g are useless to your purpose, and schemes and devices which do not demonstrate the former rather than the latter might be nets to catch the wind.
>
> If I don't stop I'll catch repentance, remorse, and a cold in the head tomorrow.
>
> With sisterly affection (one a them values),
>
> from R/[23]

Although there is only one more letter that directly discusses the problems of education, both Merle and Rosemond frequently alluded to them in future speeches. Perhaps their energy and the breadth of their interests could be ascribed to the fact that their childhood was lived in South Dakota. Merle once observed that growing up on the prairies had made him go to extremes in his thinking. On January 31, 1948, Rosemond wrote to Merle, enclosing an article from the "Connecticut College News," announcing the appearance of two college presidents who were to speak on the topic of "Reinterpreting a Liberal Education." They were Harold Taylor, of Sarah Lawrence, and Howard Lowry, of Worcester, both of whom had been suggested as members of the seminars proposed by Rosemond and Merle. Their thoughts and efforts on behalf of education were prophetic, and continue to be vital and relevant.

Even though Rosemond was something of a hypochondriac, she failed in her letters to mention any recurring physical symptoms. During the spring vacation of 1948 she underwent a hysterectomy. A friend remembered her humor regarding the gas pains that followed the surgery, comparing them to those of Dick's new baby daughter, Christine. She remarked that she wished "some one could toss her over a shoulder and pat them up," recalled the friend. It was beyond her "fondest imagination how *she* could be ill."

7

R OSEMOND WAS GRANTED HER FIRST LEAVE OF ABSENCE for the fall term of 1948. On July 15, 1948, she and Eleanor Lincoln took the first of their five trips abroad together. They sailed to England on board the *Queen Elizabeth,* arriving at the Whitehall Hotel in London on the twenty-first. Eleanor's most vivid memory was of Rosemond in a large, thickly fuzzy *yellow* coat, struggling to get off the boat where the piers had been blown up. The next day they were on a train to Oxford and having dinner with Dorothy Bethurum; a few days were spent with Eleanor's friend Mary Moore at Crossways; and on August 2 they were joined by Rosemary Park, Merle, and Winifred for a trip through Germany in what Rosemond remembers as "that little car." After a visit to Chartres and then Bauvais, they returned by ferry to London. Rosemond was on leave until February, but two days later Eleanor returned to Smith. Rosemond wrote to her from the Whitehall Hotel.

I keep thinking maybe tonight E.L. lands in the U.S. of America. Nice country but I cant say I was other than Delighted at the fact that I was getting back not to it but to London, this noon.

I didn't write at the beginning of our Separation bec. the news wasn't enough, and then it got too thick to write between, and also my hostess's typewriter got something wrong with it. But I started making news directly I left Oxon and Mary. (We'd a nice mosey time Fri. & Sat.; went to Blewbury for a large tea at a place you shd. put down in address bk.: The Triple Cottage, or Triple House—nice place. B'bury is picturesque as hell, really charming, and downs not far—we walked on one a bit.) . . .

Mig [Mignon Couser, a friend from Somerville] was in good form, and Ire. is land of milk & honey. EGGS morning after morning. Choc. not rationed! Biscuits in pounds! Hard to get right kind, but possible. Tea strongern hell! Hostess is proper Irish—i.e. uses rations right up, and big supper about 11.30 p.m., bkfst in bed at 9.30 or so. The car got fixed JUST in time to see 2 mornings-worth of the loveliest, miracle-colored sea-strands ever painted. 15 mins. drive from Helen's [Helen Roe, an archaeologist friend of Mig Couser's] with green-blue, brown-bog coloured, pink-lavendar-shadow, most unbelievable mountain-and-sea landskips. I do love Ireland. Some day, lovey. (Irish term for dogs. We had 5 Cairns in the house & a cat).

Rosemond first visited Helen Roe when she was working at Trinity College Dublin in 1933, and thereafter whenever she returned to Ireland. Helen Roe's remembrances of Rosemond, written when she was quite elderly, are probably conflated in the following letter:

"Mignon Couser brought her to stay with my Mother and me in our old home in Portlaoise in the Midlands. I remember her as young, very tall almost lanky with primrose coloured hair. We had a black furry rug in front of the fireplace on which she would uncoil herself along with a couple of dogs and the cat and lying on her stomach read endlessly Spenser's Faery Queen. At that stage she was absorbed in tracing all the herbs, plants, trees and rivers that he mentions and I remember taking her all through the valleys of the Slieve Bloom Mountains looking for them and for the headwaters of two of his great rivers, the Barrow and the Nore. Indeed during all the years I knew her Spenser's poems seemed an unfailing source of interest and pleasure to her.

"At a later stage in our friendship her interests in medieval Christian symbolism and its survival in the metaphysical poetry of Herbert, Donne etc. chimed to a considerable extent with my own interest and research into Early Christian representational art in Ireland so that we continued to exchange references and quotations until her death. I don't think she ever wrote me a letter, just postcards closely covered with miniscule and almost illegible writing would flutter through the letter box at long intervals whether from America, Oxford, Greece or wherever."

Rosemond's letter to Eleanor concludes:

> I went to the Abbey, & Kathleen ni Houlihan sure to glory is a poor play. Synge's Playboy not so allfired good either. But the place a great pleasure & excitement.
>
> This won't do; it waxes too late to make this noise & I do have to send Mig a line to her sailing-port, as she will be going from Ire. before I get word back unless I write immediately.
>
> I'll add how I feel in the morning—I bet I will feel a little mopey—you know I dont have the feeling of working yet, and have Fright at thot of serious visit to B.M.

By the middle of November, Rosemond was in Oxford again, and wrote:

> Sunday Nov. 13 [1948]
>
> Dear Eleanor,
>
> I just came back along Merton St. from College Prayers at Xt Church. They sang a Palestrina, and I put off going to Burford, that delightful Cotswold village, to visit Val Merivale at the Grammar School there, in order to hear Super flumina Babylonis. Oh me.
>
> I go to church till I have HOUSEMAIDS KNEE. Or is it the biking in all weathers. (We havent had all but only some—charming days really, and as yet not ever suffering-cold in Bodley. It's partly your Rust-Colored Sweater as does it). You see they sing something every night at 5 or 6.15 at Magd. or New coll. or Xt Ch—and I run like hare to them all. In fact I run like Hare, end of sentence. Dined at St. Hugh's and L[ady] M[argaret] Hall and St. Hilda's all within this last week (those kind women as of before, last night—it was the Mediaeval Soc. meeting there). Too bad all the people as aim to meet author of honorble book dont buy book; still I dont blame them.

[*Elizabethan and Metaphysical Imagery* had appeared in April 1947; it was a large book, more than four hundred pages, and the price of six dollars was prohibitive at that time.] I hadda give a paper at a research-tutors group night before last. Well it is easy to see that all acad. communities are very soon alike. What I really like in this one is going nowhere but just ambling on my borrowed bike down these delectable streets. And I've done that aplenty—also gone out to Wytham and to Wood Eaton and to Ferry Hinksey—and groaned that you and I could not do it together last summer. Still time.

Mary Waldegrave recalled an amusing incident, recounted by her daughter Sally, that occurred that fall: "When Sally and her next sister were at school in London, Ros who was at that time staying in some hotel there, asked the two of them to tea in her hotel. Most kind, said Sally, and a welcome break in routine. They went, and had a fine tea and then Ros, and my second daughter Jenny got into some argument, the subject matter of which Sally can not now remember. But Jenny had by then established the reputation which she still holds, of being a person you simply cannot argue with! All the family (with one notable exception) knew and knows this. (The exception being her father!) Sally expected the usual technique of simply ending the conversation to be put into execution, but not at all. Ros took her up, was surprisingly tough with her, went into an attacking position and ended by telling the young lady (who must have been 13 or 14 years old) that she had no business to adopt such a view point, nor to shift her ground in every other sentence during the discussion! Sally was surprised and impressed."

Rosemond returned to New London in mid-January 1949, ready to plunge into the second semester refreshed and stimulated by her work abroad. Her varied and singular experiences convinced her, as she would later write, that "students learn something from seeing that a faculty member considers his responsibilities to be to learning in general rather than to them as students simply and solely."[1] But this did not preclude a passionate and abiding concern for the education of her students, even their enlightenment, which was evident in all her pursuits. One of the opportunities open to her was her annual chapel talk.

During the early decades of Connecticut College, students were required to attend "chapel" at least one morning a week. On Mondays it was current events in Palmer Auditorium, but the rest of the week brief services were held in Mary Harkness Chapel, led by a member of the faculty or sometimes a student. Rosemond Tuve was one of the more popular speakers, undoubtedly because, as she prefaced one talk, "it has been my custom, and I have been asked, when this annual chapel speech comes around, to go to the poets and writers of the 16–17 century who are my field of interest, to see if they have anything still to say to us their descendants."

Her sermon continued: "When I did so, I was amazed to discover how much more attention they consistently gave, than we do, to the idea that they were *at fault,* that if something was wrong, they personally had a sense of guilt in the matter." Nor does she exclude *herself* from her accusations that we are more concerned with the guilt of others than our own. " 'Thy sins are thine,'" says John Donne, " 'out of thine own choice; thou mightest have left them undone, and wouldst need do them. They are thine, thine own —not the sins of thy fathers, not the sins of the time, nor the sins of thy youth.'" She ended her sermon with a quote from "Holy Sonnet XI," where Donne's powerful words speak of the depth of man's sin. The capitalizations and italics are, of course, hers.

> Spit in MY face, you Jews, and pierce MY side,
> Buffet, and scoff, scourge and crucifie *mee,*
> For *I* have sinn'd, and onely hee,
> Who could *do* no iniquitie, hath dyed:
> But by my death can not be satisfied
> My sinnes, which pass the Jews' impiety:
> They killed, once, an INglorious MAN,— but I
> Crucifie him daily, who is now glorified.

In the spring of 1946 her chapel talk focused on a "certain convention in mediaeval lyrical writings which one might term 'The Accusing Christ.' Like most symbols, this convention was based upon so deep an understanding that it did not die; it is the basis of a poem by the seventeenth century poet. . . . George Herbert. He calls the poem 'The Sacrifice.' . . . In the group of mediaeval lyrics which show the figure of Christ Accusing, Christ speaks from the Cross. It is not understood to be what he REALLY said; like most symbolic representations this is simply a way of dramatizing something—here the terrible and shocking contrast between the price that is paid for man's redemption, and the return man makes to those who make sacrifices for him. . . . All the long history of the attempt to protect man and bring him to good is reviewed, and contrasted with man's callous rejection:

> In a pillar of cloud I LED thee
> And to Pilate   thou leadest me.

"... The plan for drawing mankind toward good rather than evil is not one in which Powerfull Good shall magically overcome Evil, it is a tussle between those two in the free *will* of men . . . This is NOT because Good is POWERLESS against evil. It is because *until* we see the meaning of what we do and of what is done for us, Good must keep on being sacrificed until we DO see. . .This blindness is just a re-enactment of the blindness shown at Calvary. . . . We are as human beings expected to partake sufficiently of the nature of the *good,* that we TOO are expected to *make* some of the sacrifices—without even knowing whether they are deserved, without even knowing whether they will be appreciated. . . . to be HUMAN involves some tiny spark of participation in the nature of the Divine."

When she spoke the following spring, she took up the problem of technology, and how it had "got ahead of our understanding of man & of society. . . We are very efficient and clever about knowing how to do things, but we are somehow inept in our judgements about JUST WHICH THINGS ARE IMPORTANT TO DO, and WHY." Then, in an uncharacteristically lyrical tone, she asks, "How does a people learn what things it should aim at doing? What is a value? What is its substance, wherof is it made, that millions of strange shadows on it tend? And WHO makes value?" Returning to her formal voice she added: "I wonder if there's anything which individuals now *don't do,* which makes us suffer *more* from this gap than other eras have? . . .

"Some of you know that I have a professional and literary interest in Ren. & 17th c. & late mediaeval poets. The suggestion has to do with something which I discovered that *they* gave a very very great deal of time to, an incons*cio*nable amount of time, a really considerable percentage of their waking hours—something I give only very little time to. You know what they did? They contemplated. They thought about the nature of good. But that doesn't quite cover it. You can't call their activity philosophy, or study, or researching—there's something else to it; they spent a very great deal of time examining the fact that they were IN LOVE WITH THE NATURE OF GOOD.

"This is the way in which I noticed this: My poets wrote a good deal of religious poetry. I got interested in the numerous echoes in their poetry of the liturgy of the churches they happened to belong to. One was a Protestant vicar, George Herbert—that meant that he read a service, by himself, just a service in praise of God, twice daily—& that he read *every day* certain large excerpts from Christian scriptures. He was also ENAMOURED of the church music of his time, which was very beautiful, greatest period of English music. I got the calendar of readings during the Jacobean period, when he lived, and the service books he knew, & I read what *he* read, every day; day by day, *months;* I am also enamoured of that music. So I was delighted to have to read all of it that we could get hold of in the library. . . .

"Well I did learn a great deal about their poetry. But I also noticed a very interesting change in the *texture* and *focus* of my own thinking. . . . they thought about MATTERS that don't come up every day in modern life. I had to give a very great deal of my *time* to pondering on: what is man's relation to the Good? what IS good? has man any duties toward it? But this is only a small part of it. I found that they spent a very great deal of time just being ASTOUNDED, AMAZED, and GRATEFUL.

"They were in a state of WONDER—Bacon calls wonder the natural and proper attitude of man toward the divine, because wonder is "broken knowledge.' " It's incomplete. But full of a sense of marvelling, at the LOVELINESS of goodness, the *power,* and the *beauty,* of real perfection. Which men call God.

"And that's what much of their religious poetry was about; that's what constituted the greater part of the liturgical and the musical materials I read—they weren't instruction, or moralizing, they were CONTEMPLATIONS OF THE *valuableness* of good, and the attractive, pulling, endearing, adorable aspects of certain values man has seen. And I decided that one reason we suffer from the gap [between knowledge of techniques and understanding of values] I have mentioned is that we have STOPPED BEING IN LOVE WITH THE GOOD, and have stopped taking time to look at what that means."

In going to the poets of the seventeenth century for her texts, she fueled the flame and intensity of her own religious beliefs. This helps to explain how "she struck a chord in some students." Wallace MacCaffery, a professor at Harvard, who knew her and her work, explained her power to move people. "People of that era lived in an immensely sophisticated world. Music and literature were extremely complex and sophisticated. It is a different kind of imagination; the fantasy world in which they existed was very different from the one that's familiar to us. Very few scholars can get inside. . . . and she was one of the rare scholars who could get inside the minds of the past."

Sherman Hawkins, a student, later a colleague of Rosemond's, observed that "for her the life of religion and life of literature connected. Instincts and reality in religion connected in literature. Milton and Herbert were inspired. Their utterances are taken as a spirit, a living spirit." Rosemond's sermons reflected this spirit.

During the forties, few students failed to notice the distinguished professor of English riding her bicycle across the campus. For Rosemond, riding a bicycle was not only a means of transportation but an expression of her vitality as well. However, Dick Tuve was constantly urging his sister to learn to drive. And so when Robert Strider joined the English Department as an instructor in 1946 and became one of Rosemond's close associates, she found the opportunity. Strider never forgot giving her driving lessons: "Her enthusiasm for life generally translated itself into her dogged insistence on learning to drive—in 7 lessons," he recalled. "She'd looked up somewhere that the local driving schools had said that 7 lessons for X dollars per lesson—they'd guarantee you could get your license. So she said to me, 'Flat fee, Bob. I want to pay you X dollars for my 7 lessons and at the end of it I expect to get my license. Is that a deal?' So I said, 'O.K., I'll try.' So we had a good frenetic time but she was insistent she was going to get this done. And she did."

Dick Tuve was living in Silver Spring, Maryland, near Washington, D.C., and quickly found a good secondhand car for his sister. It was an Oldsmobile, for she always liked to drive a large, powerful car. Rosemond promptly named it "Siouxie," after the family cow in Canton. Dick was always impressed with how quickly she learned about the car's mechanics: "She would drive into a service station and tell the manager—'something is wrong in the differential.'"

In the early forties Rosemond developed a hearing problem and was required to wear hearing aids, a subtle addition to her eccentricity and ability to dramatize. When a student was saying something by rote, or not pertinent, she would conspicuously turn off her hearing aid. When it was interesting, she would turn it on again. Her hearing problem merely added another challenge to Strider's efforts to teach her to drive. He recalled "her engaging habit of disconnecting her hearing aid to shut out the street noises and then being unable to hear me screaming at her to put on the brakes or to stop where it said stop." The inspector passed her with a warning: "You've got to educate this woman to drive a little bit more carefully, but she's all right." Of course, one of the first things she did was to drive to South Dakota. When Bob Strider asked her why she wanted to go there, she gave the oft-quoted reply: "Oh, it's so beautiful." Bob questioned: "Isn't it all flat?" Ros: "That's why it's beautiful. Course it's flat, mile after mile of cornfields, wheat fields, and that sky—it is gorgeous."

When *Elizabethan and Metaphysical Imagery* was published, she wrote this inscription in Bob Strider's copy: "Colleague in more fields than that herein treated, and whose mastery of 'didactic theory' and 'rhetorical efficacy' is especially notable, under difficult conditions, musical or locomotive." Strider was also a member of the Palestrina Group.

In the following letter to Eleanor, Rosemond mentioned driving a car for the first time. Obviously it gave her new reasons to emote on the joys of being alive.

office Thurs. noon [November 17,1949]

Dear Nellie,

. . . The Belchertown route home is DIVINE. How can you bear to come that mouldy dull route? This other was all handsome, and most of it fresh and new to me. I of course couldn't resist going 30 mi. an hour in the good spots, and indeed I was in a String fairly frequently, of people out for Sunday drive seeing leaves—so ha, I didn't get home till 6.15—3½ hours. But it was within 6 mi. of 100 mi. I did not mind the dark-driving very much. It seems mostly luck that nothing happens to one driving blindly along like that, though. You can't really see all you need to, esp, if someone is coming.

After dithering on at length about a possible speech on Spenser at Smith, Rosemond continued:

Naturally I'd enjoy the visit with you. It is the one thing in favour.

So why don't we say I'll do it if it will *really* help you out of a pickle—but you make a little effort to spare me from it if you can, reading period having cut our class meetings down so low already that I do hate to skip *one* of the *three-only* that I have to discuss The Tempest!! (that's how it wd. fall because of our Thg. vacation).

must run,

R/

Forgot to say—I looked at *Kenyon*—naw I aint anxious to respond to that—would you?—didn't even make me cross. He did one image better than me (Marston). Wrong slant on the book's intention—but who cares—

Rosemond is here referring to an article by William Empson, "Donne and the Rhetorical Tradition," which had appeared in the fall issue of the *Kenyon Review,* criticizing *Elizabethan and Metaphysical Imagery.* She obviously felt that Empson's condescending and sardonic comments on her "massive study" were not worth the effort of a response. Ironically, Rosemond had submitted an article entitled "On

Herbert's *Sacrifice*" to the *Kenyon Review* shortly before the appearance of Empson's essay. It appeared in the very next issue, Winter 1950, with the editor's footnote: "The present essay was written before the publication of William Empson's 'Donne and the Rhetorical Tradition' in which Mr. Empson takes issue with some of Miss Tuve's interpretations of the Metaphysical poets."[2] In it, with almost the same caustic tone used by Empson, she corrected his Freudian interpretation of that poem. A lengthy correspondence ensued, and eventually their animosity was transformed into admiration and respect. Although not usually generous to other scholars, she conceded that his analysis of the image of the "gulf," or maw, of a cormorant in a poem by Marston corrected her interpretation. It also produced some witty comments about the meaning of the "gulf" from her friend Allan Gilbert, which helped to remove the sting.

Eleanor Lincoln remembered that Rosemond did give a speech on Spenser for students at Smith in the fall of 1949. It was both entertaining and serious. Her opening remarks, as was often her custom, were slightly self-deprecatory: "It's absolutely *guaranteed* that this lecture will *End*. Tell you this because this lecture is 52 minutes, so if the bell rings in 50 would you please PLAN RIGHT NOW to sit *spellbound* while I finish my sentence—I've got a couple pieces of Spell to leave out if we get behind. AND AN END is absolutely guaranteed. Quite possible that I came up here in vain. It just may be too late. Maybe *too Little* too."

After a brief story that illustrated her first important point about Spenser's *Faerie Queene*, that "Spenser IS TO BE ENJOYED *as a storyteller*," she advised students not to "agitate their minds constantly over the so-called fact that 'Una equals Truth'; let the allegory sleep under the surface of the story, instead of scratching at it all the time. Don't fuss about looking for what X equals; let it sleep—BUT WHEN IT STIRS, *then look* at it."

She proceeded to the more difficult topic of rhetoric, with a statement that "AN *ALLEGORIA* IS A LONG KIND OF *METAPHOR*." Then, no doubt, with a wry smile, she pointed out that normal human experiences "AREN'T ALL BIOLOGICAL. SOME NORMAL HUMAN EXPERIENCES ARE MENTAL. . . . It is my belief that half the time these allegorical figures of Spenser's like the figure of Despair, are not outside Red Crosse's mind at all, but are part and parcel of his nature, as they are part and parcel of the nature of every one of us. Perhaps even Una is just one part of the human spirit, who in the end wins out over some of the things poor Red Crosse has wrong with him."

Rosemond believed that allegorical writing opens the door to many and much deeper interpretations. Images in poetry are not dumb images; they are speaking pictures, and pictures in Spenser *are* the moral. In closing, as was her custom in all her teaching, she asserted Spenser's relevance to society today. "Perhaps in ten years, when you have thought some long thoughts about the predicament in which our own civilization finds itself, you will go back to Spenser's Book I and *see* that we might now live in a better world, if we'd paid more attention to a poet who knew what Sidney meant when he said that 'the grounds of wisdom lie darke, before the imaginative and judging mind, if they be not illuminated or figured forth by the speaking picture of poesy.' "

In any life there appear to be peaks and valleys, comfortable years and those fraught with difficulties. With the decade of the forties behind her and her struggle for recognition seemingly over, Rosemond's life reached a plateau.

For her chapel talk in the spring of 1950, she went again to John Donne for her text: " 'From needing danger, to be good . . . O Lord, deliver us.' That is a line from John Donne's poem 'The Litanie,' and this is a sermon on the SIN of sloth . . . By Sloth I mean in plain American, laziness—*moral* laziness: low expectations, and even those not kept." In about 1610, when Donne wrote his poem, "this had the reputation of being a Sin . . . One chief modern form of it is the setting as a standard for our own behaviour whatever our society or our group within that society thinks is the reasonable amount of virtuous action that might be expected of us."

She went on: "Earlier expectations were sterner because the standard set was not 'what a bunch of human beings mostly do' but 'what is the highest *capacity* of the *best* human being,' and making a jump beyond that to the best we can imagine, i.e. the Perfect and Divine—

what would *that* kind of being do? That is, the standards were *ideals* set by reference to what was admittedly beyond us, not *averages* set by reference to the facts of our accomplishment.

Rosemond went on to say that the people of the sixteenth and seventeenth centuries had large expectations not only of each other but also of themselves. One expectation was that "those who were intelligent or capable *owed* their services to those less endowed—since God only *lent* these capacities to them to use in his service."

Rosemond then asked, "What would happen if we expected more of ourselves?" In answer, she explained that the people of the sixteenth and seventeenth centuries, "expecting more of themselves than they could possibly ever do, they not only seemed never to have realized the extreme danger of this attitude but positively profited from it. Think of the hazards of this. Never to be able to pat yourself on the back, always to feel insecure no matter what you'd done, you'd never done enough to satisfy this impossible standard that expected fallible men to be as like God as they could."

She continued: "One reason why the thoughtful person of the seventeenth century expected so much of himself, and of his children, and of persons in colleges, lies in the fact that English seventeenth century thinking was still based on Judaic-Christian ethics. That ethics makes absolutely fantastic demands of the human being. It expects miracles. This is the manner of it:

"'I beseech you therefore, that ye present your bodies a living sacrifice, acceptable unto God, which is YOUR REASONABLE SERVICE. AND BE NOT CONFORMED TO THIS WORLD, but be Ye TRANSformed, by the renewing of your mind, that ye may *prove what is* that good, and acceptable, and perfect will of God.' (Romans 12:1–2) Do *God's* will. Take *superhuman* standards as your measure.

"I said this was a sermon about the *sin* of sloth. I therefore intend to point to moral and intellectual laziness not as *inadvisable,* but as an avoidable and wicked choice, made by a human being who is capable of being good and chooses to be bad."

In another homily, celebrating the purchase by the library of six volumes of John Donne's sermons, she cited numerous brief quotations from these texts. Donne says: "*Though* thou hadst nothing to do with God, in coming hither, God hath something to do with thee, now thou art here . . . thou are *some* kind of witness of his light. Do you wish to pass out of this world, as thy hand passes out of a basin of water, which may be somewhat the fouler for thy washing in it, but retains no other impression of thy having been there?"

Rosemond went on: "Our world has little use for protestations of faith which do not lead to real results in the everyday political and economic relations of man. So too, Donne, for as he says, 'who will believe me when I speak, if by my life they see I do not believe myself?' "

A final quotation summarized the theme of her sermon: "Man is not all soul, but a body too. And God hath divers ways into divers men; into some he comes at noon, in the sunshine of prosperity, to some in the dark and heavy clouds of adversity. Some he affects with the music of the church, some with some particular collect or prayer; some with some passage in a sermon that takes no hold of him that stands next him. *Watch* the way of the Spirit of God, into *thee;* that way which he makes his path, and by which thou findest thyself most affected, and best disposed towards him—and make straight *that* path, embrace him in *those* means." [All emphases in these sermons are Rosemond's.]

Rosemond spent a portion of the summer of 1950 with her mother, living in Dick's house while he was away. In September she returned to New London to occupy a new home that she was renting from the college. It was an odd little one-storied, modernistic dwelling, constructed entirely of steel, bordering the campus. The house appeared almost as a symbol of her new status and gave her the privacy and quiet she needed. One of her students remembered that it "was all done in sort of southwest Mexican style."

During the fifties her reputation spread across the United States, England, and Europe. More and more she was in demand as a visiting professor, a lecturer, and a critic; she received several honorary degrees. Rosemond had gained eminence as a scholar, and a special quality of her person, an enriching presence, drew people to her wherever she went.

In November 1950, she wrote to Eleanor of her move, her new house, and some gossip, and of plans to get together again. There are no further letters to Eleanor until the spring of 1952. Even for Rosemond this was an immensely busy time. She was writing reviews of books in her field for a number of scholarly journals; preparing her third book, *A Reading of George Herbert,* for publication; and then, on April 13, 1951, she was invited to give a speech titled "AAUW Fellows and Their Survival" at the annual meeting of the American Association of University Women in Atlantic City. Later, the *Journal* of the AAUW reported that "Convention delegates set some kind of record in their demand for the text of this address . . . Mimeographed copies were run off overnight, and disappeared like hotcakes. That a scholar in medieval and Renaissance literature evoked such a response is perhaps one more tribute to the value of the humanities."[3]

The day following this event the Richmond, Virginia, *News Leader* headlined the story of the convention with "Thought Tools Denied Women;" it opened with this lead: "A woman educator today told members of the American Association of University Women that college trained women are being denied the 'tools of thought.'"[4] In her speech Rosemond not only encouraged the "survival" of AAUW Fellows but also stressed the importance of a complete education for women. The following are excerpts from her speech:

"I intend to talk about something which I grant no human being can achieve with any great degree of perfection, but which every human being I respect, up and down the recorded centuries, has believed in and does believe in . . . I refer to that strange and passionate human belief: that it is necessary and good to look for the truth about things."

These ringing opening words were followed by:

"One essential: *you must have fellows* . . . What kind of a society produces persons whose primary devotion is to that peculiarly human aim which we have called the desire to know truly? . . . Not a society which puts pragmatic efficiency ahead of seeing into the nature of the mystery. Not a society which puts doing things to others ahead of being something ourselves . . ." We must have society that has a "firm and active belief in the life of the mind as a good life, and in the power of truth . . . to make men free."

Rosemond's talk continued: "It is not AAUW fellows who suffer, but society, for "a society which does not honor the life of the mind will cease to produce men who engage in it . . . We have vastly under-estimated the human being's spiritual capacities, wantonly centraliz-ing him around his less humane needs and desires." Women's educa-tion already suffers more than men's. It suffers from the underlying assumption that "the intellectual life, however rich, is somehow mere-ly tangential when we are thinking of a full life for the whole person-ality, that the life of the mind is somehow a pretty thin thing."

Society's emphasis on the biological function of women has been "to make young women think of themselves as so first and foremost female that they are lucky if they can squeeze in even an occasional glimpse of themselves as human beings, with all the complicated rea-sons-for-being that any fully alive human being has . . . If this society cannot evolve ways to let women both bear children and bear ideas, we have come to a poor pass."[5]

In early October 1951 Rosemond received a letter from Theodore Hornberger, chairman of the department of English at the University of Minnesota, inviting her to teach a seminar during the summer ses-sion of 1952: "It being the opinion of the professors of English that there is no one whose presence would be more desirable . . . "[6] As a further enticement, Hornberger offered her a teaching position for half of the winter quarter and the spring quarter, knowing her duties at Connecticut would last until the end of January (Minnesota was on a three-semester system). Telegrams, telephone calls, and letters flew between New London and Minneapolis; panic ensued in the Connecticut College English department as they searched for a replacement; and in just two weeks the trustees would meet to grant, or withhold, their approval. At last, Leicester Bradner, from Brown, was persuaded to take her seminar, the course for which it would be most difficult to find a replacement.

There followed more letters from Minnesota listing an array of courses from which Rosemond could choose what she preferred; pro-posing living arrangements, always a source of anxiety for her; and, finally, discussing finances. She outlined her preferences for an apart-ment: "Do people still live Southeast? I lived for years on Ninth Ave.

between Klaeber's house and Erdmann of Biology. I'm a country gal and love access to a yard, but despite having a car there's a *lot* to be said for being close to one's work so that one can manage afoot when there is Weather to fight, since without all my books I'll be spending plenty time at the Library . . . and also to live where I can get in touch with people, for I like plenty conversation. That sounds like near the University, doesn't it? esp. since if there's a Faculty Club of any sort, I'll probably eat at it a good deal."[7]

A few weeks later, still fretting over living space, she argued again for living "Southeast": "I guess it is mostly that I'm such a born small-towner, never learned the sharp urban separation between one's work and one's home; willing to pay for accessibility in lack-of-modern-comfort, or money. But I'll take advice."[8]

Despite her reputation Rosemond was required to suggest the names of three people who might give recommendations. Leicester Bradner was delighted: "It amuses me that Rosemond Tuve should require recommendation from me or any one else, since she is one of the outstanding scholars of our age."[9] Harold S. Wilson, of the University of Toronto, after describing her as a leading authority in the field of Renaissance poetry and literary theory, added, "she is, as well, a completely charming person."[10] And then her good friend Merritt Y. Hughes, of the University of Wisconsin, wrote, "It is a pleasure to testify to the international reputation which Professor Rosemond Tuve has won by her scholarship."[11] And finally, Dorothy Bethurum, on whom all the problems of Rosemond's leave devolved: "We lend her to you this semester with something less than delight." She admitted that "as a teacher she stimulates her best students to their maximum capacity, compelling of them a fresh organization of ideas and revealing always the timeliness of what she is teaching. As a colleague you will find her generous and courageous."[12]

Rosemond forwarded an outline of her courses, recommended reading, and possible topics for papers. Students would have their regular professors for the first half of the winter semester then be taken up by Professor Tuve. Rosemond finished teaching the first semester of the 1951-52 year at Connecticut College at the end of January. On February 7, accompanied by maps from AAA, she drove to

Minneapolis to be on hand by the fifteenth, ready to read student papers she had already assigned. Teaching at two colleges simultaneously was a trick she would repeat at Harvard in 1956.

Rosemond's problems with Connecticut College pursued her to Minnesota. Although she and Rosemary were close friends, there remained a certain tension between them. Each spring, as new appointments were issued, Rosemond was rarely satisfied. Although she protested that money was not important, she was clearly offended by the salary she received, which she viewed as an estimate of her worth to the college. And so, in mid-April, she replied to the "appointment letter" from Rosemary Park with disgust and sarcasm.

> Dear Rosemary,
>
> I had expected to write you early in the game a Mere Letter, just for news value. When I got the appointment letter, it seemed as if any epistle would have to have a business angle and I've let it slip. Out of mere distaste-for-business, and pre-occupation with Life as a Picnic—-I'm waiting for break-through in present ridiculous pattern of everything I turn hand to being a Gen. Success & lapped in smiles, 'taint Nature, but while no worm raises its head I tend to go along merrily pretty busy.
>
> I think the raises are wonderful, and I don't see how you did it. All reports are that morale is like G. of Eden before apple. [Rosemond's salary had been raised from $5,355 to $6,600 for the coming year.]
>
> I'm not dissatisfied with mine, which I note is a swatch above the mean. It is true that I am still in the group of those who are of below-the-average value, among profs. serving at C.C., even though the mere fact of what I'm doing now seems to prove value in other groups of professors, and true that if your evaluation of my worth to the college still ranges me there, this does make a difference in the way I feel about staying on. Just never can catch up I guess with Home Comforts like MXD and Gen'l MacA, and competition pretty stout

against famous etchers and sociologists and things. They hope I can (will) stay longer here. I do have to realize *when* it comes time for decision among various things what it means that I am still below the average and very considerably below the median in salary —*of* your list of professors *there* . . . The third book whose preface I've signed from C.C. comes out in July in London and Aug. in Chicago, but I wasn't thinking of this as the most typical reason why I might seem to be of equal value to you with some of those on our list who fall above instead of below the mark of average-in-value-among-those-there.[13]

She continued by relaying comments of praise, from others, for Connecticut College, and ended on a light note about the twenty thousand wild geese that "rise in patterns from the pathless and infinite plains;" and how "it would be just your ticket (except the 3.30 arising)."[14]

It wasn't until May 4 that she wrote to Eleanor of her excitement at being back at "their" old university. Although Eleanor was in her class at Minnesota, they never met.

> 2370½ Hendon Avenue
> St Paul Minn
> Good Friday
> Dear Eleanor,
> I'm having a reglar circus.
> Sorry it makes me such a bad correspnder-.
> I'm just *sunk* with letters due to the fact that *N.L.* with all its works & ways (i.e. business & friends) piled onto the usual Family-England-Business-Friends—and am behind with everyone. I trusted to DB [Dorothy Bethurum] going up to Smith soon after I'd got here, & had sent back one letter telling how the trip was not even to wet our feet, Sioux's and mine! and telling how I live in the Earth like a sort of Alice in Wonderland tale. (quite literally I go thru a bright red door, stooping the head slightly, into a house built into a hill— MODRUNISTICK—I enter on the ground level, & when I'm

in my windows open upon the ground itself, so that when I lean upon window-sills like Raphael's cherbs, in the pitcher, I look right out upon where my NASTURTIUMS are going to be.

I pay 100. a month, but it is to my mind very *amusing* place to live in, & I'd rather be amused than proper. It is what my chairman's wife says the Europeans call American Squãlor—i.e. a la ranch house has kitchen Brightnesses all red and yaller sticking out into the living room—well you'll see, so why describe. Luckily it is too small for me to entertain back the 1000's that I owe. Never been so Queen, all I do is go around like a visiting Royalty. I see the Browns and the Tates a special lot [Allen Tate, the poet, and his wife, Caroline]— Hunt Brown is chrman, and I'm much taken with his entire fmily; hear lots of music with his wife [Elizabeth (Bid) Brown, who became a lifelong friend], who is a very amusing and straightforward simple person—got me into the Bach society before I'd been here 3 days. Last night we went to Tenebrae at the St Paul cathedral together; today I went back alone to the Good Friday service but they sang nothing good. Caroline Tate saw me (as you know they're converts) ["they" refers to Allen and Caroline Tate] and I'd no sooner got home than she and her godson and a young grad. student who'd been there dropped in to tea.

Then I tried vainly to draw up some q's [questions] for Master's exam, and ran off to the last symphony concert of the season with Eliz Nissen. My object now is to get my shocking pile-up of Nylon Junk a little decreased by washing as much as I can stand, and get into bed before I catch the cold Eliz. had, me being in fine state there-for, acct. staying up till 2.15 writing a page each to my grad sem. 2 nights ago, anent their plans for papers (they're as infantile about being able to find themselves something they want to Find Out, as a bunch of seniors)—and havent caught up sleep since then or since the last time I stayed up till 2, which was to write one of my Newspapers to the various family. These occur frequently, bec. of so much family-connections in place where we were last a famly together, and run to 3 or 4 singlespaced pages; I've taken to carbons for the brothers and uncles, just can't get around separately.

I am mad about the country side; I havent SEEN IT, damn it; finally in a Revolt I just went out snow or no snow, stopping at the 3 A and making them give me local maps; ran up the Mississippi and visited ha ha to everyone's amusement ANOKA and lost myself in the mud on country roads and had a fine time & smelled Sap. Even if I did mostly go thru walls of snow, one tunelled way thru high snow walls. That wasnt long since, but now we've melted.

If S.D. gets past its flood I intend to pick up my young man cousin [Howard Cole, Norma Tuve Cole's son] and spurt out to north of Aberdeen to see the 20000 geese come sailing down over the prairie and settle and rise and settle. Elliott the man you prob. also remember as head of psych., told me about it, says "it is Cosmic"—I gotta see it if at all possible. That wd. be next Th. or Fri., & I'll just give a cut & go. If floods still, can't.

I'm looking forward no end to your coming by. I have here a study and a bedroom (bed in each) (both noisy acct. ComoHarriet car [trolley], but not so noisy as Mohegan ave.) and the livingroom-kitchen larger room. Anyhow it has 2 desks and plenty bookspace, more impt. than old Bourgeois Dining room. I'm thru the first (half)-quarter—half quarter (winter) of my stint; and into the spring quarter—so am teaching new things by now, except for my grad.sem., which continued, & is quite exciting "Image & Symbol in Sp. and Milton"—quite a good bunch, about 9 I think. Turned down 4 or 5 who wanted to audit and also same no that wanted to join in 2nd quarter but hadnt had first.

I picked a Chaucer course, undergrad, very virtuously, so's to have chance to learn more Chaucer, which I hate to forget so; quite good of me since I could have had rather a once-a-week grad sem in Drama with only 3 in it. Tired of

Drama, taught it at NL and also here winter q. I sneaked the House of Fame into the Ch course tho it is sposed to be all C.Tales, [*Canterbury Tales*] and one way & nother expect to refresh myself considerable on That Bard.

Then I do Milton, for 40 people, and about ¼ of those are grads; trying to learn to do as the men do, teach w. left hand and leave myself some leisure. Not succeeding as yet; take it as seriously as if at CC, far more seriously I took Shak than the students did. This wont do, it's past 11, pretty soon it wont be early any more. But I've composed a dozen letters in my head to you, and thot I'd get one of them Realized into Phenomenal as cf Transcendental Nature, and get it off in that clearly Phenom. engine, the U.S.Postal Service.

I hope you'd a nice vac. I put the page proof for GH [George Herbert] into the mial mail (too tired to spell) and stayed a couple days down at Hunt's (right by Lake of the Isles so a amusement to go down and stay, as twerre away for the weekend), and read Dionysius and most of the Paradiso trying to get a little brighter for the Milton stuff in the sem. Many thanks for your cards and missives just before I left N.L.—Pine to tell you all, with Details!! That will be during JUNE??? I have just a week or so between spr. and summer school, when I'll be away, but I'm sure it's too early to conflict with your stop here. I am perishing to explore Minnesota!! I nose around down the streets whenever I get going (have driven Sioux every day, ice or not) and it is all the greatest fun.

> love to you, and salute Ruth &
> Those Two Curried Chickens
> Love from Ros

The "page proof for GH" refers to her third book (fourth, if you count her thesis), *A Reading of George Herbert,* published in July by Faber and Faber, London, and in August by the University of Chicago Press. It was dedicated to Carleton Brown and Edwin Greenlaw. No doubt T.S. Eliot, who was an editor at Faber and Faber, saw the book and it may have been at that time that he became interested in learning more about its author. They met in 1959, and corresponded occasionally.

The book is essentially two essays: The first, centering on George Herbert's poem "The Sacrifice," amplifies her dispute with Empson and the "new criticism;" the second discusses themes, symbols, and metaphor in Herbert's poetry. Rosemond's thesis is that Herbert's poetry demands more than the analytical reading of modern critics. His poetry is informed, and transformed, by the tradition of Christian symbolism and medieval iconography, which must be understood if we are to fully grasp the profundity of the poetry. She writes, in perhaps her most moving statement, that "only the images a man understands as he understands his own mother tongue can work upon him after the immemorial fashion of all metaphor. Only thus will they have for him that loveliness which ravishes the understanding, and only thus will he experience what I have called the peculiar functioning and contribution of the arts: the insight into a world of values and meanings not otherwise either open to man's sight or conveyable to his fellows."[15]

Her deeply felt conclusion unifies the two themes of her understanding of George Herbert. "If we are willing to learn Herbert's language we shall hear what he says, or most of it, being made able to experience the beauty and the power which are inextricably part of it. Since he says it in the language of metaphor it did not stop being true when certain meanings it may have had to him ceased to exercise power over men's minds. Metaphors cheat time in ways beyond a poet's foresight. The meanings we find still true, even in ways he did not foresee, are yet his meanings, but at a level so deep that no man knows or could say in cold conceptual formulation the reach and scope of them."[16]

At the end of May, Rosemond sent Eleanor the following postcard:

> Dearest Eleanor: Oh shoot. How could you resist us. Get my address correct (Prob. my error): 2370 $\frac{1}{2}$, [Rosemond was in error] you have it turned round. Phone is Midway 8371. Landlord is Mr. Kerlan and office is 217 Folwell; Engl.office 219 Fol. (univ.phone no) always has gals to Inform except

Sat.—Oh frabjous day. The Bower is at the corner of Como & Hendon, right opposite the Breck school (everyone knows). Its on Como Harr.line—(cut diagonally by Hendon ave.) just below the Farm campus, about $2\frac{1}{2}$ blocks over into St.Paul and my apt. has a BRIGHT RED DOOR leading into the Earth, or so it looks. Sure we will scoot around weekends etc., I might meet you for one in F.F. [Fergus Falls, where Eleanor's family lived] or the place your family goes to, then we could use one when you are here for even fancier ideas. I havent even seen North Shore yet. Have just 1 day betw. my exams & summer sch. classes. I am cutting classes going 4 days to S.D. to get degree & revisit Childhood, today. Summ. sch. starts Ju 18.

Love—R

She wrote up the side of the postcard: "Write me when yr. dates here can be approx. settled so I dont plan w. others." Rosemond then ended her card by just casually mentioning to Eleanor the weekend she will spend in Sioux Falls, South Dakota, where she and Merle are to receive honorary degrees from Augustana College. But an earlier letter to Merle had been exultant:

I'm delighted with the idea that I shall see one piece Fambly before I leave these parts. I even like the idea that you are the Piece. . . . I am going to get away to Canton— probably my only chance to mosey up and down those streets, and sit under the Standpipe, and kill a Democrat bug in Lovers' Lane. . . . I want to Walk to the Post Office past Tobiasons and Isaacsons and Tank's, and I want to sit down on the grass and read a book where I used to herd the cow....

I expect to Purr solidly from about 30th May to 2 June. Luckily I'd a Young Broke Student riding with me on the Aberdeen—Geese Jaunt or I'd have parked the car and rolled on the prairies till I was took up by the FBI. I'm mad about Flat Country.[17]

Also, in her letter, she remarked to Merle, "I hate decisions," indicating that the efforts of the English department to hold on to her were ongoing, and that preliminary discussions with Rosemond, about a second appointment for the fall term, had taken place. In fact, Huntington Brown, chairman of the English department, wrote to President Park on May 15, seeking her permission to invite Rosemond to remain for the fall semester. "We knew her distinguished reputation as a scholar, but none of us, I am sure, had any idea of her extraordinary magnetism as a teacher . . . she has exerted a profound and salutary influence upon their point of view. They say that their courses with her have been in the nature of a revelation."[18] But another absence from the college in so short a period of time was not advisable. Rosemary Park wrote to Dr. Brown that "we are gradually getting into the position of seeming to have something in the window which we are not willing to sell. Under these circumstances, I was very pleased that Miss Tuve herself did not wish to push for a further extension of the leave."[19]

On June 1, Rosemond and Merle were awarded honorary degrees from Augustana College. Included in the ceremonies that weekend was the dedication of the new women's dormitory, to be named Anthony G. Tuve Hall. It was a poignant moment for both Rosemond and Merle. Merle also gave the commencement address and in the final paragraph of his speech he stressed the importance of poetic thinking, which goes beyond the mere recording of facts: "The basic point of my whole discussion this morning is that literal-mindedness is appropriate only to a small fraction of the total of any man's experiences in life," he said. "By far the greatest fraction, the most personal, the deepest, the most vital and treasured of all our experiences, are illuminated and transfused with understanding and import, and made significant as inseparable components of our reality and existence as persons, only by the non-literal, symbolic, associative, deep-rooted and unregimented kind of awareness and illuminated conviction which I have indicated by the term poetic thinking."

In closing, he remarked: "These thoughts I happily dedicate to the memory of my Father, A. G. Tuve."

Rosemond Tuve with students in the 1950s. Courtesy Connecticut College Archives.

8

ROSEMOND RETURNED TO CONNECTICUT at the end of July 1952. She had so captivated her colleagues at Minnesota that a movement was still under way to create a permanent position for her. Hunt Brown and Samuel Holt Monk were among her most vocal champions. But funds were scarce and her field well covered. In the end, no offer could be made. Yet, this didn't stop graduate students from forming an exclusive society of "Tuveans." Rita and Dick Gollin were already married when they attended her Spenser class. Although they knew her only briefly, it was, like so many others, a connection for life. Rita never forgot the bibliography of the things Rosemond wanted them to read that they received weeks ahead of her own arrival; not knowing what to expect, her theatrical entrance into the classroom startled them: ". . . hair flying, arms loaded with books, paper slips in all the books, and pencils stuck in her hair. She'd start talking and talking. It would gradually grow in excitement. Midway, we'd get excited by a tangent here and a tangent there, and so the drama of the class was always unpredictable and remarkable—what Dick called 'her considered improvisational flurry.'"

Rita continued: "One pedagogical tool she gave them was her own method. You didn't go into the class until you had read something and gotten excited. It didn't have to be Spenser, perhaps a poem by Donne, any poem that stirred your mind. Then you could enter the classroom with your mind flowing and your excitement and energy at its peak. She also gave a lecture on how to teach. 'One could teach like this,' she said, and sat behind the desk rather stodgily; 'or one could teach like this,' and she stood up behind the podium and adjusted things. 'Or, one could teach like this'—giving a wonderful imitation of her self teaching—coming to the edge of the platform, a step raised, and involving everyone, almost falling into the audience."

Two "absolutely imprinted anecdotes" were also stamped on the minds of Rita and Dick Gollin. On their first visit to her basement apartment, which was painted yellow on one wall, rendering it very bright, they recalled: "The kitchen–dining table was attached to this wall on one side, as the apartment was quite narrow and short of storage space. So, she would be talking and all of a sudden she would get on all fours and crawl under the table to where she had a little storage place in the wall, and still talking, she'd crawl out from under, producing the loaf of bread. Then, put out the bread board, put the loaf of bread on it, and go on talking while she sliced the bread with big whacks with the knife to punctuate her sentences. She was so large, and the basement ceiling was so low, that the gestures took on an extra dimension of heroic grandeur."

The Gollins remembered her largesse on another occasion: "Everything about her was oversized in that way. To a city girl it was alien. She drove four hundred miles to see the migrating geese. Thought nothing of doing it. Got up at three A.M. to take students. She was an inspiration in all those ways."

Then there was her love of nineteenth-century domestic architecture. Some years later, when she came to the University of Rochester as an "outside examiner," she visited the Gollins, who were teaching at the university. Rita Gollin recalled: "I took her for a drive to show her really posh glamorous sections of Rochester . . . it didn't impress her one bit. But when we crossed the river where there were turn-of-the-century houses, she would fairly percolate with excitement. All these buildings which we virtually ignored as tawdry or typical she would get excited about. She wanted to see the peculiar and eccentric—stucco, next to brick, next to wood—with weird carvings or unusual window light. What she wanted to see was the idiosyncratic, not 'Milo-like,' but original."

Whether it was eating strawberries on their back porch, the tea, the air, "there was just no element of the experience that wasn't enjoyed." Rita Gollin remembered: "Everything was so inspirational that you would like to be the kind of person she would like to share this with . . . For both of us she was one of the most influential teachers we've ever had. When she was gone, she would always be sort of a yardstick: 'am I measuring up?' 'would she be pleased with me now?' We knew her for only a very short time, yet she encouraged us in the most profound way."

The Tuveans were like a distinguished society. Whenever, or wherever, you met someone connected with Rosemond, it soon became apparent that he or she had known her. Sherman Hawkins, whom she met at Princeton, said, "It's a world of Roz Tuve lovers who find each other." Many of her students from Minnesota went on to academic success. Earl Miner, who was her student assistant, later went to Princeton to teach seventeenth-century literature. Paul Ramsey, continuing his work in Shakespeare, went to the University of Tennessee. Nancy Streuver, a graduate of Connecticut College, who took her degree in history at the University of Minnesota, remains a staunch Tuvean.

Earl Miner was not in her Spenser course, but, he recalled, was "doing research for her and used to dog her books for her and help her rest up." Her teaching, he remembered, was a "kind of conversation with students about ideas, about knowledge. It wasn't any ordinary lecture style. It was just being Ros. Also, there was nothing sectarian about Ros. She appealed to everybody. In a sense, what is important about my knowledge of her is the depth of impression she could make upon somebody in so short a time. She wasn't anybody for small talk, and she wasn't very good at it. Ros always talked about what mattered to her, what was important, so it didn't take long to be impressed."

Miner remembered this anecdote: "Ros really liked good food, but never bothered to cook. In 1952, at a meeting of the MLA in Chicago, Dick and Rita and I were in a taxi driving to a French restaurant where Ros ordered herself a really fancy dinner, including snails. An event occurred in the taxi which was characteristic of Ros. Rita and Dick are Jewish and there was a lot of anti-Semitism in those days. The driver said something like he hadn't been in a temple or synagogue since his Bar Mitzvah, and it wasn't a good thing. And Ros gave him something like a lecture—'Young man, we all come from somewhere and we must all honor where we come from. I come from South Dakota and you come from an important and ancient heritage and you should value it.' It was the kind of remark that she used to make: at once cultural and human."

Miner went on: "When we were at Williams we had a party for her. She just bounded over those Berkshire Hills. She had great physical stamina as well as stamina of personality. People were drawn to her for a combination of reasons. If people had heard about her, they were curious. But if somebody didn't know her, they could see that those who did know her thought she was someone special. Some people were envious of her, but none of us thought of ever trying to rival her, or ever felt any envy. We were just happy to be with her."

Although Rosemond preferred living in the East near her family, she missed the attention and recognition she received at Minnesota. Shortly after returning home, she drove to Vermont to visit the Browns at their summer "camp" in North Fayston. She would maintain a close friendship with Bid Brown until the end of her life, her letters to Bid revealing yet another aspect of her persona. In October, she wrote the first of many letters to Bid Brown.

Monday night after my seminar.
Sitting by the desk, on the New Rug, of which
Dutch says 'Dead Leopards'. Hurry & come give
your Judgment.
Dear Bid,
      Note example of Poifect Courtesye—lined-paper responds to lined-paper. One degree 'umbler than Woolworth's; i.e. college blue book. It never occurred to me, till I sought the *papier juste*, this minute; from henceforth is my chronic family-stationery problem solved. I can't find ANYthing ratty-looking enough to prevent my Mama from saving my epistles for their HISTORICAL INTEREST. Maybe this is it.
      I have written a dozen letters in my mind, usually in the Bath, wherein my mind is inordinately active. They were going to start

Dear Bid and Hunt

but blest if time didn't catch up with me and today I got Hunt's letter thanking me for the book and therefore Delicacy prevents me including him by name (both of you have such fine fillings you would understand this in a trice), so he is not getting a answer to his letter herewith, *that* will probably come up out of the well of unknowing about December and will start Dear Hunt and Bid ASSUMING that you will write in between somewhere and tell me the news. Such as: do you walk around the lake Saturdays, and who. Is Mrs. Edwy nice. Have you and Caroline been to Collegeville. Does SAM [Monk] miss me (wring his neck if he don't). Is Chris [Bid's youngest son] going to be confirmed. Who has slept in my bed. When any of you go past the Bower on your way to the Elliotts do you see ghosts (if you don't you are a passel of dead fish). What's the Bach society singing. Who from Mpls. in next year's Freshman class at C.C. is Jon [Bid's son] going to come down to see next fall when I'll lend him the study to sleep in and the house to have his friends over to. *When* is Howard's oral so's I do the orguliest possible praying for him. WHY didn't anybody tell me Hunt was going to have a operation is that any way to act a person's friends to be on the Table and no worrying done the *idea*.

Are Henry and Eleanor in the house yet. Does Henry look Rested. Is John still adamant on the Resurrection of the Body. Did Elizabeth take it ill that I parked your mirror on them and are you and Hunt sorry you lent it me considering I couldn't fizzically get it back as I should of. Has Leonard got jolly. What colour are the trees along 24th Street.

oh SHUCKS. it makes me lonesome.

Life here is rich likem blum cake (oh HA HA that touch was unintended. Call up Freud.) I am in up to my neck after plums the whole time. We go to things incessant. They are good things, all of them; only trouble is how they crowd out the plain simple seeing of one's friends. We had Gropius last week and he was excellent; so was the string quartet the afternoon and the night before, three dinner parties the same week (only here we don't have the sense to stay and talk after dinner parties, we always have to get in a car and all go to a dance recital or a reception-for-new-faculty or something). One thing I do find myself re-enamored of: being in the country. I get into Sioux at least twice or thrice a week and in $3\frac{1}{2}$ to $4\frac{1}{2}$ minutes am setting on a hill with 42,476 stones embedded in it covered with red poison ivy, looking at olde whyte cottage and grey shingled barn 4 cows assorted sheeps and a red gate. Then I correct student essays. Coffee in thermos. I especially like this when it rains. Then I amble slowly home and cross the Thames with Irish light over it and a coupla rainbows just as the sun comes out in order to set. (Sun very meticulous about this here. Yankee methodicalness). My students are charming. I scare hell out of them by telling them I'm not used to any immature dependences and inadequacies, standards formed at University, on MEN students. They listen like I was oracle. They're quite good.

This won't do. I have to read two whole books and correct 10 essays by 10.30 and it is nearly 11.

> Love to you all.   Ros

I NEVER wrote and thanked my Host for a visit in Vermont.

I am a Pig for manners.

Later, in a long, meditative letter to Merle, she confided her feelings about being back:

> "A little lonesome and Grim here in the Nurses Ward after Minnesota (infinitely less dutiful and more swarming-with-interested-and-curious), yet when I see them in Boston at the meetings 2 days after Christmas I shall beat on them to please have no notions that would give me anything to decide, for a couple years. I cannot live in a city. The country here has been ravishing, & all that ails the people is the 20th century."[1]

After spending Thanksgiving and her birthday with Eleanor, she wrote again.

Dearest Elianore   [December 2, 1952]

. . . I have been drownded in the new Psych man's pro-posals for His Offerings, before Inst. [instruction] comm. today; they are shocking—new courses, & we had decided to STOP dividing our 850 into innumerable fractions, AND so much psych. for his majors that they must go out as illiberal as all the usual psychologists.

This is not the only set-to since my return which has fed me up with the unhappy results of Ambition in Human Beengs. It sure is the Apple. I think all this may be related to sense of Euphoria I get when visiting you. Get cheered up abt. Human Race, acct this big Respect I feel when I see an actual person who has turned down the flesh-pots and the Sense of Power because actually prefers to think and read our Poets. I get disillusioned seeing so much accepting of synonymity between Live and Strive. Big deception. I will be condemned to the latter entirely if I dont stop this & do lessons. I havent said thank you yct, but I guess you can gather I had a Pleasure in the visit, so I will close now, with regards to All . . .

                    love & thank you
                    R/

According to her cousin Norma Tuve Cole, the months at Minneapolis were "the happiest of Rosemond's life." Her return to Connecticut College proved difficult. The melancholy and loneliness expressed in her last letter to Eleanor carried over into a letter to Merle about Christmas with her mother. As we learn, even her physi-cal health was affected. (Her gallbladder was removed the following May.) It is the only time Rosemond admitted difficulties with visits home and painful relations with her mother.

No mention is made of the overwhelming success of her book *A Reading of George Herbert*, which filled the windows of Blackwell's bookstore in Oxford when it was published that past summer. Of all her writings, it comes closest to expressing her own religious beliefs, which so nearly matched those of Herbert. Sherman Hawkins, a colleague and friend, recognized the connections she saw between religion and literature. For her, the literature of Milton and Herbert was inspired. "Their utterances," Hawkins remarked, "are taken as a spirit, a living spirit, and her gaudiness is the vehicle by which it remains in the memory. She was a presence, not a particularized presence; a Platonist, moving through appearances to reality. God-man is made in image of God, filtered through personality."

During the first three months of 1953, a series of lengthy letters were written, first by William Empson, then, in response, by Rosemond. Empson was publishing a new book and wanted Rosemond's opinion on some of his ideas, expecting that her views might influence his. Initially, the tone was courteous, but later Empson became vituperous; Rosemond, although not giving in, tried to remain warm and tactful. Empson's condescending remark that "she suggests to me a powerful secretary, determined not to let the reporters write up what is actually said by her lunatic millionaire" [2] was, in Paul Alpers's (a former student and colleague) words, "wickedly accurate."

Meanwhile Rosemond was still battling for recognition from Connecticut College. In March 1953, just a year after the previous exchange of letters about salary, Rosemond wrote again about her "appointment letter." There was also a suggestion that the University of Minnesota was still interested in hiring her. Only the cover letter remains.

> Dear Rosemary
>
> I never get over the feeling that dear miss park is terrible cold and despite greatest respect for your Office can never quite dissolve you *into* your office. Therefore all letters require a covering note w. more love and less awr.
>
> It seems to me that I am *still* left in my pickle, how to act if.
>
> For a person that's sposed to be worth something for their writing it will prob seem to you *as* to me that most writ-

ing is letters. This may take long to read but it took a lot longer to write. It's interesting, though, and all Nice.

> yrs,
>
> Ros [3]

Rosemary's reply was swift. "Dear Miss Tuve," she wrote, "I should like to acknowledge your letter of March 14. I regret that there is still doubt in your mind as to your value to the College.

"You realize, I am sure, how difficult a task it is to weigh different types of merit and to repay in various ways with leave, salary, etc. There is no question in my mind of your value to the College, nor do I think anyone else connected with the College has any doubt. I have said this to you many times and I anticipate saying it again.

"I realize, however, that in your present situation this is not enough, and I shall be glad to recommend to the Trustees that an additional increase of $400 be made in your salary for next year."[4]

Rosemond's salary jumped from $6,600 to $7,200 for the 1953–54 academic year. The following undated letter appears to be Rosemond's response.

Dear Rosemary,

I am airing my brains on the Chesapeake, very healthy bay fulla sea-nettles so people are sparse; give me nettles any day. Organ mentioned is fully aerated now and I am about to turn back. It has been in the back of my mind about your Father and operation, and I am hoping that it went well.

I don't know how you carry everything . . .

Now I still seriously think of you as free without remark to make any adjustment you find proper or necessary, before April meeting, in connection with your last letter. The different *feeling* (feels good anywhere to stand up straight among yr. peers) having been conveyed, I think you should do what you need to. There's one point I forgot: please would you tend to it just without speech that I do not by chance or happenstance ever get up too close to two people I ought to be 'way under: D.B. and D.B. [Dorothy Bethurum and Dean Burdick]. I shall never know any figures, nor do I state any, but would cut throat if that proportion were disturbed, and would always rather be Peter, you remember how they paid Paul, when not enough to go around.

The grass is growing fine. That was a generous kind image, and worth mints.

Merle says McCarthy is no.1 Communist he bets. Since he said same in usual louder voice than chemins-de-fer-d'etat, in the Wardman Park, I spose we'll all be testifying for him presently; get ready. You were seen enroute Chartres with this pink.

So as I learned to say from my betters,

Regards,

Ros [5]

In May, after months of experiencing a variety of troubling symptoms, Rosemond had her gallbladder removed. Six weeks later, she drove to Mexico, going part of the way alone. Since her Vassar days she had been fascinated with Mexico. With her books and thermos beside her in Siouxie, she could glory in the scenery and mull over whatever book of literary criticism she might be currently considering. (During the fifties, she was invited to review many books for scholarly journals.)

Before leaving for Mexico she wrote to Bid and Hunt Brown:

Mexico—July 20—after that—N. Fayston, VT—the Brown's place. I shall have some company in the car for 1000 miles or so, so I won't get any good communion with Nature like as I had in 1952 in the West.

with love from Dowsabel.

Dowsabel is a character from Drayton's "Eclogues," a country lass who is very dumb.

In a letter to Leicester Bradner, after learning that he had undergone the same operation, she wrote with great gaiety of what must have been a painful procedure. Bradner saved the letter until the end of his life.

C.C. 11 Aug. Just back from Penna.
Dear Leicester,
    Hooray!
    It's a wonderful operation. I didn't know what Eating was like till after I'd had mine. All kinds of bras I thought were too tight began to be unnoticeable, and innumerable annoyances that I thought were part of the course of Human Life turned out to be nothing but PEBBLES out of place, camping in me instead of rolled round with earth's diurnal course the way rocks & stones SHOULD be . . .
    I am partial to operations anyhow, as cf. being Ill. Op's get *done,* and all you do is slowly and surely feel better, while reading. Whereas sicknesses cannot be cured by an *act,* and therefore have no shape or logical form, and are one damned succession of try-it-and-watch-it. I am devoted to the system of flinging out the offending member and then just waiting for the system to discover with delight that the offense has really departed. You will see; System will find this out and you practically can't hold back its enchanted rush into plain unconscious *health* again. Everything takes on new charm, as if the world had got a quite new light over it. I became absolutely enamoured of the tastes of things. I drove to Mexico about 6 wks. after mine, and will also report that this op. does not have that hang-over as with some, a sort of psychological getting-over-the-disturbance-to-the-community. The Gall Bladder seems to have no standing, and all the rest are simply elated when she moves out.
    Just to cheer you in any sinful wayward selfishnesses you might commit under the Influence of illness, I will confess that my little ego found time to say to itself during the morning, what luck I got Ast to Saunderstown [the Bradners' summer home in Rhode Island] before they had a invalid on their hands there. I had such a nice time I could not help thinking how much better that L. shd. suffer a few extra weeks as compared with me not introduced to those boys, chicken dinners, bathing-clubs, chipmunks, kitchen-gardens, and views.

Now there is a fine Open Breast made of human depravity for you to rest back on and think upon your Virtues. (Maybe Guyon had just had his gall bladder out and needed to meditate upon his better Side). [Guyon is a knight in the *Fairie Queene.*]

Get those boys to drag in books you hadn't expected to read, by the DOZENS. I read over forty getting over my G.B. extraction. I never seem to have any sendable ones, and anyhow I think since you've got fetchers, it is better to just jar the deadened mind with unusual suggestions. If you havent read some of these get Boy to look for them at Brown: the letters of S. MacKenna not the novelist but the translator of Plotinus. (scrumptious).

The *Journal and Letters of Stephen MacKenna,* edited by E. E. Dodds, which Rosemond was recommending, had been loaned to her by Rosemary Park, whose father, John Edgar Park, at one time president of Wheaton College, had loaned to her. Rosemond wrote: "I was much impressed by this man, and much moved. It is not a book one comes upon; unfortunately."[6] She often recommended the book, not just for the beauty of the writing of this extraordinary, witty, and eloquent Irishman, but also for the deep spiritual insights of the first person to translate the *Enneads* of Plotinus into English.

MacKenna had been forced by deep "abysses" to search for a deeper solution of his personal religious problem than was to be found in a merely disciplinary Catholicism. During the last period of his life, his strongest interest lay in the attempt to "discover a creed which both his reason and his heart could approve." [7] He wrote that he could "no more doubt the existence of a divine mind at work (or at play) in the universe than I can doubt the existence of a mind in humanity."[8]

One excerpt from a letter to Dodds's mother perhaps best illustrates his "credo": "Religion, always very deep indeed with me, has never . . . been an insurance against peril in this world or another—but simply an intense desire after goodness in myself and in others, and also a craving, morbid at times, for something like union with the

divine in whose personality—or some super-correspondent to personality—I have always believed. This union not at all in the sense of
the mystic achievement: that doesn't tempt me one red cent's worth;
but in the sense of being worthy, being high so to speak; in fact I don't
know how to speak—just I suppose as certain heroic souls have wanted to serve their country, artists their art, hobby-imbeciles their imbe-
cile hobby."[9] MacKenna gave a good deal of his life to Irish politics
and social activism. As he continues we understand how Rosemond
was moved by his words: "I want also everyone to be good . . . by sheer
delight in the beauty of goodness . . . there's one God, and every man
may be and should be his gay prophet."[10]

To conclude her letter to Bradner, Rosemond listed many more
books—biographies, memoirs, and novels, then, "Love & Kisses. I'm
just delighted." In pencil, at the top of the page, she added: "Dear
Hallie—When he's through maybe you could get leprosy or sleeping
sickness & ask for Return of Tender Love."

Rosemond expressed her devotion to Connecticut College in
innumerable ways. When she returned to the college in September,
she wrote a letter to President Park, following through on a promise
made in a letter the previous March to donate $150 to Connecticut
College anonymously.

Sept. 17, 1953

Pretty One,
            This is you-remember-what.
    NOTICE DATE. As per original statement, is dated after
second salary payment—account I'm on the 10-month system, and no Foresight known to man can make Sept. like
other months. But I'm so scairt I'll forget it; so, anxious to
send and be able to destroy the Notes to Myself that I find
scattered in all my drawers reminding me. Is made out to you
personally because it is utterly Anonymous forever. No
Strings. President's Basil Bed or Auerbach Commemorative
Lunch, for alla me.
    My Cancelled Cheque is My Receipt; save the office-letter

for Mr. Rockeyfeller, & some present involving more Pure
Cash and less Pure Gefühl [feeling].

my gefühls are always real Pure,
they fizzle loud but they is

> pure
>
> as
>
> yours
>
> with
>
> Love,
>
> Ivory Sope[11]

After spending the summer of 1953 on this side of the Atlantic,
Rosemond was unable to resist the pull of the libraries of Oxford and
London. As she said earlier in a letter to Merle, "that's where the
Spring flows from," the capitalization of *Spring* giving it allegorical
significance. Rosemond's brothers were concerned about their mother's deteriorating heart condition and urged her not to leave at this
critical time. But she was already at work on a book on Milton, despite
her resolve never to write again, and was not going to allow her mother's health to keep her in this country. Consequently, as soon as college was over in June, she departed for England, not returning until
early September. Although her correspondence with Mary
Waldegrave seems to have ended, it can be assumed that she did at
least run out to Chewton while she was in England. Their home was
her home, and she loved the family atmosphere.

On her arrival home she went immediately to Washington to see
her mother, returning again to New London in the midst of another
hurricane. She threw a brief thank-you note to her family before leaving for New York City and a meeting of the English Institute, of which
she had recently been made a member of the board.

Rosemond's mother died on November 20, 1954. She had been
suffering for several years from a heart condition, troubling in itself,
but a constant concern to her children, especially Dick, in getting her
the best care. The following letter is in response to one of condolence
from Eleanor.

Sunday evening   [January 17, 1955]
Dear Eleanor

The lovely feeling of classes being over until early February. (Now that Xmas has been spoilt and we don't have any vacation then.)

Many thanks for your letter. It is not so much painful as engrossing, and extremely serious. I am so glad to have mother not in pain and trouble any more. But such discoveries of loving thought over the years, as one finds a person has left behind—people would be so good to each other if they knew all the intentions of the heart and the trials of the mind.

I would not give anything for having had my attention drawn more to religious matters of the last ten years; water in the dry land . . .

In the following fragment, which was found enclosed with the previous letter, Rosemond revealed more feelings about her mother's death.

. . . over my sense that all that goodness that pushed those loving hearts through day after day, year after year, just does not stop existing. It is just as strong a sense now as two years ago. If there is any such differentiatable thing as "good" then I just do not think it is annihilated though I've no notion of the mode of its continued existence—nothing we can figure out I'm sure. So I have a good deal of happiness, and had especially during the first weeks and months, out of gratitude and gladness that somebody should at last be able to be what they tried to be, year after year, decade after decade. Love just seems stronger than death to me.

Bid Brown felt that Rosemond did believe that in some way life goes on after death, that "her heart told her more than her mind could express."

In January 1955, Merle was invited to participate in a symposium with Susanne Langer and F. Edward Cranz at Connecticut College.

Their lectures were to be on the subject of "freedom and creativity."
Dr. Langer, professor of philosophy, and Dr. Cranz, professor of history, were preeminent members of the Connecticut College faculty.
Merle's notes, in preparation for his talk, indicate the thrust of his
remarks: "methods and problems of physics from any angle, but left
eye occasionally directed to the problem of Freedom."[12] Cranz
remembered his emphasis on the "importance of the wild guess, or
dreaming—the mysterious, poetic, creative activity which precedes
the scientist's articles in journals. He might have influenced
Rosemond." In a moving letter to Rosemary Park, accepting the invitation, Merle related this event:

"When I last visited New London I spent an hour and a quarter
sitting in the speaker's chair in the darkened chapel while the
Palestrina group singing their hearts out echoed from downstairs.
There is a simplicity to that action which is far too rare in the world of
today, with present emphasis on materials and progress. That hour was
a precious one to me. I had not thought of an honorarium for speaking to your students, and I have no intention of allowing you to make
me such a gift, but if you chose instead to make some small gift to the
Palestrina group . . . I am confident they will find it useful. If they lift
their voices in worship just once because I troubled myself to put
together a talk for the students, it will be more pay than I deserve."[13]

The quiet beauty of listening and the generosity of its outcome
illustrates how Merle and his sister are branches of the same tree.
Before she knew of Merle's gift to the Palestrina group, Rosemond
wrote to him, her emotions still high, her mind churning.

Dear Merle and Win:

I write you jointly because I wouldn't be sprised if the
second named is partly responsible for The-Merle-As-At-
Present, which is the subject of this discourse and the current
astonishment of this institution.

Richard said "you've no idea what a pleasure is in store for
you," and he was quite right. I haven't had a more continuous
experience of delight, unmarred by any reservation I can seem
to scrape up by trying to think of one, in a very long time.

I seem to find the roots of this in the fact that all the conditions and preoccupations of my life over a period of years have caused me to take extreme pleasure in a particular human experience: to watch the play of a mind, over materials and among questions which I have found important and complex, when it is not a compartmentalized mind, but is a whole human personality actively and transparently functioning.

There is a kind of daring which comes with the willingness to put the whole person into an activity, which is absolutely recognizable; I've very seldom seen even the youngest student fail to catch this, it's some kind of Mana; and though they tend to call it "sincere"—a word I would gladly scrap for good—and we older ones call it "honest," there is something outside both these words. The something is whatever makes this activity somehow *lovable,* of all odd things. I detected before Merle had been on the platform three minutes that curious quality of relationship, he had the *love* of his audience. And this has been the consistent element in all the constant bombardment of remarks which people of all sorts & ages keep running up and grabbing me to make.

Now I am not half so convinced of the il-logicality of our emotional reactions as you-all are, and I only see this happen when there is the best reason in the world for it, the one given above; human beings respect the Humane in others, working at full speed and with unself-conscious, unself-centered, generous completeness.

It has at no period of human thinking been absent, its connection with human "dignity" is patent, I aint never see it in a Dawg, and if it hasn't some deep and *logical* connection both with what religious call the Divine Spark and with the relation between "love" and "sacrifice," I am a cockroach.

Now I knew Merle would be good, but I didn't know this other element was going to shine out so pure, and cause the dramatic valuableness that everybody felt, so that everyone kept saying at this phrase or at that "*OH! yes,* that is it!" "oh,

GOOD!"—and smiling so, and laughing at the least sparking of the match. The fertility of mind I and friends of mine enjoy and expected was a pleasure to watch, always is. This humility-of-the-enquiring-mind-in-action was equally obvious, causally connected with both the fertility and the dramatic interestingness, and so clear to the most immature (if my experience of others is any index) that they simply don't need to be *told* what a scholar's attitude in the search for truth is. They could smell it . . .

Now I surely hope no Thinking IS wasted, for damn it I see by the clock this done took me an age to put down. But it is all part of My Province. My field is the Enjoyment of what comes under the Aesthetic Component. Like all responses in this area, it is impatient of measure. So to hell with Space & Time, and let them as don't enjoy things with Abandon be hung for a precision and a miserly smudge.

Well, I have to run up & view a candidate & write 20 business letters & decide what to say first about Sir Walter Ralegh, so good bye with love to all parties.

from Ros[14]

Ten days later, as she casually mentioned to Merle, Rosemond drove to Harvard to give a talk to the Graduate English Conference. She had been invited by Harry Levin, a prominent professor at Harvard and for many years chairman of the comparative literature department, and his wife, Elena, to stay with them. Levin recalled meeting her at the first Modern Language Association meeting he attended: "I remember one of the highlights was meeting her. I knew and admired her work and I found her immediately a most attractive and congenial person, and we had a very lively conversation."

Now Levin wrote to Rosemond: "The students tell me that you are driving up that day [of the Graduate English Conference] and will probably be having dinner with them. Elena and I hope that you will be able to stay on for at least another day or two, and give us a chance to have some of your Cambridge friends in to see you." Rosemond's reply was written in her best midwestern colloquial style.

Dear Harry,

That will be lovely. I wrote the boys that I'd go over from Widener to your house in time to be fetched by them around six. Don't bother to write again; I'll just turn up, and in case you and your wife come to dinner too (boys' expressed hope) please tell her to support me in the wearing of wool; won't bring no tiara unless advised. One extry dress.

It's awfully nice of you to put me up, and I'm looking forward to it. I had thought I ought to run along home Sat. night, but it does seem a bit breathless (besides tempting the gods in the matter of snowy roads by night) so perhaps if I plan to nip off while you are still having you first cup of Sunday morning coffee, that would be safer. I'm real convenient to have to stay, rather like the first 8 weeks of a baby, as I can be deposited upon any vacant bench in Widener and do not fall off but can just be picked up off it again when desirable.

I expect they told you I'm going to try out some parts of a piece written on certain large and ancient images in Milton's Nativity Hymn. I'll try to make it decent for non-readers of the poem, but it's probably rather firm going. Well, these are students; we'll try it.

Yours, Ros

Three days after her return from her weekend in Cambridge she was writing to Merle again. Paul Laubenstein, director of the Palestrina Group, had just received word of Merle's gift, his honorarium of one hundred dollars, and phoned Rosemond's office to tell her. When Laubenstein wrote to thank Merle, he admitted that "nothing like this ever happened to us before. It goes to show that one never knows when one is entertaining 'angels' unawares . . . It was worth the price of admission to hear her [Rosemond] 'Whoop' over the phone when I told her what you had done."

Esteemed BENEFACTOR

You could have rolled me over with a common-pin when Laubenstein rang up my office as I was just rushing from door to committee meeting yesterday—and asked for your address; "you know what your brother did, I spose" I sez "which brother" thinking one of you has shot somebody or called McCarthy a Pig.

You never heard anybody so jubilant as L., and as for me, I rescued entire Foreign Students' Comm. from a doldrums by saying, oh there is LOTS of Good in the world, listen to the deed of one who is no better than One of the Wicked—really it was a delicious action, inspired from on high I am entirely sure.

The most delicate aspect, your not mentioning it to me at all, so that my obvious astonishment creates much mirth and shows it up for Pure Love, devoid of gain or smirch . . .

You'd not believe how Mama's not writing me where everyone is every week makes Space very much more like space.

I must fly.

thank you, archangel

Rosemond[15]

Rosemond's response to her first visit to the Levin's home was a full page. Her enjoyment of both Harry and Elena, and the spark of intimacy ignited, is evident, and her wit is in full play.

Tuesday 22 Feb.
so it is DOWN WITH TYRANNY
Dear Harry and Elena,

I am still filled with wonder and amaze how you could be so generous, squander away two your good days making me have a lovely visit . . . I'm sure it was a pleasure to me from start to finish, and that you are unconditionally responsible. They were the nicest parties, I liked all the people, nobody else ever gives me tea at night, my bedroom view sits in my head tasting for some reason of Henry James (must be those houses), I love your Dog and your Daughter.

Elena said of Rosemond: "In our home she was a very good

guest—bubbling over, accepting of everything. She would come back from the library disheveled, so many ideas coming to her at the same time, that she said her cheeks would begin to burn. That was what would happen to her in a museum— her cheeks would begin to burn. That was physical. It was excitement. But she had a tremendous capacity for relaxing and entering the family life. She was really quite remarkable—a unique human being. Her letters are eminently quotable."

In a letter to Merle on March 18, Rosemond told him she was off to Kingston, Ontario, to be part of a team that would decide on grants for thirty-six applicants for an International Federation of University Women fellowship. "I am struggling with the applications and my income tax and 2 quizzes and 17 essays to correct and my seminar to teach at Univ.Toronto to which I drive goody goody *New Road* NO MERRITT PARKWAY NEITHER on Sun. 3 April."[16]

Northrop Frye, University Professor at Toronto, and perhaps one of the most eminent scholars of this period, remembered her visit. "It was certainly Professor Woodhouse who arranged the visit . . . she stayed with us, and drove us around (we don't have a car) the suburbs of Toronto. We showed her nineteenth-century houses full of gingerbread, which she loved, and of course being in a car with Rosemond was something to write epic poems about afterwards. I remember her getting pinched for turning up Columbus Avenue in New York the wrong way, but she charmed the cop out of his ticket." Frye also remembered the "alleged seminar which was actually a long dialogue between herself and Woodhouse about Milton. He had started out as an eighteenth-century scholar, she as a medievalist, and the curiously different assumptions from which they collided in the middle was quite an education in itself."

On July 1, 1955, the *Hartford Courant* ran an article on the presentation of the $2,500 achievement award of the American Association of University Women to Rosemond Tuve. The article went on to say that the award was given to "Dr. Tuve for her research and critical writing—chiefly on the poets Spenser, Milton, and Herbert—as well as for her teaching." In the introduction prior to the presentation, Rosemond was acclaimed, as her father had once been, a "giant in the earth." It was also noted that she "served as a trustee for the American Society for Aesthetics and on the editorial board of Publications of the Modern Language Association of America and the governing board of the English Institute. More important she is a teacher of rare power both to inspire and to train, so that her influence with students is great both on our general culture, in these times so critical for the study of the humanities, and in sending able women on to scholarship and teaching."[17]

To justify her announced title, "The Race Not to the Swift," Rosemond began her talk by declaring that the subject of her speech that night was the pursuit of truth. "At the heart of every discovery and every piece of scholarship there is one key ingredient or component: an indispensable human mind, working without thought of reward or gain or of anything except finding out. Lose this, and no amount of money can buy you another."

She continued: "Scholars in the fields I represent keep our past alive. And it is true that without a past a human race, like a human being, is a poor thin thing. Consider your own life, and see. Imagine yourself confined to thoughts of your own thinking, religions of your own finding, symphonies of your own writing, language of your own inventing, landscapes of your own pruning, even trees of your own planting." In defending her own pursuit of truth she admits that "intellectuals generally support what looks useless to others. What earthly difference does it make if I don't know exactly what form Spenser read a mediaeval romance in? Only this, that I might make some tiny little error in trying to figure out how he got in the habit of using romance situations to symbolize certain important moral problems."

She goes on: "Am I going to make a big contribution to literature and morals by knowing this? Not at all. I'm going to see whether some ideas about symbols and allegory that came out in somebody's book nineteen years ago, and which I've been gradually questioning over a period of eighteen years, might need a little adjusting and correcting. That little adjusting might turn out to make us realize that the great power of allegory in the Middle Ages results from the fact that allegories were understood as vast metaphors . . . When we understand that, we read the great Spenserian metaphors as figures of our own state, and suddenly he is more beautiful than he ever was, and more gripping."

But she admitted that AAUW members have to work their fingers to the bone to support scholars for what often appears to be useless knowledge. And then she became almost lyrical in her explanation of why this is necessary:

"Your faith has to be in the great postulate that there are relations between things which it's good for us to find out, because in the great super-web of truth, especially historical truth, . . . a knowledge of mul-titudinous relations will sometime lead someone to see *pattern*.

"To see that pattern, significance, what we call 'meaning'—that is the end in itself.

"You can't sell a 'meaning' in the market; yet you know yourself that those moments when you have suddenly thought you came upon something of the significance of life are precious beyond rubies. That is the human experience par excellence."[18]

She continued with a thought that led to two of her favorite quo-tations: "I should think most of you are anxious that at least profes-sors in universities and colleges give your young people some notion of what can be seen in and from the Tower of Ivory, some notion of what it means to transcend this small and transitory life, how a man can get past being 'confined and pestered in this pinfold here.' [Milton's *Comus*, l.7.] "'And be not conformed to this world; but be ye transformed by the renewing of your mind, that ye may prove what is that good, and acceptable and perfect, will of God.'" [Romans 12:2] She closed with a final plea. "This then is what I assume you and I honor tonight—nothing we possess or achieve, but something we know exists and have seen men die for in the past: knowledge, a store-house of truth that attests to the glory of its creator, and that asks every student old or young to give account of his gift of reason to the benefit and relief of man's estate."[19]

9

A S SOON AS THE AAUW CONVENTION WAS CONCLUDED, and despite a previous letter to Eleanor saying she would spend the summer in New London, Rosemond left for England and the Continent. Her brother Lew and his wife, Helen, were also in Europe. It is difficult to guess where they had met when she wrote to them from London in mid-July: "It's so wild to think that I last saw Lew's handsome departing back amid the eucalyptus & the desert airs." The letter continues, revealing again the warmth and caring she always felt toward her family.

> I worked *hard* in Oxford (after the 3 days in the country near Wallingford, picking black currants & weeding the broad beans—old friend of mine recently had a stroke, so I turned to & helped in the garden). In Oxford, I went to the Bodleian every day, even if I was a little staggered by just how to make best use of my time when I got there. I had *written* so hard in June that I never went abroad so ill prepared to make good use of the libraries . . .
>
> I'm working in the British Museum these few days— always meet people there, have an odd meal or two, & walk my feet off—to church yesterday up in the City & then walked all thru' the bombed parts looking at specters of old City churches behind St. Pauls'; & in the afternoon walked all over Hampstead Heath w. a Univ. of London friend [probably Kathleen Tillotson].
>
> Best day in Oxford was with a JESUIT. Geoffrey's nephew, whom I knew first as a school boy, then a Univ. (Cambridge)

undergraduate—I wd. visit him & dine in his rooms with the best College white wine. War banged him about & he became R.C. & then went into the order—& is a lovely, serene, utterly successful human being, full of love & sweetness & tranquillity. We walked and talked & ate sandwiches (they have no money of course—give it all up); I thought how nice people can be when they are entirely delivered from self centeredness & ambition.

I still do feel most grateful to you for the lovely Parties & entertainment. Not fair on the Oldest but anyhow vastly appreciated.

I say *do* write me a note—I had one from Rik (graduation gifts, so *Enforced!*) [Rik is Richard Larsen Tuve, 2nd, her brother Dick's son] & feel I may not hear again from "family" all *summer*—so melancholy. Addresses at head of letter. Any little note is enough.[1]

Elizabeth Chapin, her old friend from Bryn Mawr, now married to Holden Furber, a professor of history at the University of Pennsylvania, had persuaded Rosemond to join them in Portugal. Dr. Furber saved one of her letters from Lisbon, which was written on the back of one from his wife. He explained, " 'Ha-Ha' was Elizabeth's pet name for her aunt (the explanation is that whenever the aunt came to the house, she laughed as she talked to the child, so this was E's first memory of her)."

Dear Mr Chapin and Aunt Ha Ha (one of my favorite names)

Here we are as if 30 years had never passed over us and the magical planked steak & baked Alaska of Norristown were still as digestible as if we weren't MIDDLE-AGED. [Elizabeth's father used to invite the two to lunch whenever he had business in the vicinity of Bryn Mawr in 1925–26.] Imagine Elizabeth & me being solid & dependable—we are, though. We keep that wild frisky Holden down. The views are very close to being as good as the ones on the Marblehead Christmas cards that I count on each year despite not having sent a Xmas card since 1927. Your children are very sweet & kind & good, & we're all having a famous time. Every corner of this town is worth sitting on a bench & memorizing—the colours and 18th c. shapes of things are a delight to the eye. We *eat* a good deal I'm sorry to say but we were scrawny & needed building up (or at least out). A swim today—the same drops of Atlantic that you'll look at toward about next Monday.

   Love to you   from Rosemond

Immediately on returning home, she wrote to Lew and Helen again, mailing her letter from Dick's home in Silver Spring, Maryland, on September 12, 1955. She had gone there in order to drive with Dick and Maxine, who were taking their son, Rik, to Pennsylvania State University.

   It was all-powerfully nice of you to have a letter meet me at home; George [Lew] Gets Prize in family for this summer for I have been a thirsty soil as regards those other Buoys, and kept alive by eldest. I carried it along in Sioux and read a second time enroute Md. by the roadside, and Richard read it when he took his sabbatical from driving and Maxine had the wheel, as we rolled along about McConnellsburg. We were going to ring up Sunday from State College and were so wound up with doing what surrounds the depositing of an Egg (or is it Sperm) that we were home before even our postcards were mailed or our hairs tied back, and it was too late. Not that we'd anything to say of import. Quite hard on the parents to put thr. firstborn out to graze . . .

   Rik has a good view from his room, a room-mate who proved likeable, and is this a.m. signing up for engineering but since he is not sure (with interests ranging from architectural drawing to meteorology and forestry & *anything* Out of Doors) he *is* a Engineer [Rik became an architect]. I do hope he has been allowed to have one 'cultural' course, likes history awfully but is discouraged from it by his Papa. We drove home Sun., Richard packed hastily and off to Mpls. Mon.

early by air (arr. safely); he will take your boy & girl out to dinner, and expects to hire a car and mosey around old haunts while Am. Chem. Soc. isn't in interesting session; there is a foam day on Fri. and he gives a paper.[2]

Richard Tuve achieved a large measure of distinction for his pioneering work in chemistry and engineering, particularly in his research into flame-control phenomena and fire-extinguishment methods. For more than thirty years he was the principal technical consultant to the Navy Department in fire engineering, where he developed a foam to fight fire on water, of enormous value during the war. In addition, he created a substance that could be used in the event of an attack by sharks. Rosemond's letter continues:

> Merle phoned on return from Alaska last night . . . he's so THIN but says he is better. He came over and we talked an hour. So we are all picked up together again and I will run back & start the year and hope Inspiration will carry me through until I'm used to the subjeck again.
>
> I was so delighted to see yr handwriting abroad, it was so thoughtful, knowing that I missed having Mama's "family" letters—but in the end got one whopper from Richd, and from Maxine, so all ended up Happy Ending. I guess the entire Tuve Clan now starts its Schools so life will be full as usual, such a blessing to like one's work. I must run & buy groc. with Maxine now,
>
> love from all. Wish I were with Richard in Mpls. We was going to go all over his paper route and everything. Not there for 29 yrs., since age 14.
>
> Rik is a nice boy, and budding interests—it wouldn't hurt to give the child a word from Uncle Engineer once in a while.
>
> Love and hugs, God Bless Baby Lew [3]

Rosemond was unable to restrain herself either from her interest in Rik or from her excitement about her brother's trip to Minneapolis. And so, one week later, she wrote to Maxine and Richard with a carbon to Lew and Helen.

I'm just back from the first faculty meeting—anyhow I didn't cut *that*; I'm in my usual autumn state of terror lest I forget a class or omit a condition-exam. It *has* happened to me. I'm so curious about how Richard felt as he gazed at 1203 7th St. S.E. [their address in Minneapolis] that I can hardly bear it. I think that little boy, whose ghost he surely saw about, lived to do honour to the spot. Who would know he would re-visit it as an eminent chemist for the navy? We didn't turn out as near perfeck as we might 'ope, but still the worst fears our parents must have lived through have not been realized—Maxine wouldn't you say he at least passes as a husband? Absolutely SHINING success as a Brother. Far exceeded the modest expectations I had when our common address was as above.

On a lower level, the restfulness of having untorn-curtains in my bedroom for 1st time since 1953 is *marked*, and the fact that I GOT some CLOTHES and needn't worry so about Hartford trip just when I'm starting college—oh that is scrumptious. I know my things are all right if M. has seen them on me, and there is *not one* person here whose taste I trust thus; hence a great assistance, esp. since I'd had no intention or hope of accomplishing this . . .

I am disappointed that Rik cannot take advantage of the interest in a "humanities" field—history—as a side-issue to his more professional courses; *nothing* is more exciting than the chance to discover just in the first flush of Being At Last Responsible to Oneself Only, that some field of "study" where one is not professional but just learning something interesting, is as good as a sport or a car or a girl. I hate to think he may get in the rut of "Studies are WORK" "Soccer and Dates are PLEASURE" before he has a good chance to happen upon the other experience . . .

I had such an interesting conversation in the back seat with Rik, impressed with his budding interests (*not* distressingly narrow or imitative); and he is *such a nice* young man. M. and R. both you should feel well-rewarded and grateful—

I won't say proud because I don't believe in that attitude. But young people can be such wash-outs, and have such personal difficulties or obstacles, and such nasty arrogance and unlikable selfish mean streaks—really quite a few of your prayers has been answered reel satisfactory and I do not mean only the fact that you just don't have to worry about something that would bring you to shame like lack of integrity or honesty, wenching and drink and cheating.

Well, I think about Rik a lot, with so much fellow-feeling; for our Freshmen are all around and I meet my own in a day or so; it is a very endearing stage, and one of the most valuable moments of the 4 yrs . . .

love from R[4]

In an interview with Rik, he talked enthusiastically about Rosemond: "I can still remember to this day when I was eight years old [1946], going across the country with her. She was fascinating. She would just get so excited about—oh look—over there—she was always interested, active. Merle in his prime—you had to tie him down. Unbelievable, unbelievable. Very vibrant individual—different way than Rosemond. Much more physically energetic than Rosemond, although Rosemond was much more like Lew, in a sense of really talking with you and fun to be with as a person. She was always interested in art and architecture. She was interested in iconography but then that would expand into why a building was as it was. She would expand her thinking into all areas around it.

"I can remember having to do a paper in a baroque architectural history class and she sat down with me and simultaneously translated three books—one in Italian, one in German, and one in French—to try to tell me what the subject was—a baroque church in Rome. Her intellect was mind-boggling. The first impression was not as a stern taskmaster. She was very close to me. We had a great relationship. I never remember being angry with her.

"Later, sitting in a cathedral and asking her about the stained-glass windows, and what was that all about, and out it comes. She knows the whole thing and I'm fascinated with this. You have to have a kind of energy behind what you're doing or it just doesn't make it.

That's another thing about Rosemond that I was always fascinated with—her boundless energy in all sorts of things. She burned herself out, turned her body off. She didn't realize how badly her body felt because her mind took over. She was the first real hippie I have ever met. She was a liberated female, but she didn't say anything about that. She just did what she wanted to do. I especially enjoyed her uninhibited character.

"I occasionally remember as a child sitting down to the piano with her and playing. She just liked to do that. I mean lots of people would be too uptight to sit down with a ten-year-old and bang out whatever it was. She'd sight-read the music, play the piano, and I'd play something I was practicing. That was a very warm thing for me, to have somebody actually interested. Her interest and excitement about life was fascinating to me. There wasn't a thing that she wasn't interested in. I would ask her crazy questions as a kid but she was always interested. We had a special kind of chemistry together."

The following January (1956), Rosemond was writing again to President Park, requesting leave for the entire 1957–58 academic year. With so many "matters involved for so many people," she was anxious to make plans early. She argued that she felt that with the "so-called Achievement Award" it was incumbent on her, and she was eager, to use the grant for research "on some possible connections between literature of the late Middle Ages and the Renaissance." She added that she "began working on a few ideas in 1952 when teaching a Minnesota graduate course, and became re-interested in them when teaching Prof. Bethurum's medieval course during her absence . . . It appears that a small Milton book may develop on me; if so it might be finished before the time I have asked for leave."[5]

There was no mention of her invitation from Harvard University to be a Visiting Professor during the fall semester, the reason being, perhaps, that no permission from the trustees was needed. But in her next letter to Eleanor, of which only a fragment remains, she explained that she had arranged her teaching schedule at Connecticut so that she can keep her seminar and still give two courses at Harvard, and thus not "get out of line for leave."

In 1956, the graduating class honored Rosemond by inviting her to deliver the baccalaureate sermon. It was both profound and moving. Quoting first from Donne, a passage she was to return to again and again, "In the great Ant-hill of the whole world—I am an Ant. I have my part in the Creation, I am a Creature," she asserted. The way to be a creature starts with gratitude. Then, to be a worthwhile ant, "you must be a *servant* of good." She confessed that she is so "old-fashioned as to think all sermons require a text. We need a text because we do not understand the precise nature of our error when we find ourselves unable to accept what it is to 'Be a Creature,' and because we do not see what shall be our remedy, so that we can understandingly say with Donne '*I have my part* in the Creation.' A man has to learn his part; he does not know it by nature."

She went on: "The text is from Ephesians iv. 1 to v. 17 (I have omitted intervening verses): 'With all lowliness and meekness, with longsuffering, forbearing one another IN LOVE. That we be no MORE CHILDREN, tossed to and fro, BUT speaking the truth in love, MAY GROW UP INTO HIM which is the head.' Earlier ages *had* a remedy. Not the remedy of self-sufficient stoicism; Stand and TAKE the world's inability to value you truly. Not the well-known "accept yourself"—*who could?* Here earlier ages had a hope that FAR transcends those we grasp at. They said, you can Be Another Self. They didn't believe a human being was ever finished; they said CHANGE. And they thought one could, and pointed out HOW.

"They thought it was NATURAL for us to be alienated from the life of God because of the ignorance that is in us, but not NECESSARY—because we could take on another nature."

Rosemond offered suggestions for transforming "our proud selves, to 'put on the new man, which after God is created in righteousness and true holiness': I believe in reading."

She continued: "Instead of pushing the conscience and the feelings to deal with issues that are alien to them it has been my experience that a gradual fructifying takes place if we allow ordinary secular intellectual curiosity to carry us into *materials*. I believe certainly in reading the Old and New Testaments, but if piety and belief seem like an alien world, I believe in every kind of tangential approach to religious conceptions—from being steeped in medieval sculpture on Roman facades, to interest in Platonic elements in the literature you read. If going to church, go for the music. If you are cold to religious feeling, read theology. If alien, let it get to seem possible by filling mind with ideas that become familiar, especially John Donne's sermon number 711—let it blow on the coals. Don't worry the matters; let them come unharried into the mind and see if they have power in themselves.

"When Donne said 'I have my part in the Creation,' he meant that it was Possible, even my proper destiny, to 'walk worthy of the vocation to which I am called'—*as* a creature, and that that vocation is to walk not as a fool but as Wise, to walk as a Child of Light. Who would not wish to be numbered under so lovely a phrase? and we are told HOW. Now if I were to be at all complete in telling of this remedy for our blind alienation from the Good, this is the place for a sermon on Grace, & I have neither time nor competence to preach it. But I would call your attention to the fact that the ancient passages I have quoted have all ended not with condemnation nor despair for man, but HOPE, hope for that radical transformation I have mentioned which gives men a totally changed centering of their lives."

It is clear from her many sermons that the words of the poets she taught gave impetus to her own beliefs and power to her preaching. Like her grandfather Gulbrand, and Luther before him, she could not do otherwise—"Ich kann nicht anders."

Two months later Rosemond wrote to Eleanor again, this time on reminiscent old writing paper picked up at Douglas Lodge, Itasca State Park, Minnesota, probably on a trip there with Eleanor the summer that Rosemond was teaching at the University of Minnesota. It was mailed to Eleanor at her family home in Fergus Falls, Minnesota, during a rare summer that Rosemond stayed at the college. It is less breezy, more meditative than her usual letters to Eleanor, possibly because she was alone and more relaxed that summer.

DOUGLAS LODGE   [July 28, 1956]
Itasca State Park   Douglas Lodge, Minnesota

Dear Eleanor,

I am so astonished at how little one gets done when one does it every day. I go to the library—but I go late acct. of picking the petuniers and I leave early because of going to the dentist. My teeth crack and my bones squeal and my books don't find Favour with the great. I think better of yours every time I look into it. Forget what I consulted there tother day but I know I thought oh damn if *I* could write Clear and Proper I would have less wounding encounters with them as reads and judges me. Ah well, it is only This World. Won't last.

I believe more and more in the shortness and triviality of this little inter-lude. If your family, esp. youthful family, is all around you you will not have this sense of unreality. But it was not just two years ago with mother's death that I got it; yet all one's brushes with modes of reality which are not noticed in our daily come-and-go sharpen up the sense that we live very superficially, and when any death brings one up against the naked *real* and the question of what lasts and what does not, I do not find the daily traffic of life sufficient. If you have any of this haunting dis-ease, and un-comfort, and weight of the Pity of the human adventure, try what I tried; I read the New Testament epistles, two chaps. a day. I never read such courageous audacious conceptions in my life.

Rosemond Tuve was the first woman to teach in the English department at Harvard. The September 25, 1956 issue of the *Harvard Crimson* announced her appearance on campus with these remarks: "Professor Tuve from Connecticut College presides over readings in non-dramatic Elizabethan literature in *English 121*. There's some talk of courtly love, Neoplatonism, and skeptical currents."[6] Her second course was titled "Romance, Allegory and Pastoral."

Armour Craig, from Amherst, also a visiting professor at Harvard that year, later expressed his admiration for Rosemond: "I first met her in 1936 [at Connecticut College] when I visited one of her classes. I was visiting the young woman who was to become my wife, and accompanied her to some of her academic engagements. If I don't remember Ros's topic on that winter day in 1936, I do remember her style—eager, direct address that singled out this student then that, her wry awareness that not many of the young before her cared about her subject as she did, her absolutely unqualified sense that care about it or not it was THE subject. She was a teacher, and her performance encouraged me to hope that I was on the right track, for me, in hoping to be a teacher myself one day. Behind her words one felt a strong person—knowing, imagining, distinguishing, celebrating, believing, and finally loving person."

After a party in their rooms at the end of the Harvard term, Armour Craig and his wife recalled speaking "mainly of religion. Ros declared herself, not at length though positively, and expressed her sense of the connection between her belief, and her subject—her main subject—the literature of the Renaissance."

Northrop Frye was also in Cambridge that semester. He remembered: "I still see her bustling into the room she was occupying at Radcliffe with her hair full of pencils and carrying four ice cubes on the back of her wrist, about to fix drinks for my wife and myself . . . I remember her Lutheran background, her fondness for her brother, who was in physics, (they sent each other mutually unintelligible offprints), and the profound religious feeling that kept bubbling up inside her . . . We went to visit her in New London . . . she was the kind of person with whom one could simply relax and talk intelligently."

Possibly the most extraordinary result of her Harvard experience was the group of young scholars who were forever changed by her presence. Wherever she taught graduate students, her effect on them was profound and lasting. Leicester Bradner once said that she was "wasted" at Connecticut College. But she remained at Connecticut, no doubt, partly because of the loyalty she felt for the college, and also because of her conviction that women should have the same quality of education as men. In addition, she couldn't help but be aware that she was instrumental in sending more students on to graduate school than other professors. There was also the emotional support she received from women friends there that added a dimension to her life she might not have found elsewhere. When it was mentioned to Douglas Bush that one of her colleagues at Connecticut had heard that she was the "darling of the aesthetic community" at Harvard, he replied, "She carried heavier guns than that!"

Robin Winks, who went on to become a professor of history at Yale, was on the faculty at Connecticut for one year. He observed Rosemond's significant position at the college in another light. He recalled that although he was "utterly junior and in a department different from theirs," she was one of three faculty members who went out of their way to make him feel welcome. Rosemond, "though she and Susanne Langer were clearly the two very famous members of the faculty, took the time to single me out, have lunch with me in the small faculty dining room, and respond (when I asked) to my questions about how best to deal with certain matters of Renaissance literature in my European history survey course. I think it was this element of welcoming everyone into the college as though it were a genuine community that was most impressive about her, and it led me to sit down and read her work that year simply in order to get to know her better. That she had passed up opportunities to PERMANENTLY locate at 'more prestigious schools' was commonly known, and frequently used by the senior faculty to induce mild guilt in any junior faculty who thought to look elsewhere for employment."

Her sense of community extended beyond faculty associations. She was known to visit freshman dorms, prior to the beginning of classes, to meet the incoming students and talk about their interests and concerns.

Helen Hennessey, now Vendler, one of the foremost critics of poetry during the second half of the twentieth century, was undoubtedly the outstanding student in Rosemond's Harvard seminar, "Romance, Allegory, and Pastoral." Originally a chemistry major, she had switched her focus to English before entering graduate school at Harvard, and was invited by Rosemond to join her graduate group. Rosemond confirmed for her the value of poetry when she assured her that it was "okay to be a poetry person." Vendler acknowledged that the title, *Part of Nature, Part of Us*, a book of essays on poetry published in 1980, alludes to their shared connection to poetry.

Professor Vendler, who now teaches at Harvard, was struck not only by Rosemond's sensitivity to beauty and metrics in poetry, but also by her keen observations, whether of natural landscapes or illuminated manuscripts. Vendler understood that for Rosemond, religion, literature, art, and music were all one gestalt and the clue to allegory was her religious beliefs. That she was a harmonious person came from a central selfhood.

But she also observed that she was "like a big grown child." Rosemond once acknowledged to Vendler: "When your last remaining parent dies, there is no one remaining for whom you are a child." Rosemond never lost her childlike qualities, some would say "childish," or the power of her intellect. She liked to wander through museums eating her lunch, so that she would not waste time chewing. Occasionally she asked Helen for advice about clothes, and Vendler remembered a short, green, satiny dress she bought at Filene's basement and the fact that she special-ordered her size twelve shoes. Rosemond once remarked on "the vacuous faces" of the female models that appeared in newspapers modeling clothes. Mostly, Vendler remembered her as a "generous" person.

In October, even under pressure from her long hours at Harvard and the stress of commuting, Rosemond wrote again to President Park, repeating her previous request for leave during the 1957–58 year. It would be the first leave (with pay) since 1948, and she would combine the $2,500 achievement award with a half year's salary. She wrote:

> I have been working for about five years in the general area of relations between romance and allegory of the late Middle Ages and the Renaissance, matters which enter constantly into my way of presenting the literature of the later period in courses. I am not sure that this will become another book, and do not regard that prospect with pleasure—a jaundiced view which characterizes all persons with a book currently in press. [The book then in press was *Images and Themes in Five Poems* by Milton.]
>
> In case my activities at another University this first semes-

ter make the request for leave seem at all out of line: you will
recall that I came in December to inquire about "chances" for
a leave, before declining two year-long Visiting Professorships
(one the Berg chair at New York University, the other
Wellesley, although of course I wish this to remain unknown
out of courtesy to the incumbents who did take them). When
the Harvard semester-appointment came up, I made it a condition with them that I should be allowed to retain my seminar here, the only course other than Freshmen and
Sophomores which I was to teach, and the one whose relin-
quishment would make difficulties for my department. I felt
that a year away would quite understandably take me off the
list for coming leaves . . . In order that the Harvard teaching
should not present the same problem, I kept my seminar here
(actually, teaching currently a similar course there and here is
having the most gratifying effect upon the attitudes and
accomplishments of my C.C. students). I could have refused
the Harvard offer like the others, but I think we agree that this
would not have been to the best interests of our own College.

I shall of course be here full time in the ordinary way next
semester, and to the best of my knowledge no institution or
person, including myself, has any designs that would get in the
way of my return, rejuvenated and re-charged, in the fall of
1958. None of these invitations has seemed to me to bear any
of the signs that characterize institutions looking about with a
view to permanent appointment later; and if the present one
gave the *slightest* inkling of any such complication of motive I
should certainly communicate this to you with speed.[7]

Rosemond's several references to the possibility of a permanent
appointment at Harvard may confirm the observation of one friend
that she was "wounded" when the offer was never made. Harry Levin,
for many years chairman of the comparative literature department,
offered this explanation:

"It is surprising how much she meant to us considering the hours
[very few] we spent in one another's presence over the years. She had

a very successful year here . . . Reuben Brower and myself were very anxious to bring Ros to Harvard on a permanent basis and I don't think there was any serious opposition to the idea, or to her personally. She had the respect and admiration of most members of the department. But it would have been hard to swing because at that time Douglas Bush was active and Herschel Baker worked in that area. We would have had to make a case because the field was already covered. On the other hand I think she was willing to stay at Connecticut College as long as she did because they gave her a very, very free tether. She was an ornament to them . . . But it was increasingly clear, that it was just a loss not to have Ros available at an institution which had a Ph.D. program."

Levin's wife, Elena, offered these observations: "She really liked to teach men. The experience at Harvard was good for her . . . She liked the dynamics of her relationship between herself and men students, and this is what she did not have until she got to Pennsylvania."

On a personal note, Elena recounted this story: "I once asked her . . . 'Ros, how did you escape marriage?' And she said, 'Whenever they came near, I fled.'"

Harry Levin then said, "I think she made a conscious choice between marriage and a career." Then to Elena he added, "Do you remember when she said, as she was fussing around her apartment: 'What I need is a wife'?"

During that term at Harvard, Levin sent her his recently published book, which she acknowledged in this letter.

> Dear Harry,
>
> It is such a delightful book! when discovered on return Thurs. night I read 15 pp. with such mirth, late or not, & have since re read w. unabated glee & gone onward to be serious . . . But oh how I agree about ballets-of-bloodless-images. Well, thank you & embrace that living quiddity-est of all q's Elena, whom I love.
>
> Ros
>
> a) saw *Cocktail Party* [a play by T. S. Eliot]—what POSSESSED him

b) why have we never talked abt. Geo Moore, just finishing *Mummer's Wife.*

Despite the continual pressure for leave that Rosemond put on
President Park, and the difficulties it caused, Rosemary remained
her loyal supporter; nor did it prevent her from praising Rosemond
when an opportunity arose. In her report to the board of trustees in
1955, President Park quoted Rosemond's assessment of an ideal college faculty:

"Our distinguished Professor of English has phrased it well when
she says, 'Students learn something from seeing that a faculty member
considers his responsibilities to be learning in general rather than to
them as students simply & solely . . . I think it is the duty of a college
administration to see that the faculty as a whole represents a fair division between the productive scholars and artists, and those whose
gifts are more marked in the area of teaching alone. The scholar may
lose sight of the pupil in the nobility of his devotion, the teacher may
become dull and a little sentimental if he sees nothing but the human
problem in the pupil. Fair standards of work are established only by
concern both for the magnitude of the task and for the restricted
capacity of the human being. So a faculty which sees the two aspects
labors to set educational goals which are realistic and which nevertheless disclose the vaster areas of knowledge awaiting further disciplined consideration.'"[8]

David Kalstone, a graduate student in Rosemond's Renaissance
course at Harvard, confirmed the validity of these words in describing how she galvanized him. "Part of it is this absolute dedication she
had—first of all to her own work. And to see that in action was so
stimulating. She didn't spare herself and she was an author. She came
to it with a kind of freshness and a release of energy. "Suddenly
Harvard was filled with these fascinating people from the outside
world, who were far more interesting than almost anybody I had met
there—Ros, Northrop Frye, F. W. Dupee, Armour Craig. Ros Tuve's
presence there *was* so extraordinary because it suddenly made
Harvard seem an entirely new and different world. Our course was
built around Spenser and conducted at a very high level with no con-

cessions whatever to the failings of any of the students. It was wonderful. The course was built around books of the *Faerie Queene*. If you
were given book three of the *Faerie Queene* you were given Sidney's
sonnets. She just threw us. But what I remember was the physical
appearance—so striking. Often a bright yellow sweater, pencils *stuck*
at very odd angles, and she was up there kind of like the Medusa, a
very benevolent one. But no tolerance for laziness, and no tolerance
for ignorance."

He went on: "She's responsible for *very* important books in
Renaissance literature. Tom Roche's book on Spenser; Paul Alpers's
book [*The Poetry of the Faerie Queene*], for which he got no encouragement from the Harvard people, but he certainly got a great deal
from her. In it, he wrote this dedication: 'In Memory of Rosemond
Tuve—Miss Tuve's powers and disinterestedness are apparent on even
the densest pages of her writing, but one had to know her to realize
fully how penetrating and flexible her mind was, and how profoundly she was motivated by love of the literature she studied. By her
friendship, as well as by her example, she made you want your writing
to be worthy of its subject. I hope this book is, and in being so it is
worthy of her.'"

Rosemond is also acknowledged in Kalstone's book, *Sidney's
Poetry: Contexts and Interpretations*: "It was the late Rosemond Tuve,
with her learned regard for Sidney, who first taught me to value his
poetry and helped me to undertake this study." Kalstone admitted he
would "never have written about Sidney if it hadn't been for her." He
also believed that part of her students' admiration for their teacher
was "her colorfulness and inspiration. She kept track of things you
were interested in, things that you had forgotten you'd expressed some
interest in, in some little paper. So I would get postcards from all sorts
of strange places with bits of information that she'd just come across
and file away, you know, and something that she'd found on bas-relief
in a French cathedral. I think I'd written this little paper on Hell and
figures in Hell. Now and then, and ever after, she kept bombarding me
with these vivid postcards."

He continued: "The complaint people usually make is that the
books are too difficult, too knotted. I found it *[Allegorical Imagery]*

the kind of book I like to go back to. [There are] sentences that you didn't understand when you were twenty but understand now. *Allegorical Imagery* is a very difficult book. I think her interest in allegory was really because she had an allegorical temper herself. It's not like somebody who comes at it from the point of view of literary theory. It's more like somebody who's trying to understand his own attitude toward the world. I think that her genuine love and immersion in medieval literature and her religious temperament made it natural that she would find allegory the most congenial form of expression. Allegory was just her language."

Merle made precisely the same observation: "For her, allegory was just another language."

Paul Alpers concurred with David Kalstone: "When I was writing my dissertation at Harvard, I didn't have one friend whose literary tastes or intelligence about literature I had any interest in or respect for, who had anything but contempt for Spenser. You can't believe that now, because anybody sees now that he is a very great poet. He is immensely teachable. Ros was the one who was saying that he was a very great poet . . . I met her just before she left. I just stopped by and we just hit it off. We really just liked each other. The only formal connection I had with her was when I finished my Ph.D. thesis, which was a very tangled, thrashing out of how to read the *Faerie Queene,* which neither of my thesis directors had liked, and had given me a very hard time about. I was very discouraged about it. I guess I asked Ros if she would read it and she said sure. I mean, anything for the cause, as far as Spenser was concerned. She was going out to Berkeley that summer. She took it and read it in motels across the country. I saw her that Labor Day weekend at the English Institute, and we sat down next to each other and she said, 'That's a good book. There isn't a silly sentence in it.' She was the first person to see that I was saying anything about anything."

In January of 1957 Rosemond received a letter from the Reverend John W. Pyle, Canon Pastor of the Cathedral Church of St. John the Divine in New York City, confirming her appearance there, in March, for a series of Lecture Forums on Anglicanism and English Literature.

"One of the purposes of the forums," he wrote, "was to effect fruitful dialogue between academic disciplines and theological enterprise." Reverend Pyle had been moved to invite Rosemond after reading her article "On Herbert's *Sacrifice*," which had appeared in the *Kenyon Review*. Her lecture at the cathedral, titled, "George Herbert and *Caritas*," was published two years later in the *Journal of the Warburg and Courtauld Institutes*. It was undoubtedly the most profound and deeply moving utterance of her career.

Herbert writes poetry, she asserts, as a theologian and, like Augustine, "he thinks of our love for God as God's gift . . . Defining the nature of love is a central problem of Christian theology [and] to examine it, we must discuss outright the Christian doctrinal positions enunciated or implicit in Herbert's poems—which to my way of thinking does not preclude our looking at them 'as poems,' as the phrase goes." Carefully developing her theses, she affirms that "the place to fix our attention in Herbert's poems is upon their revelation of the nature of man's love of God." She speaks of man's reasons for loving God and the true bestowing of *caritas:* of the necessity of suffering; of adoration as "inseparable from a love which the creature (twice-created) has for the Creator"; and for gratitude, "the *basso ostinato* in all this music of gratitude, which to Herbert is truly a grace."[9]

Charity is not for our good, but rather for the good of the Creator, who, through his love for his creatures, teaches us how to love. Herbert knows that "only divine Agape in the heart can by grace enable a crumb of dust to love, which will be to will, as God does. That this could happen—transforming man's entire relationship to other men into one of love, and making all his service to Christ 'freedom'— he does believe, and his poems seem to me to record how man loves when it does."[10] At the conclusion of the forum Reverend Pyle wrote to Rosemond: "I cannot thank you at all properly for the brilliant lecture on Herbert this past Sunday evening. It was exactly the kind of thing I wanted for this series of lectures. The way in which you used the literary materials involved to communicate some finely drawn theological discussions was superb. We are equally appreciative of the graceful way in which you participated in our picnic-style seminar discussion after the lecture . . ."

Rosemond's return to teaching full time at Connecticut College in February may have been somewhat awkward for her. Her recognition by the academic communities both in the United States and in Great Britain, although never advertised, created a certain amount of jealousy among some of the women faculty. Her fifth book, *Images and Themes in Five Poems by Milton,* was being published that summer by Harvard University Press and Oxford University Press. Her invitation to speak at the Cathedral of St. John the Divine, although kept to herself, was certainly known by her colleagues. And in June she received her second honorary doctor of letters degree, this time from Wheaton College. It was accompanied by this citation: "Born in South Dakota of pioneer stock,....yours has been a life devoted intensively and zestfully to scholarship at high levels and to the instruction of college women. Your studies of English Renaissance literature have brought you coveted honors at home and abroad, and in your thirty years of teaching you have skillfully infected the youth of Goucher, Vassar, and Connecticut College with your own love of learning and your excitement of cultural things at their very best."

It is likely that whenever Rosemond received acclaim, her answer, whether voiced or not, would be the same as Herbert's and her father's, "Praise God."

In *Images and Themes in Five Poems by Milton,* Rosemond used a similar patterning of rhetoric and imagery as that which she employed in *Elizabethan and Metaphysical Imagery,* but on a larger scale. Less polemical than in her Herbert book, she shows how Milton's great themes are bodied forth through the use of images: "truth in a metaphor as in a proposition . . ." In other words, each group of images, weighted with historical significance, is woven into one great tapestry, revealing profound conceptual meaning. The book is dedicated: "To my three scientific, contemplative brothers."

10

Rosemond's long anticipated, and carefully planned, year's sabbatical began on July 11, 1957, with her journey to England and the Continent. Because she would be receiving her salary for only one semester, she had applied for, and was granted, a Fulbright Fellowship for the period of her leave. In a letter to the Fulbright committee, Rosemary Park wrote that she could "recommend her with complete enthusiasm."

Eight days before her departure, Rosemond decided to write a will, enclosing copies with individual letters to her brothers. The will was devised in her own words and signed by her friend Edward Cranz and two librarians, but apparently was not even notarized. To Merle she wrote:

> You will be amused to get this piece of Foresight. Just to avoid legal nuisances. So far's I know, we ought not to need it for a few years yet. Not that I own anything much, no house, no furniture worth saving. But there's always a car, and bonds, and that stock from Mama. Actually if I would die this year you would all get lotsa money; what with Minn. and Harvard and the 1500. prize I got all which I saved up mostly in N.L. Federal Savings & Loan, there'd be good cash all around; but I probly won't have the grace to clear off till after your children are all past the needy stage. In this condition I had enough margin to add the note asking that Dutch get little nest-egg in Perpet (and in case I should inadvertently stick some more in there put a ceiling on gift, as I am likely to forget my arrangemts and might build up that account, forget-

ting destination). For of course I wouldn't give away out of
the family what you boys needed. D is retiring after 1 more
year; is not very well, and worn to pieces with demanding job,
extremely close to the edge financialy & it takes much
courage.[1]

Added to the bottom of the will was the note she mentioned:

I wish to append the following personal wish, easier to
convey thus than to intrude in the body of will: In addition
to funds at N.L. Federal Savings and Loan, I keep a smaller
fund of savings at Perpetual Bldg.Assn.Silver Spring, Md.
Will you please give to Dutch Burdick the contents of the
Perpetual Bldg. Assn. account in my name *or* $2000. (two
thousand), whichever is smaller. It is to assist her in her
early retirement plan."

Not long after arriving in Oxford, Rosemond learned that
Christopher Brown, the son of her good friends Bid and Hunt Brown,
had been diagnosed with leukemia, and had only a brief time to live.
She wrote immediately, filling the "air letter" completely, even up the
sides, with meaningful words of comfort, striving to connect to their
pain with every resource of her heart and mind.

Dearest Bid and Hunt,
Oh dear people, I am so sorry. I do not know what to say
to you but I want to write you—make this as wordless as you
can; I would just embrace you both as hard and long as I was
allowed, if the Atlantic didn't prevent, instead of words, that
are so busy *talking* and such a loose inaccurate garment for
the heart to travel in. It is the boy himself I think most about;
I should have been so unfit to hear such news when I was 18.
But Chris was always gentler and inwardly readier for life
than so many are, and I have confidence in him. I do not
know if he had some of the affection for church and Christian
things that was here and there in your big family, but if he had
it will help him. It doesn't have to be so Special and

Particular; the sense of the (*probable* even) *reality* of an invisible order of things is a big start if one is suddenly in trouble of the kind that involves dealing with that order of reality, where all our little competences fall to the ground; sometimes I think that if people just got used to liking church music and taking kindly to reading the New Testament it's enough, for being in basic trouble takes care of the rest. I'm never over being astonished at how *much* that strange genius of a Paul said about the exact things that knock over a person, and what a peculiar applicable power it takes on to just comfort one's forlornness, being so full of hope and speaking straight out of the *lasting* things, instead of the grand secular technique of Distraction. It just may not be Chris's way. But I don't myself know any other route out of our wildly insufficient tendency to think that a "complete" and "full" life here is such a *summum bonum*. At 80 or 95 a life isn't "complete" no matter *what* was in it; our lives are *radically* incomplete. Before he goes Chris may have had a deeper and clearer experience of what it is to be a human being than those of us who waste and hurry through year after year of the wild chase to evade what the human self-consciousness was really put down here to discover. Though it hurts *me* to think of what he will not see and feel and have a taste of, I don't *believe* in tasting-the-world as an end of human existence, nor do I think anybody does after they've tasted a lot of it; I do not think there is any such thing as an obscure, or a short, good life; there isn't any Time where a loving life is concerned, nor any Quantity when it comes to the eternal ideas, lovingkindness and beautiful things or action, nor do I think death can defeat them; I feel as loved by my mother as when she lived, and find myself caught up with gladness that we can be delivered from the self-engrossed body that *tries* so hard and *never* succeeds in sharing perfectly in these eternal realities, and be made part of the very eternal things themselves and be *fulfilled* at last. My ideas of what people refer to as immortality are dreadfully unconventional but of the eternity of the light we have little glimmers of and reflect so faultily, I just do not doubt; there is just too much proof around of how good and lovely things do not die when *people* have been doing nothing else *but* die ever since anyone began to notice. Oh dear it all sounds pie-eye and preachy and oh-sure-that's-fine-if-you-aren't-in-it—but anyway it is what seems to me true, and if it didn't I'd never teach a poet or bother to tell a child to listen to a symphony. I spose what I mean is, what drew me to Chris won't stop, just be where the rest of it is, the source it came out of. But we love the shapes it comes in here, and that part is so bitter. But not for *him.*

I haven't any more place to write this time about Oxford; it is full of Permanencies, and that is what I exult in, being here. Lovely things that death-doomed men have kept alive and passed on down and down and down, surround me on every side, and I am in a constant state of gratitude—especially because I go to hear a great deal of music, especially in the cathedral, 2 or 3 times a week, and it is much borne in upon me, the *impossibility* of killing that in man which throws himself away in thinking how best to praise whatever gave him the gift of being, and loving others, however transiently. I feed daily on the results of that reckless throwing-away, none of it got lost at all, and I am so grateful to be one of the endless stream of those who will go but the things remain for all those yet to come. Chris has held and conserved and passed worthily on, & that's all anyone does. I have heard of 3 cases here where predicted dates simply proved wrong. But what I have been saying is as much about 1975 as 1958; I was talking about us all. You two passed on lots to me, so I was just speaking of all dear loved people and how they may die but you cannot say they aren't living.

Excuse everything in this that is not as you would have it and retain what you cannot but be willing to let me send, warm and constant

love, to you all—from
Rosemond

In a similar letter of condolence to her Oxford friends Daphne and Robert Levens some years later, she quoted Ben Jonson:

> It is not growing like a tree
> In bulk, doth make man better be;
> Or standing long an oak, three hundred year
> To fall a log at last, dry, bald, and sere;
> A lily of a day
> Is fairer far in May,
> Although it fall and die that night
> It was the plant and flower of light.

After thirty-two years of demanding, devoted service to Connecticut College, and with deteriorating health, Dean Burdick announced that she would retire at the end of June 1958. No doubt at Rosemond's suggestion, but also because she was greatly admired by President Park, Eleanor Lincoln was invited to come to Connecticut College as dean. She declined, stating that they needed someone "brisker." Both she and Rosemond were now fifty-four years old.

Rosemond received news of Eleanor's decision while she was in England.

> 10 p.m. Fri 6th Dec. '57
> 8 Longwall St., Oxford
> Angel-face,
>   I didn't know how grievously disappointed I'd be. I expected it so melancholy-ly that I wasn't surprised, but somehow it was just as sad to me as if I had thought you'd come. I didn't. When you said all those "*ought* I to" in your letter, I knew it was a lost cause. I do not myself do many things of permanent or crucial nature because of pure Oughts. I would have written and teased you to come, but I didn't think I should. I was too fearful that it would prove to be a disappointing decision. I had a bare hope that the adventurousness and the knowledge that we would just Pedestal you within an inch of your life (a calming position at our age)

might just pull you to us—but I absolutely understand "just do not want to be a Dean." Because I shouldn't . . .

Oh shucks I wish they'd some scheme by which a Dean could come and give 5 years and then call it a day. WHY must we be so *permanent* with everything we do. I spose you wouldn't have been willing.

I should so have liked to have you in my Daily Life.

Love & big hugs Roz

Apparently it was impossible for Rosemond to quietly pursue her research and writing exclusively while in England. Wherever she went, she was in demand as a lecturer. Kathleen Tillotson, a friend from her Somerville days, and herself an important scholar, remembers the "memorable lecture she gave to her students" at Bedford College, part of the University of London. In May, Rosemond lectured at Cambridge, after which C. S. Lewis sent her an enthusiastic letter.

"Dear Miss Tuve," he wrote. "It was a great pleasure both to hear your lecture and to meet you afterward, and of course I was proud and surprised to hear that you had "sat under me." Your dissent from me in the Milton book is more gracious than most critics' agreements. I still feel it is unavoidable in making the *map* of an allegorical work to use what may be called "equations." I never meant that if "Rose = Mboinis [illegible] Love" one shd. then dismiss the Rose from one's mind. The contours on a map are not a substitute for the real mountain.

"I am normally home with my wife and family every week-end . . . How long will you be in Oxford? I should much like to see you in our house and discuss many things. We have much to discuss. For instance, *Comus* . . ."

As always, Rosemond was glad to take a break from the intensity of her work, and to travel, always searching for unusual, ancient churches. In July, Eleanor Lincoln met her in Lyons, where she recalled awaiting her friend's arrival until 6:15 in the evening. Friends who made plans with Rosemond often expressed annoyance with her difficult and unpredictable behavior, but afterward she would apologize. Eleanor remembered that they "cruised little Romanesque towns looking at churches, and Rosemond taking pictures of high crosses with her Brownie." Before leaving France they had visited almost twenty towns, among them Le Puy, La Chaise-Drew, Brioude (where there was a Pilgrim shrine), St. Flour, Conques, Aurillac, Cordis, Orcival, Clermont, Feraud, St. Nectair, and Mauriac, before spending a few days in Paris.

On arrival in London, there were new dramas and histrionics. Rosemond had been asked to speak over the BBC and she urged Eleanor to read her paper. Then, during dinner at the Whitehall Hotel the next night, with another friend, Frances Yates, Rosemond lost her voice. Somehow, the next day, she succeeded in giving her talk on John Milton, titled "A Name to Resound for Ages." There were reverberations in the press from critics who took issue with some of her remarks on the profundity of Milton's imagery as opposed to the modern habit of searching for symbols. To illustrate her point, she recalled an experience from her childhood, no doubt one of the first to suggest to her the power of images and allegory, when she spoke of "the marvellous precision and restraint with which Milton slowly commands our attention to large complexes of meaning through images perfectly suited to their task, as a wind will blow unseen over a prairie and show itself only in the obedient bending of the grasses."[2]

Sometime during her year abroad Rosemond visited the Waldegrave family for the last time. Near the end of her life, Mary Waldegrave expressed regret that she "lost the opportunity of getting on to confidential terms with a very interesting and distinguished personality." But their lives had taken very different paths and their interests—Mary had raised a large family—were quite opposite.

Rosemond returned to New London in the fall of 1958, her ties to the college gradually beginning to fray. While abroad she received word that she had been awarded a NATO fellowship, one of only four offered from the United States. This meant that during the first semester of 1960, in less than a year and a half, she would be on leave again. With these plans only an undercurrent, she began preparing for the Gauss Seminars at Princeton, a prospect that had been of continuing concern for over a year, and would eventually move her one degree closer to severing her remaining connections with Connecticut College.

When E. B. O. Borgerhoff, of Princeton, invited Rosemond to deliver the Christian Gauss Seminars in Criticism in the spring of 1957, she was going abroad and had to decline. It was her second invitation. Her reply to Borgerhoff was characteristic: "It needs no saying that anyone asked to do a Christian Gauss Seminar is in a state of astonishment, pleasure and humility, with a strong dash of wholesome dismay and an equally strong one of excitement."[3] Although Hannah Arendt was the first woman actually to give the series of six lectures, Rosemond was asked three times before she was able to acccept. She followed both Arendt and Mary McCarthy in being so honored.

In March 1958, while in Rome, she received her third invitation, this time from R. P. Blackmur, to deliver the Gauss Seminars in the spring of 1959. She wrote her acceptance from the American Academy in Rome: "Of course it frightens the life out of me that you are all that sure you wish to have me hold forth and discuss; you're sure to wonder why, later." Then she added: "I've been working this year on late mediaeval ways of reading allegory—particularly texts—and relations therewith to Elizabethan allegory, most especially Spenser."[4] As the correspondence between Rosemond and R. P. Blackmur developed, it became, like her previous relations with like-minded colleagues, both playful and witty. In May 1958, Rosemond wrote again to Blackmur: "I'm as scairt as ever, but I've put it behind me (in front of me?) while dealing with the more immediate scares of talking to these wretches over here—luckily it did not occur to them to run the risk *you* run, of a row of six thus draining the jug quite." She closed the letter with: "I'll be curious as to what kind or whose faces I'll be looking into."[5]

Back home in October, steeped in medieval literature, she assumed the voice of a damsel in distress in her next letter to Blackmur: "I'm perished till I hear something of who might be there. Fright now forces the lady to close with greetings (faint)."[6] Erwin Panofsky, the eminent art historian, whom Rosemond knew, replied to his invitation to the seminars (attendance was by invitation only) that, though "having the highest possible opinion of Miss Tuve,"[7] he was unable to accept.

Rosemond cared deeply for the quality of education being offered not only by Connecticut College, but also at educational institutions everywhere. There was no question that at age fifty-six, wearied by concerns and the pace at which she lived, her patience had begun to unravel, and a tone of bitterness crept into her letters. The following letter to President Park was an illustration.

23 January, 1959

Dear President Park,

I write in much distress of mind and presume on long friendship to speak quite uninhibitedly, upon learning of decisions taken to allow students to split the Reading Period in two by absenting themselves from the College.

This obviously sets at naught our entire policy of securing a period of uninterrupted time for more leisurely, more independent, culminative reading. I had thought we were at last achieving the original conception of a true period of quiet independent experience of what it is to be a student, and facing down for ever the slot-machine interpretations, by students and faculty, which have increasingly bedevilled us. It becomes humiliatingly apparent to those who have defended Reading Period, as a valid trust in our students' capacity for maturity, that we were unwittingly putting up a sham and leading others also to mere satisfaction in the pretty statements of our neat-on-paper theory—through all the long constant struggle for well over ten years to get more departments and courses to keep the time unbroken by class engagements . . .

The spectacle of a community of candidates for the Bachelor of Arts degree who cannot face one week of study, nor reside quietly in a place of learning for three weeks, is so absurd, that one feels that no faculty member can easily forget it, in his necessary attempt to grasp what are the working assumptions of the College touching the kind of persons we teach.

The hollow sound of our simultaneous talking about changing "the intellectual atmosphere" is too apparent, when it is obvious that even one or two such requests for relief, if granted, would do more to destroy the idea that such an atmosphere is expected here, than can be built up in scores of discussion groups or years of faithful insistence on maturity in classes and courses.

I would attach to this debacle of the idea of a period of tranquil and enjoyed reading, the fact that one has heard also that the possession of cars may be allowed for one reason or another. If Princeton can say categorically, "No automobiles," Connecticut College might find it possible to maintain this last one remnant of the idea that the pursuit of knowledge makes some demands unfitted to American suburban living. If practice-teaching is to bring in its train the inability to hold the line on the undoubted fact that study goes ill with free mobility, many persons must see that we are selling our birthright for the pottage once again. No more votes for pottage for me. But the real and unmendable crack, that comes with all these things, is that a faculty whose hope is broken, how tough soever it was in the face of daily disproof, will in the end not fight but accept. People will sweep the ocean back with a broom for years, and actually keep one little spot dry enough to keep in the fire that will start the next man's to come, but let them once be convinced that the broom is a joke and everybody but they realizes the wood's wet anyhow, they'll take to riding the waves till their time's out, like the rest. The younger give in first; only the older are idealistic enough to Buck a Trend. They die . . .

Amen. Don't miss Palestrina. Ighest possible standard. Pour la monnaie.

Ros[8]

Rosemary Park replied, with what she termed "relatively cold comfort," as soon as she could assess the Reading Period problem: "This seems to me a most regrettable situation and I am only sorry that I did not know of this fact until I received your letter." She told the "Schedule Committee to be sure that we do not set up a similar program in another year, whereby the Reading Period can be so misused."[9]

In response to Rosemond's second concern, the possibility of students being allowed cars on campus, she added: "Please do not be unduly concerned about the automobiles. The matter was thoroughly discussed and, as far as I know, has been definitely put to rest . . ."[10]

The Christian Gauss Seminars in Research, consisting of six lectures, primarily for faculty and graduate honors students, were held on consecutive Thursday evenings, in April and May. The title of Rosemond's six lectures were: "Spenserian Allegory and Some Medieval Books:" "Guillaume's Pilgrim and What Kept Him Alive"; "The Virtues and Other Sevens, Not in Aristotle But 'The Rest'"; "The Double Knighthood"; "Imposed Allegories"; and "Paradise Lost." Rosemond stayed at the Nassau Inn in Princeton, and received a stipend of fifteen hundred dollars, plus expenses. More important, it gave her the opportunity to mingle with graduate students, and to engage her colleagues in intellectual discussions, the exact nourishment that most animated and filled her. Two students, Sherman Hawkins, who helped her with the slide projector, and Tom Roche, who also assisted, later became valuable friends. Tom Roche recalled that later assessments proclaimed Rosemond's series of lectures one of the better ones.

One of the amusing things about this one, according to David Kalstone, was that both Mary McCarthy and Hannah Arendt, each of whom had previously given the seminars, were in attendance. "They were rather mystified because the general implications of what she was saying she never bothered with that much," remembered Kalstone. "She just went right into her missiles." It is rumored that Arendt and McCarthy walked out. This reaction is partially corroborated by a graduate student, Elizabeth Turner Pochoda, after another lecture Rosemond gave: "At this point she was working on *Allegorical Imagery* and she would give those lectures with slides. The analysis was so subtle. The scholarship was so imaginative and so complete and so convincing. They were absolutely wonderful. I said to her afterwards, 'These people have no response to your lecture, did you notice that?' She said, 'Yes, they just don't play in my gardens.'"

Just before Rosemond began her grueling but exhilarating trips to

Princeton, another agonizing problem presented itself. On March 18, 1959, Rosemond received a letter from Robert W. Rogers, chairman of the English department at the University of Illinois.

"Dear Professor Tuve," he wrote. "In order to put on paper what I said on the phone yesterday, I am writing to invite you formally to serve as a Visiting Professor of English at the University of Illinois for the second semester of the academic year 1959–60. As a visitor, you will be asked to teach two courses on subjects of your own choosing, one a course exclusively for graduate students and one a course open to graduate students and advanced undergraduates. The salary for this position will be $7500 for approximately four and one-half months of service.

"I frankly hope that during your stay here, you will come to like Illinois, its students, its library and my colleagues so much that you can be persuaded to stay permanently. Professor Harris Fletcher is retiring September 1, 1961; and you are the person I would most like to have take his place. The salary of the permanent position would be in the neighborhood of $14,000 and the teaching load for a regular member of the staff is three courses each semester."

After all these inducements, Rogers outlined additional generous incentives: "Should it be possible to make a permanent arrangement next spring, you could return to Connecticut for the year 1960–61, or take up the appointment in Scandinavia for the year, or remain on the teaching staff here as a visitor for 1960–61, at the end of which time the permanent position will be available. Or I will try to arrange a research appointment for the year which will give you time in which to do your own work.

"I realize that I am complicating your life with this proposal; and you should feel free to take as much time as you need to make a decision that is to your own best interest. Time is of no importance."

Rosemond, who often expressed her hatred of making decisions, found it did complicate her life, but only for a brief time. She was strongly tempted, first bringing the problem to Rosemary Park, and then to Merle and Dick during her Easter recess in the Washington area. Another two-page, single-spaced, typewritten letter was immediately launched to Rosemary.

I find unpalatable the idea that you have to go to bat and do any pleading, in order for me to do the kind of things I have done and contemplate doing. The actions of the Trustees toward me have been unexceptionable; I was really angered by what you quoted to me of their attitudes.

It makes considerable difference to me in my weighing of relative advantages of this post and the one up for present consideration. Such attitudes indicate that they judge it to be not a service to the College, to go and do a term of graduate teaching at Harvard and return here, or to meet Princeton's request to go and do the seminars for faculty. I would rather know it if others on the faculty turn down these things, and if this is what the Trustees would prefer. If there are four NATO professorships in the United States, and Connecticut is asked to provide one of them, it may still be true that they prefer keeping on the faculty here those who do not trouble them with such irregularities.

In our general need to establish this younger college among those institutions whose prestige and greater age encourage better applicants both for studying and for teaching here, it has not been my experience in the academic world, the learned world, or the outside world generally, that my activities away from this campus have harmed our standing.

Many kinds of service are provided to a college by many kinds of persons. If the kind I can peculiarly provide is not regarded as one, but largely as a favour to me, others could be found who would teach here uninterruptedly. I have not felt that you agree with them in finding this so preferable to what those can do who go out to bring back the fresh air into our own system and teaching, or re-introduce the disturbing element of connecting what we do here with values as the greater world of education and learning understands them....

If the Trustees do not see these kinds of contributions as commensurate with the flexibility which is the way of paying for them (rather than direct financial outlay), I need to be aware of this. I am not interested in some hard-bound deal, nor in getting official promises. But I am interested to be a little surer about a point of view, for if every four years or so one of these non-cost releases comes up, I do not care to be put in the doghouse (excuse it hermann) while you try, unsure of success, to persuade persons with other ideas of the kind of contributions they want, that I have a right to make such and such a request ..

I hope you realized that I haven't even a thought of raising any money-finger. Chiefly I am tired of being afraid to open my letters all spring. I would like to be thought valuable enough here that some of the sackcloth and ashes could be seen as not necessary. You personally are always a relief and an uncomplicater to go and see . . . It is the policy that worries Ed Cranz too . . .

Rosemond's thoughts and feelings were stimulated as she wrote, reminding us that she had accused the typewriter of running away with her words. She exaggerated the "every four years or so," which now seems to be every year. In the last paragraph it appears that Rosemond had already persuaded herself not to go to Illinois.

In this instance there are several factors for me. Colleagues there, and graduate teaching, are for it, as well as a clear $40,000 greater security for old age totally without family resources; geography and roots are against it. I am not going until Friday early but I think I ought to answer during the vacation; but Dorothy is still not well from a cold and I hate to face her with any blow before tomorrow. It does certainly come into my set of factors to be weighted that the trustees do not consider my outside activities to have been of value to this College and the course of education here, and would therefore not be likely to be amenable if I thought of flexibility to leave oftener than others, at no cost, as one of the inducements to remain.[11]

From Dick's home in Silver Spring, she responded to Professor Rogers's letter with complete honesty and gratitude.

Despite the generosity of your arrangements, I am afraid geography is too much against a move to the Middle of the United States, for me to accept your handsome offer. As I told Professor Pratt, I am tied to this part of the country partly because "home" has come to mean convenient nearness to the family households. It is also true that roots grow deep in thirty years or so, and the connections and friends and habits one makes during one's professional life—and all of mine has been spent in the eastern part of the country—exercise a stronger pull than a person is quite conscious of until permanent change is confronted.

It was a temptation to think of helping to maintain the high prestige Illinois has kept, in a field where you have been eminent, and my conscience about putting my full strength behind graduate work may begin to hurt me, whatever solace I try to take in our wellnigh perfect departmental conditions of work and the quality of highly selected undergraduates. I rather look forward to the Danish NATO visiting professorship in the spring of 1960, feel obligated to my department for its willingness to release me three times during the past four years, and all in all believe I had better remain in the setup I find myself in, for the present. I should have enjoyed the colleagues I would have found at Illinois, and certainly the generosity of your offer and your attempts to meet me in the matter of date and leaves was most outstanding.

Robert Pratt, to whom Rosemond refers in her letter, was a medievalist at the University of Illinois, and obviously better acquainted with Rosemond. He wrote to her as soon as he learned of her decision. Of interest is the knowledge that she took seriously his request, and that of Robert Rogers, that she help them find someone in her place. Arthur Barker was hired on her recommendation. Pratt's letter: "Dear Ros," he wrote, "your news is a heartbreaker; we need you, and I'm terribly sorry for us that you don't need what Illinois has to offer; but I sympathize completely with your decision. Now that the ice has been broken, I hope Bob will have you out here now and then to talk to our graduate students; its a fairly short flight from Boston (or N.Y.).

"Meanwhile I'd be grateful for any suggestions you may have for us. Our need: a teacher; and someone to use the great collection of renaissance books . . . Someone who will use the books and guide students to their use . . . Well, all good wishes. It was a wonderful idea while it lasted!!!!!" He signed it "Yours cordially, Bob."

Robert Rogers also wrote in the same vein.

As soon as Rosemond returned from Washington, she wrote to President Park:

> How good you are. I came back today still unsettled, one brother saying Go another Stay. But Geography on this rain-and-sunny day is very speaking, and your letter like those things they throw on fires and they become quiet and have bright colours, a thing to make one feel contented about one's decision instead of gnawed and merely making one out of weariness.[12]

This was followed by a long, melancholy letter to Merle:

> You looked tired to me, and I was distressed by those images of your going around with pains. Also (based on I don't know what similarity of experience) I have a quite acute sense of that ambiguity of feeling about Lucy's simultaneously being lost and being safe. [Lucy, Merle and Winifred's daughter, was married, it appears, while Rosemond was in Washington, at Dick's house, where she often spent her vacations.] Americans live the most *without* the necessary balms and velvet-layers (of convention I spose) placed between them and the pain of the human condition, of any nation born. We are too rational, and throw too much out. Every English life I know from inside has so much more in the way of coating. Some call it pretense and some call it a false slavery to the idea of "duty" but the net result is to avoid this lone and naked individualism that we have come to think of as human "nature." They live at a lower rate, but more in concert...

I decided that the *English* secret was an ancient but almost universally regnant notion, very oldfashioned and I bet riddled with falsity, that they Ought To Be Good. People were so good to me I nearly died of it; I simply couldn't make it out. They *conspired* to be good to me. I'm sure it cost them much; but they didn't ever tell.

The upper classes I guess still believe in Grace. I found it an improvement on Nature. I figgered I'd import it and retain this marvelous undercurrent of surprised gratefulness (I *met* it as much as I *had* it; I was *incessantly* thanked for just existing and going around pleased). But I must say it's a damn sight harder to put in practice where everything is going past like a millwheel turning and nobody takes time to pick up each other's handkerchief. Why do I find it so much less practicable to do a thing or two for anybody in my own country? And so noteworthy when I do? like a remarkable event. It's a terrible way to live. Well I have got going on the ramifications of what I think is a national blind spot, but the start and spring of this was, that I thought looking at your face in repose so like mother's, that's such a good kind generous boy and I've known him all my life, I wish I weren't so far away, I'd MAKE him move over and holler or not I'd see if he drowned in a bath of unintelligent affection, the usual sisterly sort, insufficiently qualified and half phony but very resilient.

So you see what you've escaped.

Not entirely. For in the end I decided not to go that far away. I don't want to come home for reasons, but for *nothing*. And the same is true with the whole network of relationships from Widener at Harvard to the Folger at Washington, top of my normal ladder where I run up and down to bottom, north to south; I have long ceased to plan my personal relationships and intellectual peregrinations but let them happen to me. I go to libraries and institutions all up and down this habitual gamut, to work, then since each one is a sort of ant's-nest of ancient warm ties, Delights are always happening to me. I'm getting so easily tired by planning; I'll do it if some utter

Whopper comes along, but I'm a little fearful of the Factory element in a department like Illinois. Yourself 2 yrs and 5 months ago is the amount of Pep I've still got to remould existence. I'm real old. Have to be sure remoulding would in truth be nearer to the heart's desire including nearer to what my conscience says I shd. do for English Studies in the U.S. before I stop off. I had thought of all the points you brought up, and I went through them all again after you spoke of them too,—especially since I have rebelled for 23 years against colleges, and women's education in particular.

So it may not be so smart. But this particular alternative might not be so smart either. You wouldn't *believe* the enslavement to inadequately trained and immature-hence-dependent *hordes* of persons seeking graduate degrees which I have seen my friends stagger under. Perhaps English gets them nowadays. Well, I'm not sure. But it seemed dangerous as I perceived what a good time I had at Princeton (I saw Willard [Thorpe] for lunch and reminded him he used to practice in Alexander Hall—remember? I worked at Pn. all day Sat. before Easter; had long talks with the two young instructors [Tom Roche and Sherman Hawkins] who loomed up to "help" me, and sometimes think I do most for "the future teaching of English" in these legions of connections I keep going at Brown and Cambridge and Yale and Smith and Amherst and what-not, but who knows). And as I perceived what a pull it wd. be to stop going to Harvard for a day's work, and looked at Dick's head singing in his choir on Sunday morning, thought it might be dangerous . . .

I have to go to bed. Thank you for coming over tired though you were. We are once more singing a mass reproduced through the monies you put to the Palestrina account. I wish I'd seen Winnie but I'm sure she was near dead with the excitements; and it really filled the days going each afternoon to Emily's. I start the Princeton weekly treks in a week & a half, really expect to learn something off my select auditory; then when that closes in May, drive to Rochester to be

an outside examiner, Bob's old spot and 2 old grad. students
of mine from Minn. [Rita and Dick Gollin] plus a Britisher I
lectured for at Hull last April. I like best that flowery drive
alone through the ravishing villages of the Empire State.
        good night. Don't get sick any more.[13]

   Despite Rosemond's anxiety about what she felt were transgres-
sions against the deeply serious purposes of education, there were
lighter moments, moments when she could genuinely enjoy her inter-
changes with students and gain some real satisfaction. Nancy
Donahue, who went on to be a playwright, was a student in more than
one of Rosemond's classes during this period. Her memories were
dramatic and vivid: "I had steered clear of Miss Tuve like the plague
because I had heard that she was difficult, and I don't think I could
have managed her before my junior year. My first feelings about Miss
Tuve when I saw her were—she was so strange to look at. She was
lovely but she was odd, really odd. Not peculiar, not weird, and not
spooky funny like some teachers. What was odd at the heart of Miss
Tuve was not that she was separate from the rest of us but that she saw
things very clearly—in a way that went far deeper than the rest of us
and she was so involved with them that she simply forgot about everything else. And it wasn't that she was absent-minded. I don't mean
that. It was easier to put on whatever came to hand and keep your
mind on what you had to do. She had a vision that was so comprehensive. That was both mystical and comprehensive and *very* learned.
And because it was all three of those things and not just one of them
she must have been like the only one on earth who could think that
way and so she must have been very lonely. She had friends who
adored her, so that when she was with them she wasn't lonely. It's just
that I don't think anyone quite saw the way she did. Miss Bethurum
said "Ros was a mystic." Anyway, she loved us students and she loved
the work and she loved our interest in things.
   "Her overriding passion was to transmit somehow a little bit of
this vision she had to us—to get us thinking along lines that maybe
would bring us to have a little bit of it on our own. Not just simply to
stamp it on our minds or to just hand it across. But to try to make us

think in a way that we would begin to see how everything was connected. "The tissue of existence" was how she put it. She would come into class, it was as if she would leap into class and try to get right down into things. She would look abstractedly at the table or at an object, or something, and she would talk while her mind focused visually on these things that she saw and she wanted us to start looking for. She would make us talk about a stylistic element or something and she would make us talk about the truth or non-truth of a certain footnote, a real, real tiny specific from which I think now, that I follow the same path. I believe that in a deep and passionate, and immediate and sensory connection to specifics you begin to get a sense of the way all the little specifics hang together in order to form the whole big general number . . .

"I'll never forget this particular class," she went on. "It was one of the seminars and she had been talking about the different connections, the different levels of reality that things exist on all at the same time. There is this image of a person being dragged in a cart. On one level it is a human being in a cart who is going from one place to another, and on another level, which is also true, it means a person going into death because that's what it has come to stand for. The person traveling in the cart is shamefully being taken into death. If you stop to think about it, it is borne out by the men going to the guillotine, like an animal being taken to slaughter. There was that level. There were two other levels. She was talking about her perception of it and it was a stunning perception. I remember physically, having a sense of my head being shot up and widened. And it was like as you stand at the top of a hill and you take off down the hill. It was breathless. She veered from point to point to point and again she suddenly arrived at stylistics. It was all connected.

"She would be passionate about ethical things. We loved her and we were afraid of her. If we ever angered her it was in innocence and she had the compassion to know that. And then we had these weekly papers. In the drama course one day she quoted a line from Marlowe's *Faustus*, and she said, 'See, see where Christ's blood streams in the firmament, one drop would save my soul. Oh, half a drop—Oh Christ.' I've never forgotten it. She had that kind of passion.

"Two of us were invited over to her house to discuss music. It astonished me because it was all done in sort of southwest Mexican style. At one point she said, as we were discussing a specific point, 'Nancy, go into my bedroom please, and get me the book, etc. etc. It's on the bookshelf by the window, on the far wall.' So I went. The bedroom was four walls, and maybe one-half foot in from the four walls was a double bed, on all four sides, except for the one side of the wall in which the bed was actually flush with the wall. There was absolutely no way to get to the bookshelf. The bed filled the entire room. I stood there a minute and I didn't know what to do and I thought about it and finally I came out and I said, "Miss Tuve I can't get to the bookshelf." She said, "Oh, no problem." And she went into the bedroom and walked across the bed. I mean these great strides across the bed with her tent-like skirt. And I remember thinking she partly did that on purpose and I love it. I love it.

"I think I've tried to connect things up in my mind. I think I have an ability to connect extraordinary things you might not think would get connected. It's at the root of the best part of my writing, and I think that was something she appreciated and fostered in me in a way. Ros did that herself in her own exalted sphere. Somehow, I felt I had cottoned onto an enormous mother who was on a shopping trip and my legs weren't long enough and I kept running after her, as fast as I could. If you'd asked me what visual, sensory, physical, sort of picture I would have of her which is totally unconnected with anything that actually happened, it is that of being a very small child behind an enormous and very loving mother, who has her mind on a thousand things—with one hand on the child's hand and is racing on ahead in these great boots, and you're running after her. And you love this mother so much and all you could see was the back of her skirt and these great boots. And then she might pick you up and look at you and then you would see this wonderful sweet face, which knew everything and you didn't know anything yet. And yet she knew things that you were going to know."

During a brief lull in the complications of Rosemond's life she found time to write to her brother Lew about her plans to go to

Aarhus, Denmark, the following February. The letter is written on University of Minnesota stationery, saved for seven years.

25 May [1959] or anyhow Monday
Dear Lew & Helen,

I never could bear to use the last of this stationery. It smells so fine of linseed oil. Helen will remember Folwell's smell—maybe the engineers had pure air. I am through with my Princeton jaunts and all went very well, so they said. Princeton Press wants me to make a book of the 6 lectures, [the book is *Allegorical Imagery*] so my heart sinks; books are so hard. Anyhow they were just *talks*. Oh shucks.

I write esp. because maybe nobody has said that I am evidently going 2nd half of next year to DENMARK. Long time ago I got a letter, did I want to be a NATO Professor. At "Aarhus." I never heard of it, but since there are but 3 such prof-ships and the other 2 were Belgium & Greece I figgered it out. My Viking blood of course boils at the thought with great fervent zeal to run to land of forefathers or roughly so. Not that I forget them Danes had us enSLAVED until syttende mai. Anyhow nothing got done for ages while I stipulated I must teach not Amer.lit but my own stuff, must talk in English, and must not go till Feb.—then Fulbright people wrote and said all that was all right by Danish Embassy and I shd. hear from the Univ. soon. I havent but they said it was evidently a settled thing, so we've planned here on my absence. I had an offer from Illinois, very large luminous and lucrative, and part of my turning it down hinged on CC's willingness to let me out on strings for my ADVENTURES— so I have leave. I am only one in family hasnt seen scandinavia, so you can imagine I am having all sorts of pipedreams. I do like scooting about. I had a lovely time at P'ton, hosts of new friends, all Joy and Luve.

My duck of an asst. was transported with my Relative. Says we are ALIKE. Claims GLT's KINDNESS was supreme and exalted, thinks smile is angelic and hair Beautiful.

Altogether a Beautiful Character I gathered and I am said to be LIKE him.

Rosemond had previously written to Lew, who was teaching at Case Institute of Technology, telling him that during her spring vacation, "you'll be having a call of greetings hot from griddle by my entirely *charming* young student assistant, who lives in Cleveland . . . I told her she shd. with my blessing go and bring my love in person, and could ask where she might go to ask about a job on Case or WR [Western Reserve] campus this summer . . . Do you think real broke girls shd. try for *factory* jobs in Cleveland to earn *lots,* or stick to nice atmosphere of a College? I was as you recall a *atmosphere* gal & you defended me in it."[14]

On June 7, 1959, Rosemond was awarded a doctor of letters degree from Mount Holyoke College. She had refused one from Smith College, which was to have been awarded on the same date. The citation she received was spirited:

"Rosemond Tuve: Valiant champion in the endless battle of the Ancients and the Moderns, in your teaching and in your writing you have upheld stoutly sound historical learning and disciplined imagination as the true basis of all fruitful interpretation of literature. You have brilliantly defended the poets of the past from their audacious modern detractors. The vigor and wit of your work, and its deep seriousness, have brought a new excitement to the study of poetry. Your hearers and readers, whether students or professional critics, follow your lead, breathless and exhilarated."

Eleanor Lincoln attended the ceremony, in nearby South Hadley, after which she invited her friend to return home with her. Rosemond wrote promptly to thank Eleanor for her hospitality, expressing again her longing for congenial companions with whom to share ideas. Except for "Dutch" Burdick, who was now retired, she was wary of her friends at Connecticut College. Intellectual discussions were, as she wrote to Merle, "the breath of life." They reinforced her hours of loneliness, hours in which she must have had some bad times, playing for high stakes; yet it was a loneliness not necessarily for people, but rather an inner craving, spiritual hunger. It was a desire for transcendence, or, as Eleanor put it, "divine revelation."

Saturday   [June 1959]

Dear Eleanor and Virginia,

>   The brightest thing, I have done
>   this spring,   (POEM)

was to get myself ast to your Country House.

I keep thinking how amiable of you to not retreat in a PANIC from merest notion of a guest, plopped into your post-commencement businesses . . . Goodness me I had a lovely time. My head is full of images of bliss. I have really learned your house; so different to stay more than 1 night in a place. I think it is a triumph, and just your way of taking it is my notion of the Perfect. You're almost my only friends who don't FUSS, driven by possession of mansion to a slavery. I was filled with admiration. And all so pretty.

The Marie-party was a special high point.

Oh dear I did enjoy the silent libry. It was all so easy to the mind—so I thank you special for that for it wd. have been so natural for you to carry over some of your own THINGS AREN'T DONE to my psyche. Instead I just had a delicious sense of freedom and delight.

One pleasure you might not know about or realize is, somebody in lieu of nearby family, to be glad about things one gets handed. I find socalled honours almost worthless of late years; there is literally *no pleasure at all in them alone.* Unless someone is pleased, what earthly fun is there in being handed anything? It seems so funny to walk about with nobody to tell anything to who will be glad about it. It seems too mixed in at this end with invidious comparisons, or with being suspected just slightly of Putting One's Value Clearly Forwrd. Or what not. So in the nice warmth of having given somebody else a little pleasure I gleamed away at the laurels all the way down in a Content.

Then your conversation is so good . . . .

Many many thanks for everything. It isn't so much the special nameable gifts and courtesies; I just like to be around you since it is a pleasure to admire people and not have reservations to make within about the unfortunate nature of the human spirit.

So cheering . . .

love from Roz

Rosemond was elected a Fellow of the American Academy of Arts and Sciences on May 13, 1959. When T. S. Eliot was awarded the Emerson Thoreau Prize by the Academy, in October 1959, Rosemond drove up to Cambridge to attend the ceremony with William Meredith. Meredith was at that time poet in residence, and lecturer, at Connecticut College and most certainly an acquaintance of Eliot's. Twenty-five years later he recalled the event:

"Rosemond took me and somebody else, and we went to her induction to the American Academy of Arts and Sciences, which is now outside of Boston. It's an old and very distinguished professional society founded by, I believe, John Quincy Adams, it's that old, and she was made a member the year they gave the first Emerson medal, their annual prize, and they gave it to T. S. Eliot. The thing that struck me about that event was that as we went through the reception line— I went with Ros—Valery Eliot, who was looking very young and English peaches and cream compared to Mr. Eliot, was giving him names and he was talking to somebody. Ros gave her name to Valery Eliot, and Valery Eliot *beamed,* and said, 'Darling, it's Miss Tuve.' Eliot had wanted to meet her. Apparently that was one of the things he went for, a chance to meet this remarkable lady."

Meredith added, with obvious affection, more recollections of Rosemond. "She always was cheerful and an extraordinary person, in spite of the severity with which people remember her in the classroom and outside. She was never anything but personally very gay and light-hearted. But I was always aware that her standards, that she applied to herself, were visible and tended to work as a reproach, whether she had meant them so, to students or colleagues, if their standards were less than hers."

He continued: "I was very fond of her and interested in her conversation. She wanted to know about modern poetry and I knew a little more about it than she did. We would walk home from the campus to her house which was down on Mohegan Ave. and my house was across the street. I lived on the top floor. Ros came home with me and we would often have a drink and sit around and talk and it would get to be supper time and I would say why don't you stay for supper and I would cook supper and we would eat together. And this went on I suppose as many as ten times in the fall semester. And one night as she was leaving she seemed to have something to say and I thought she was going to say, next time you must come to my house, but what she said was, "You shouldn't waste your time cooking all the time," was all she said. Once in a while I went to her house and we had something like tea and graham crackers. She knocked herself out.

"My impressions are of a bird-watcher," he said, "who could tell sort of what she was up to. Her thought was as eccentric and original as her style. She was the only person who probably would have thought those things that got thought about Renaissance literature. In that sense the eccentricity is a form of being a misfit, where geniuses are misfits. I think that was her creativity, scholarship, in its creative form. Some women cook and some women make poems, but I think for Ros she found this form of creative activity very early. It was absorbing because I think she read a great deal that was of no use to her to make sure that no relationships escaped her that she might be able to discover. But I think the reading was creative. She listened to people and thought about it and made patterns in her own mind. She was very nearly too eccentric to be wise, but wasn't too eccentric to be wise—that is, as Eliot says about experiments: "They are valuable in proportion as they go very near or over the edge and discover where the edge is of usefulness." Ros's imagination is at the periphery of respectable scholarly speculation."

Meredith went on, "About her beauty: It was a kind of radiance of intelligence. This capacity to listen resulted in her almost unbroken eye contact with you and she was like a very attractive girl in her eyes. The indifference to her dress and hair was real, but before she left the house she put on something pretty and fixed her hair but after that it was on its own. I think she never worried about being attractive. She knew people liked her. She never would have been thought of as a Cambridge lady, the dried up stereotypes that we have in scholarship.

"When Robert Frost visited the campus he didn't know who she was because he wasn't interested in that sort of scholarship but he was a man who could tell by looking at somebody that they were somebody. Everybody loved her and that tempered our fear of her. Ros had a great sense of the wittiness of things. Not an ordinary sense of humor, but a polite perception of the ridiculous, not at all like the absurd, or the dark sense of the ridiculousness that we have. She had an Elizabethan sense of the ridiculous.

"Everybody had a domestic life except Ros—shopping, cooking, and entertaining. I swear to God I don't think Ros ever had a party. In the summer she had that little garden and people might have been allowed in. No white Russian princess knew less about the kitchen. I never heard this one first hand but I truly believe it. Where she lived on Mohegan Avenue, it was not as it is now, it was a tree-lined street, and she was feeding the birds and she decided to feed the squirrels that would come and eat except one day she noticed that they didn't have bushy tails. She was feeding river rats.

"The only insight I ever had into her private life was when we drove once to the opera in New York and had a lot of time to talk. She had been reading Lawrence Durrell's Alexandrian Quartet and she asked me what I thought about it, and I had bogged down quite early. And she said—and it's to be remembered that in the late fifties when those books came out there was a sexual frankness in them that was not common, it now would look awfully tame stuff—she said something so charming— 'There are things that don't lose their novelty in the doing that surely do in the telling.' Also an epigraph to modern pornography in its sameness."

Rosemond's next official honor came on November 9 at Goucher College, where she was invited to fill the Isabelle Kellogg Thomas Lectureship in English. Each year distinguished writers and teachers were invited to participate. (Rosemond's personal remarks prior to the body of her talk were quoted earlier when she described her life as a student at Goucher.) An article in the Goucher Weekly, the student newspaper, attempted to explain Rosemond's topic, "Some Mediaeval Illustrations and the Fairie Queene." The report concluded: "Dr. Tuve's pet anathema is people who find mediaeval texts 'quaint.'"[15]

Annette B. Hopkins, a "formidable" Quaker lady, who was chairman of the English department at that time, recalled the lecture as a "tour de force," punctuated with "pyrotechnics."

In less than a month Rosemond returned to her alma mater at Bryn Mawr to give a lecture titled "Pilgrims Before Bunyan." The occasion, sponsored by the department of English, was in honor of the college's seventy-fifth anniversary. The *College News* had this to say: "The theme of the English department's Anniversary lectures is 'Literature and Knowledge', or 'what must one know in interpreting the literature of the Past?' For Miss Rosamond [sic] Tuve, the answer is, 'You can't tell.'

"It is the student's responsibility, not his teacher's, to find out what he must know, and most of his early reading, interesting or not, is done without knowledge of where it will be useful. 'A scholar must take a passionate pleasure in what he is doing: no other approach can leave one free to find one's own questions.'" [16] This is the only time that Bryn Mawr College recognized her abilities and achievements.

Three weeks before her departure for Aarhus, Rosemond was again writing to President Park requesting leave. She had just learned that she was the recipient of an award of ten thousand dollars from the American Council of Learned Societies, which would be announced at its annual meeting on January 20, 1960. She was one of ten scholars in that year, and only the second woman, to receive the ten-thousand-dollar prize. (The first woman to receive the prize was Mary Hamilton Swindler, professor emeritus of archaeology, Bryn Mawr College, in 1959.) The prestigious award was given "in recognition of the distinguished contributions they have made to humanistic learning," and Rosemond was eager to make use of this extraordinary gift.

The following citation was published in the *ACLS Newsletter*: "Rosemond Tuve—Student of the literature and thought of England in the middle ages, the Renaissance, and the seventeenth century, who brings to her work the grace and ease of the accomplished literary critic together with the learning and the accuracy of the scholar, and who thus corrects the influential dicta of critics who have more grace and ease than of scholarship; who, when she presents a lucidly composed and quietly written paper at a learned meeting, is probably in the act of exploding a generation of literary misconceptions; whose familiarity with the intricacies of literary and philosophical ideas in the past and whose attachment to the best literature of the present enable her to explore both the similarities and differences, the continuity of one with the other and the integrity of each; who illuminates one matter as she corrects another, and thereby gives scholarship the substance that enables criticism to proceed in insight, and herself offers shining examples of both."[17]

> 13 Jan., 1960
> Dear President Park,
>   In pursuance of our conversation of 9 January, may I make formal request to absent myself from teaching in order to make use of the award which will soon be made public, from the American Council of Learned Societies?
>   Since it amounts to more than a year's salary, and though said to be given for services to the humanities, undoubtedly is given in anticipation that one will continue these services. I feel it incumbent upon me to put the monies to use in further researches; I cannot well do this while teaching my usual program.
>   Because it comes so uncomfortably close upon a previous generous release from the College I have devised the plan we spoke of, of putting off use for a year and a half from the time of granting, thus asking to be released for the academic year 1961–2.
>   It is probable that I will spend the first semester in this country, meeting the request of Princeton University (to assist in developing a program of studies—though this parenthesis should not be put into print). I would there be a Senior Fellow of the Council of the Humanities, Visiting Professor of English, and would be able to continue work on a book which the Princeton Press has asked me to complete. I should thereupon (in January) go abroad for further materials.[18]

As with all her honors, Rosemond passed over them lightly. But what she was actually confiding to President Park was that not only had she become just the second woman to receive the achievement award from the ACLS, but also that she would be the first woman invited to teach in the English department at Princeton.

If they were looking her over for a possible permanent appointment, the old-boy network couldn't agree. Later, Thomas P. Roche, one of the young instructors she had met during the Gauss Seminars, recalled this story: "One of the reasons that Ros was not hired here the year she was teaching was that our benighted chairman was unable to see this was a remarkable person. And the other thing is that Ros went into her Rabelaisian phase. Sam Howell, who has done all sorts of things—she gave him a very good review and liked him—and several others used to have lunch up in the library tower, and Ros was the only woman on the faculty at that time—visiting. And there was Sam Howell and Carlos Baker, more uptight men you have not met I can assure you. And Ros said, 'Oh, let's talk about Faulkner.' And she started talking about his latest novel, *The Hamlet*. None of us had read it. And I thought since I was the 'youngest angel' on the platform I'd just sit by and watch. She turned to Sam who came from upstate New York and said, 'Of course we understand Faulkner's humor, don't we, because we know all about these 'stump-broke cows.' What happened was, Sam got scarlet; Carlos looked into his tuna salad. And she gave a great slap to her thigh and then realized she had made a rather nice point but it had fallen like a soufflé."

~ *11* ~

ROSEMOND LEFT FOR NEW YORK en route to Aarhus on Wednesday, the third of February, 1960. Immediately on her arrival in Denmark, she wrote to Dick and Merle, instructing them to send copies of her letter to Rik and Lew.

> Dear Family,
>   Here I sit. (Luther had to stand! No pun on HERE I STAND was intended.) As usual, it all seems like a *picnic*. A week ago correcting exams in New London, and today what did I do? Raced off after my bkfst was brought in (tea and GOATS CHEESE and 3 kinds of bread, & jam) and caught a bus on Vestrestrand-allee down to the Domplads, i.e. the cathedral square, and went to a LUTHERAN church that was started in the 900's and was adorned up front ha ha by a Coronation of the Bl.Virg.Mary in gold & pearls and covered with mediaeval frescoes up and down all the inner sides of huge great Romanesque arches. In the middle of which a person sits and sings the *Canton* hymns with Danish words, meanwhile staring at a vast baroque pulpit ½ cupids and ½ angels, I hardly had time to address the Lord properly regarding His extreme thoughtfulness in my direction. It really has been marked . . .

Regardless of where Rosemond landed in Europe, she was soon in demand for speaking engagements. By mid-February she was in Köln (Cologne) for one lecture, then on to Bonn for another. Her talks centered on Spenserian allegory and medieval inheritances, but each had an informal introduction slanted toward the group to whom she was speaking. These were her remarks prior to her prepared talk in Köln:

"I had certainly never thought, as I turned over these texts and these illustrations in the Bodleian and the British Museum, to make my remarks upon them in so august a university. I come from an institution some 530 years younger, whose President holds her degree in German literature from the University of Köln, and I can only say that she happens never to have heard me expound these ideas, so that in spite of that *general* recommendation I cannot be said to be presenting ideas which have had an *echte Kölnische* übersicht [stamp of approval]."

In a few sentences, Rosemond simply and accurately described her life's work, the motivation behind her long hours alone in the silent libraries she loved, anywhere in England or the Continent. D. C. Allen, in writing a review of her *Allegorical Imagery* in the Journal of English and Germanic Philology, made this observation: "She combined in her nature a love of learning and of intellectual adventure. She was never halted by the fact that an important book might be old & dirty and in some strange, foreign language."[1]

In Bonn, Rosemond's introductory lines were even more humorous: "It does not seem very fitting to me that an American should come to tell *Germans* anything about writing in symbols and figures. Not that Americans are quite as literal-minded as you may have concluded from some you have met—but still, the history of such writing in Germany would keep any American running as fast as he could (which is very fast)—just to understand the meanings of what he has read. Hence, though I am *surprised* to find myself where I stand—and also delighted—I will at least reveal to you the spectacle of an American running fast. She will run about one full hour—don't get nervous—but go if you must."

Whatever heights her international reputation reached, the tone of her letters to her brothers never varied—it was humble and caring. She wrote to Lew in March:

Dear Lew & Helen,
    A terr'ble thought strikes me, sp'osing that wretch Merle

did not send on the letter which was marked: ON TO LEW, then you wouldn't have heard my first impressions in Feb. You just ask him for it! One of me can't get round to 3 of you so I took the course of carbons and round-robin-sending. I am in conniptions of delight at Scandinavian surroundings—mad about it, and lamenting the near approach of May 31 when I will be packing up to do 2 wks or so Norway & Stockholm and then on to Paris to work . . .

I want to report that your little Danish dictionary that you gave me at Xmas is the companion of all my hours from 8.30 a.m. when I look up words to tell the breakfast-bringing-maid that the weather has improved, until late night when I finish my Danish articles on MSS. I must see in Copenhagen. ALSO the maps of Norway proved most extraordinarily convenient when I had to hurriedly check on the trip planned by Dorothy with no reisebureaus open to study out what she had booked us for. So I am most extremely grateful.

I can't forbear trying to learn Danish as it is just around the corner of comprehension—though I spose I'll never use it in this world! I'll come back. I do not get the spoken words when people talk to me. I can manage lots myself, and I regularly read a Danish paper mornings, and of course work in the library constantly on my own stuff, in Danish—but it is the literary and art vocabulary—and the religious one! that I can do, and daily nothings are hard to phrase.

Can you beat it, one student who comes to both my lectures offered the fact that she too—when I said I was a South Dakotan—had been in S.D.; I said WHERE??? She said at a little college in Sioux Falls called Augustana. She spent a year doing English there! I guess besides liking everybody & everything she also found the Puritanical aspects of Mid-West Lutheranism a poser; no smoke no dance no talk to men after 5 p.m. or so—I had forgotten how odd such things wd. seem to a girl who is accustomed to the Danish habit of *co-ed* DORMITORIES quite deprived of anything in the shape of a warden or Housefellow, and complete absence of snoops from the side of any profs . . . ARE YOU WELL?? My head still full of lovely Xmas memories. Ach there's not room to say ANYTHING, but in truth I cant get round to my letters. With much love—& send me even a scrap of a line to say you aren't sick—R

Writing around the edge, she added in her tiniest handwriting: "Did Mig Couser forward the Prize Writeup to you—or was her handwriting too illegible to get it successfully forward? This means yr. after next (1961–62) in Princeton and Europe."

In April, as planned, she stole an extra week of vacation to spend Easter in Greece with Eleanor Lincoln. Before she left she started a letter to Merle, which she finished in Greece, asking him, "Please do give to Tryg & to Richard & make each *swear* to pass on to the other !!"

She wrote to Merle:

> 3 public lectures in May & no time.
>
> I had all your pictures (i.e. you boys & your families) out to show my favorite colleague, a young Nottingham M.A. who's done his teaching variously in Italy, Jugo Slavia, and Denmark, and is the only one in whose kitchen I stand around on one foot while the beefsteak broils (Not done w. Danes), drinking my Bourbon that I expended the Nato monies upon and carry with me like a talisman. And I got so fond of the family I was showing off that, coupled with a long letter from Lew, and Richard's with the news of his new award—like two great beautiful solid meals—I aim to induce you to write me too. Meals are sposed to come in Threes. Vor Daglige Brod [for daily bread] . . .
>
> This is the most BEAUTIFUL little city. I have me a noble Palfrey of a bicycle, with gears, so that I stroll up hill on my wheels, and explore all the back streets, and commonly eat my knaekbrod and ost in some garden at noon, just to sit in the sun. I ride every morning—it seems always to be sunny, but dashed cold, and windy like Viking saga . . .
>
> Holy Sat.: Usual continental absence of Ink. I've been to *Epidaurus* & *Mycenae* & am quite over come with common

enthusiasm of all visitors to Greece—cannot think why anyone ever goes anywhere else. Also long lazy days on the
Acropolis, reading *Iliad* behind a stone wall & looking out. I
spent 3 hrs. with the Byzantine mosaics at Dafni & think I've
got them by heart. We go to tea this p.m. with old head of
Amer. School in Rome who has retired here, WHERE ARE
YOU RETIRING? Please make it some agreeable place to visit
such as Bangkok. Wd. you *show this around* to family? I do not
get around to all 3 families. I keep [envisioning] Winnie
climbing Acrop. with her stick—some hill! My knees creak.[2]

Rosemond returned to New London just before the start of classes in September. One month after her return she received a letter from
Marshall Clagett, director of the Institute for Research in the
Humanities at the University of Wisconsin. Clagett was inviting her to
be the Herbert F. Johnson Visiting Professor in the humanities for the
year 1961–62, with a stipend of approximately $15,000, a prestigious
and lucrative offer. The "only requirement," the letter states, "beyond
the pursuit of your current research project is the delivery of one or
two public lectures during the spring term." Rosemond first telephoned Clagett, as he suggested, then wrote, revealing her genuine
disappointment that she must refuse the offer. Even though writing to
someone she had never met, she employed her usual informal and
friendly manner. "Dear Prof. Clagett," she wrote, "I can think of few
things I would rather do."

She then explained her prior commitment to Connecticut
College, which precluded taking yet another leave.

> None of that is to your purpose, for as you see I am con-
> tracted to use 1961–62 otherwise than in the delicious way
> you propose; but it is easier to explain the whole.
> I have thought the Wisconsin Institute a thing of beauty
> ever since I first heard it described; it seems incredibly gener-
> ous, and fruitful of great things to come. The more attractive
> to a Middle Westerner like me who thinks the country stir-
> ringly beautiful, the people my people, and everything hand-

some about it. So I think with great sadness of how I shall not be there. The only consolation I can worm out is that you'll have done up the Renaissance for so long that either your money will run out or it will also be so long hence that I'll have done my Term of Pious Devotion as above described and could be in the running again—but by then doubtless Renaissance scholars will have multiplied, or my next book years hence won't be any good, or something tiresome. This was a horrid painful letter to write, and I have only grace enough, barely, to say thank you.

On the same day she put a note in President Park's box. Rosemond's salary for the 1960–61 academic year was $10,200.

for the record. (have to make myself look Worth Supporting) never rains but it pours, oh for a nice comfortable drizzle. Turned down Univ. of Minn. [Another Freudian slip? Does she mean the University of Wisconsin or did she receive an offer from Minnesota also?] on the phone 14,000 Prof. Just thrust this back in my box. Never *will* get to get my cushions recovered. I have to go to Wash. to screen them 60 Fulbrights, 60, am filled with Pity how the poore strugglers from Utah and Mississippi got to not get one. What a country. Both too rich and not rich enough. Imagine Wisconsin, where the Injuns were running loose 100 yrs back—now Archimedes in the Middle Ages, and the Myceneans and next year the Renaissance—I love the American imagination. Cheese into Dreams—I believe in it too.[3]

As soon as possible, Rosemond was off to Cambridge to use the Widener Library and visit friends. One colleague she called on was Douglas Bush. While there they surely discussed her recent article, "George Herbert and *Caritas*," which had appeared in the *Journal of the Warburg and Courtauld Institutes* earlier that year. Professor Bush wrote to her on October 19, 1960, after she had stopped by to see him and his wife, Hazel:

"It was a great pleasure for Hazel and me to see you, although you always leave me feeling, in the words of one of George Eliot's villagers, 'no better nor a hollow stalk.' This painful feeling was tripled by the reading of your article, which is so immensely learned and so subtle in its discriminations and insights that, after two readings, I am only beginning to get hold of parts of it. I got out my revised section on Herbert to see what I could do with it, and found I couldn't do anything; it is too elementary to be revamped. So I am reduced to the desperate state of Parolles— 'Simply the thing I am shall make me live.' But I wish I were brighter. With our affectionate good wishes, Douglas"

Rosemond's letters over the last eight years revealed a subtle change in her attitude toward students at Connecticut College. Her increasing associations with graduate students, both at home and abroad, contributed to her irritation. In December she wrote a long, angry article to the student newspaper, *Conn Census,* under the column heading "Free Speech." It was as strong an outburst of what she felt was wrong with undergraduate students as anything else she previously had written.

"I have found 'Free Speech' this autumn thoroughly shocking and disillusioning," she wrote.

"One comes back home expectantly, from places where students are wont to express their concern with public affairs of moment, intellectual dilemmas, or artistic experiment, to (or so it seems) a community of 'students' whose mental temperature rises to boiling point, and over, only when some social privilege is in question, some world-shaking matter like number of nights, or men in their bedrooms, or who arranges the sign-out rules. Defending my countrymen to other young men and women, against the charge of American misdefinitions of 'freedom'— . . . I can only be glad I did it in ignorance of what trivial losses of freedom would turn out to cause most uproar among those I was defending . . .

"Two things are riddles to me. One that my own students in my own classes seem so different in maturity and manners from these sizzling individuals met in the college press. The other, that if these restraints and privations such as have always characterized lives lived for deeper purposes, are so galling to those who fill the columns with them, why not go away? Why suffer in an alien environment? The life of the mind is not everyone's dish, and need not be. Those eagerly waiting for the vacated places might take fire from the kind of flame we are supposed to generate in a collegium."[4]

On the occasion of its Centennial Humanities Convocation [1961], Augustana College invited Rosemond to accept its centennial award, given for distinguished service to the humanities and to education. In conjunction with receiving the medal, she needed to prepare a speech for the occasion and arrange time to fly to Sioux Falls. But nothing would give her more pleasure than a chance to return to South Dakota and to visit her Minneapolis friends, the Browns. She had written a note to Bid Brown the previous November to warn her of her possible arrival.

> Dear Bid,
>
> Are you going to be home to Aliens on Sat. night 15 April? I'm about to conclude with the people at my Papa's old college (you remember, Sioux Falls) who are celebrating 100th anniv. that I'll give em a talk. It means inserting plane trip to your far parts into class schedule here, but I do figger I can get to Mpls. from NL by train and plane (not very early Sat. of course) on the Saturday. Have to spurt off onward to Soo Falls earlyish Sunday to get in the requisite jobs and short drive to BIRTHPLACE. But imagine SITTING IN THE SPECIAL CHAIR!! I cdnt. leave the decision till I'd writ & asked—but DO not be gone just that very one day! I am too feeblehearted to telephone, scairy; so I just Hope. I have to return after 2 speeches really & bankets [banquets], all in a day Tues. 18th and teach here Wed. 19th. Wonder what you are reading. Will borra it. Love and all as usual, and to Hunt, from Roz

Bid Brown was a wonderfully energetic, intelligent, and intuitive woman, who admitted that she was "born happy, with a great appetite for life, and the most simple expectations." In speaking of her friend-

Rosemond Tuve at home in New London wearing the centennial medal awarded by Augustana College at the Centennial Humanities Convention, April 1961.

ship with Rosemond she once puzzled over the question of friendship—"what it takes, and why occasionally one recognizes a stranger
as someone you are deeply related to. I think that's what I recognized
in Roz the first time I met her. Without speaking one knows we speak
the same language. Mysterious and wonderful!" For Rosemond, Bid
was a trusted friend with whom she could share confidences as well as
some esoteric literary tastes. Bid recalled that they both adored
Victorian children's literature, particularly the writings of Charlotte
M. Younge, Maria Edgeworth, and Juliana Horatia Ewing: "When the
learned, rather condescending men were not about we would read
aloud to each other with the sharpest delight from the *Daisy Chain* or
Flatirons for a Farthing or even *Rosamond and the Purple Jar.*"

Rosemond's relationship with Bid was less inhibited than with
colleagues at Connecticut, without fear of gossip, so the two could talk
freely together. Bid remembered that "she was often lonely, and said
so explicitly," and speculateed that this was for lack of a close human
companion. She also acknowledged that Rosemond was "an eccentric,
but a gentle one, and not a bizarre one. I think she was the only
woman Hunt [her husband, Huntington Brown, who was chairman
of the department of English when Rosemond was at the University
of Minnesota] could bring himself to admit was a true scholar." It is
not surprising that Rosemond felt comfortable about writing and asking if she could come and stay with them.

Again, in March 1961, Rosemond sent a check for one hundred
dollars to Rosemary Park in commemoration of the 50th Anniversary
Fund of the College:

> This of course is of a size to be only what they call
> Symbolic (a nasty denigration of a good word)—impulse
> mostly related to images of you travelling all over and getting
> 50¢ from the White Carpet fellas, so I guess sent personally
> so's you could whack it in next time some Incident makes you
> think, oh Hell; rather than any feeling this time of secrecy.[5]

Rosemary's reply was swift and very warm. "I was always in favor
of symbols and it was only Connecticut College that takes a material-

istic attitude toward them, but the poor old place really clapped its paws this morning when it found that nice note from you and the very generous contribution to the Anniversary Fund.

"It gave me the greatest pleasure to turn it over with smiles to the proper authorities, who received it with smiles, and we hope same was on your face when you wrote it out.

"Many, many thanks from the corporate entity and the little fellas who work for it."[6]

Before leaving for her adventures in the West, Rosemond spent, as usual, a spring weekend with Eleanor. Despite an almost impossible schedule, she took time for the relaxation and refreshment she found with Eleanor, and, as usual, wrote a long, bubbly "roofer."

On Monday, April 17, 1961, Rosemond attended the Centennial Convocation Dinner at Augustana College. Following dinner, and various toasts, prayers, and musical offerings, she gave her address, titled, "Viewpoint of an Ant." It was gleaned partly from previous sermons delivered at Connecticut College and partly from other lectures, but slanted toward the gathering and peppered with new thoughts. Her theme (an old favorite) was, "In the great Anthill of the whole world— I am an Ant. I have my part in the Creation; I am a Creature." She spoke of the need to be humble and do the work of a creature, not to assume the role of Creator. It was wise, witty, and, as always, a moving exhortation for people to do their part in this marvelous creation we find ourselves enjoying. She closed her talk with these reminiscences:

"I wouldn't blame you if you were now saying to yourselves, 'Large talk for an Ant.' But of course I couldn't describe the pitfalls so well if they weren't my own holes; everybody knows his own back yard best."

She continued: "And then besides, there's another reason why I can talk so bold and free. This is my own father's piece of anthill. I was a little ant under the shadow of this name and these colors. I've licked more envelopes with Augie catalogues in them than any secretary since hired. There was a time when the money Augustana had was needed for so many other important things that the best way to get the catalogues out was for the President's family to lick the envelopes as the President typed them. There is no virtue in this condition. But it can teach a child—not how to live so hard a truth, for I can't yet either, but the truth of the fact that our part in the Creation is, to be a Creature. We put ourselves at the service of, not at the head of. So that though I never was an alumnus of Augustana, perhaps I can say that, like former students sitting here, and like students now in the college, and like students yet to come in another 100 years, I too learned from Augustana what true values could be, and some of "how to be a good worthwhile Ant."

It was probably the next day that she gave a lecture on "Milton and the Humanities" to a group of faculty and students. The talk revealed her firmly established ideas about Milton's imagery and thought, but in addition it was almost a sermon in the tradition of Hauge, or her grandfather Gulbrand, or even her father, in the almost passionate pleading for her listeners to consider themselves part of nature, not arrogant rulers of it. And she used both the poet and the scientist to illustrate her point. Moved as she is by Milton's writing, she becomes the vessel from which his, and her, profound beliefs are poured.

She began by asserting that even though in *Paradise Lost* "evil and destructive forces stand no chance against the forces of light . . . the *great* example of Milton's insight into the pride of the Stoic unconquerable will, and into the heroism of the man who slowly learns not to dominate but to serve, is Samson." And then, in a deeply felt and solemnly spoken evocation, she confessed her creed. "In what is probably Milton's last written work, *Samson Agonistes*, nothing in the human condition can take man's freedom from him; he can be a slave to himself, but when he learns what and who he is, nothing, not Death nor all demons, can defeat him."

What is so complicated is that she is speaking, as Milton did through Raphael, about "what surmounts the reach of human sense." This can be done only by "using symbols, 'spiritual forms' likened to corporeal ones. It is the power of such modes to reach into significances impossible to direct conceptual language, and it is the timelessness all metaphors have, so that all great literary works are contemporary, for it is *we* whom the characters portray and *we* whom the action concerns."

Freedom was a "key problem to Milton—perhaps the possibility and the nature of Man's Freedom is the *one* problem of the Humanities, having Freedom as Man must, only within Nature, and as some disciplines of the Humanities assert, having it Under God." Rosemond closed with this: "Milton didn't SAY these things, as I have had to. HE says them all in images, in what Sidney called speaking pictures. Without their beauty of sight and sound, the pictures would be dumb. This is a major accomplishment of the humanities, that loveliness should give a voice to truth."

A week after returning to Connecticut, Rosemond wrote to the Browns. In retrospect, it is one of the most poignant of her letters.

Dear Bid and Hunt:

This Paiper is my version of Bid's ruled Scratch. [Bid often wrote on lined pad paper.] I've been home a week & a day—but not so's you cd. notice I was exactly sedentary—for the Renaissance conference at Harvard was last Fr–Sat and I took a horde of 5 up in my Sioux. I seem therefore to have just clung to the rock washed by tides, & couldn't write till now. I've inserted also two faculty mtgs changing the curricular set-up, one dept mtg., and two exam-committees plus the mere matter of teaching Keats; Burton & Browne; and the *Prelude*, with 58 student essays corrected in the interstices.

Wish to report that my native Air cured my sinevitis & I have flang the arm-sling into the corner. It got better the minit I hit S.Dak. & its dry prairies. Oh dear I had such a delicious four days! Your part (it seems like a full week I was there—so crammed with affections & sensations and re-unions with my loved objects like My Chair, the room I always slept in, St. Mark's windows, Mpls streets, Lake-un-moved).

Your part (to start again), was magnificent. I was so egregiously sinfully inordinately proud as I rose into the air out of Mpls. at being so welcome to everybody; my character is ruinated, for I felt like the Queen, & I'm sure it is not healthy.

I do thank you from the bottom of my heart. Nothing could have been more like IT ALWAYS WAS and that is my idea of happy circumstances. Time fell out down through the sieve & you are exactly my same old delights as you always were. In the first place I think you are both beautiful to look at, and your voices are dear to me; in the second we did JUST what I like best and in the third you made it all seem as if I weren't being any trouble so that pouncing down in the middle of school was not even on my conscience.

S.D. was a love-feast from start to finish. Old Cousin Norma that I was a baby-child-young-girl with, *met* me with Pres. Stavig, and off we went to my darling Canton and turned-over every blade of grass and there sat the houses of my babyhood and the standpipe where you have the picnics, and we got in the church where I was confirmed and my father was buried from, and its windows and altar there as I used to puzzle over them (things like Alpha & Omega, all the old wild puzzles of my childhood, like symbols of the Crucifixion and bits of Greek). The sun shone & the prairie stretched out for ever and the sky was ALL OVER, horizon down under I'm sure below sea level. I never care about living in the world especially long *except* when I get on a prairie, then I wish life would please last. Maybe this is because I think you all and the rocking chair and the lake will *be* in the next world but recognize a Prairie as definitely confined to this one. I lived in Tuve Hall; the speeches went fine; I got a meddul hung arount my neck, my relatives all turned up at the Dinner, my First Love (a cousin named Stephanus now 71) we went to see in a Rest Home, and I could hardly bear to see Soo Falls vanish under the plane. I HAVE to come West more. But you come east just when I get free to drive out. But John & Bobby would be there, and all in all I am going to not give up these delights so much as I get older, I am going to come and drive around and Sing.

This won't do I have to go to bed. DO not pass my door un-speaking. My love and gratitude to you both, and

thank you for all the fetching and the
cooking and the Love & Friendship
After Sept 10 or so Ill be
very on the Main Line: Princeton,   Ros
with I feel sure an extra Bed!

But Rosemond did not have long to wait before returning to the Midwest and another reunion with Bid Brown; it all came about because of some quiet diplomacy by Rosemond. Lew, Merle, and Rosemond had each received a letter from Lawrence Gould, president of Carleton College, offering them honorary degrees on the occasion of Carleton's commencement on June 2, 1961. It was surely the first, and perhaps the only, time that such an honor had been bestowed on one family. Rosemond's letter in response is a consummate example of tact, humility, and love.

Dear Pres. Gould,

I must first thank you for your confidence, and say that I am captivated by an idea so ingenious, in fact so all but poetic. You have contrived to get around the chief dissatisfaction accompanying honorary degrees, which is that sense that someone else should have got them.

I do not immediately give a clear answer, because I am disposed to act in concert with my brothers in the matter, rather than singly. This is not entirely a result of the awkward fact that, besides a lecture trip to Minnesota and S. Dakota about a month prior to this and necessitating indulgence toward my desertion of duties here, June 2 comes exactly when I am examining and may take special permission for me to manage. It is also a result of the fact that the triplicity is so much a part of the quality of the thing that if my brothers cannot go I should be inclined to ask if you did not want to 'save us up' until a year when they could. I am myself not only pleased by your expression of confidence but greatly attracted by the idea; and hopeful that things may go as you wish.

Having said this, I am about to set forth an explanation of why I think *I* should decline, and ask you to confine your honour to two. The reason for this is so curious that I shall be very precise in stating it. You see I have another brother, whose work in his own professional area has been of a distinction equal to that of any of us. I shall have to state a reason or two for my making this statement, if I am to escape the suspicion of sentimental-sister. I should say first, that of course I am not implying that you should stretch to a fourth Tuve; three is troublesome enough, and of a generosity quite abandoned. I am thinking rather of the escape mentioned above, or if you like a trinity, that they be as is the accepted thing in Western culture, all male deities.

Her letter goes on:

The brother 8 years my junior, Richard Tuve, is still Head of the Special Research section of the Chemistry Division of the Naval Research Laboratory, despite efforts of the Dept. of Agriculture to give him a couple huge labs to run in the West, for he is a fire-fighter, with more calls than he can handle to key-note or advise in all circles or conferences that face fire problems (military, civic or other). The foam controls and the fire-fighting jeeps and plane-carrier chemical fire-protection inventions and discoveries which you have seen publicized of late years are his work, though because he works under naval anonymity you have known less about this Tuve than the others. The last naval award of $5500. for 'pioneer work in applying scientific methods and techniques' in this area was in 1960 and brought his awards to the legal maximum, since two others of equal size had been presented in 1958 and 1959.

Rosemond continued:

The awards for life-saving inventions and chemical devices had started actually back with the 'shark chaser' research he directed (and had to write up for the US Naval Institute Proc. in 1947), and there had been also the fluorescent 'sea marking' rescue dye, and fighting of oil-tanker fires in the war. These are the reasons why he never had time to

Rosemond Tuve and her three brothers each received an honorary degree at the Carleton College commencement in 1961. Left to right, Richard L. Tuve, Merle A. Tuve, Rosemond, and George L. Tuve. Courtresy Carleton College Archives.

proceed to the Ph.D. though of course he directs 8 or 12 of those creatures, in the 'group' with which he shares all awards, in the anonymity which is common (and necessary no doubt) for civilians in the laboratories of the services. Internationally, (interchange and sharing w. Britain, Germany, Scandinavia) his work has not been so anonymous.

You see my problem. In sum, this brother's work is of a distinction so clearly on a par with that of the other two men, and in my opinion so clearly outranking my own in its value to human life and its pioneering character, that I could not concur in the seeming differentiation between the four of us by accepting your invitation to be one of the three.

On the other hand, the satisfaction of having one's eminent brothers recognized is so vastly superior to that felt in one's own recognition, that I would co-operate in eternal and complete silence with any "out" you chose, from the awkward situation posed by the numerousness of professional Tuves. So of course would my brothers, for there is no one of us that is not accustomed to take more pleasure in the honours accorded any of the others than in our own, and none would be disposed ever to reveal any fact or previous action that could cast a shadow of chagrin.

I wish to add my personal remembrance of our meeting at Carleton, my thanks, and my hope that you see some comedy also in this novel instance of the embarrassments which attend a Population Explosion.

But the die was cast and the stage set for another first for Rosemond. For the first time in academic history, four members of one family would receive honorary degrees at the same commencement. It is an extraordinary day for the Tuves. The ceremony opened with these words from Professor Reed Whittemore:

"MR. PRESIDENT: We see before us a covey, a gaggle, a swarm, perhaps a tribe of Tuves. I am speechless (nearly) before this challenge. The Tuves descend upon us here today from Ohio, Connecticut, Maryland and Washington, D.C ; but they began their trek toward this platform a long time ago in South Dakota, where they were born to a music teacher at Augustana College, and her husband, the president of Augustana College, who were married on this very remarkable day, June 2, 68 years ago. It is not often that a family, one family, does what these Tuves do."

He continued: "There is George Lewis Tuve, a graduate of Minnesota, who is Chairman of the Department of Mechanical Engineering at the Case Institute of Technology, the author of textbooks and contributor to many engineering journals, and the winner of the F. Paul Anderson Medal for his contributions to the world of heating and air conditioning. There is Dr. Merle Tuve, also a graduate of Minnesota with a Ph.D. from Johns Hopkins, who has been associated with more educational institutions than I care to mention, who is Director of the Carnegie Institution of Washington, and who was a member of the Executive Committee of the International Geophysical Year. There is Dr. Rosemond Tuve, also a graduate of Minnesota with a Ph.D. from Bryn Mawr, who has frequented easily as many institutions as her elder brothers, who is the author of several books of literary criticism including a fine new work on Milton, and who is professor of English at Connecticut College. And finally there is Richard Tuve, the youngest, the only Tuve without a Minnesota degree who did, however, play a violin in the University of Minnesota Symphony Orchestra at the age of twelve. Richard graduated, a chemical engineer, from American University in Washington, and became head of the Special Research Division of the U.S. Naval Research Laboratory at Anacostia, receiving there three U.S. Civil Service Awards (the maximum allowed) for developing foam-fire-fighting and crash-rescue techniques on aircraft carriers."

He went on: "I think it is apparent from this bare evidence—and it is too bad I can give so little—that the familiar sociological unit, the family, has not yet disintegrated in these parts; further, that with a few more such families we would probably not be faced with a national shortage of brain power in either the sciences or the humanities. It is an honor for Carleton, Mr. President, to be able to recognize such a family—by awarding George Lewis, Merle, Rosemond, and Richard Tuve with a fine assortment of degrees which will now be described."[7]

The degrees he described were: George Lewis Tuve, Doctor of Science; Merle Antony Tuve, Doctor of Laws; Richard Larsen Tuve, Doctor of Science; Rosemond Tuve, Doctor of Letters. The minute the formal ceremonies ended, Rosemond eagerly stepped down from the flower-bedecked wooden dais that had been erected on the college green, to greet friends and relatives in the audience. One friend was Bid Brown, who had driven up from Minneapolis for the occasion. She recalled, in her typically imaginative style, that Rosemond, "who cried at the drop of a hat, cried for days beforehand and practically every minute of the ceremony while wildly searching for a handkerchief down her bosom, with her brothers trying to look patient. 'It's all so beautiful!' she sobbed."

Soon the Tuves were saying lingering good-byes, apparently to go their separate ways. Rosemond stowed her degree in her suitcase and started for South Dakota, some two hundred and fifty miles westward, where, early the next morning, she reached her childhood home. As she crept around a bush, hoping not to disturb anyone inside the house, she saw a "Mexican" with a wide-brimmed hat. She thought to herself, "That's funny—looks familiar." It was Merle. Rosemond hooted with surprise and pleasure. Now they could reminisce about their early years here, renewing the source of their physical and spiritual roots, connecting once again with the earth and the vast sky that had nourished them.

Rosemond had the summer to complete her professional and personal duties before leaving for Princeton and her year away. Two more articles had been published in 1961 and there were future publications in progress. "Sacred 'Parody' of Love Poetry, and Herbert" had been published in *Studies in the Renaissance,* and "Baroque and Mannerist Milton?" appeared both in *Studies: in Honor of F.H. Fletcher* and in *Journal of English and Germanic Philology.* It was likely that there was one more trip to Washington, and perhaps elsewhere, before her departure, as Rosemond never remained in one place for long.

As she anxiously concluded her last-minute preparations for her departure from Connecticut College, Rosemond corresponded with Tom Roche and Sherman Hawkins, who had volunteered to help her in her move to Princeton. It appears she had remained in contact with the two young men, whom she first met during the Gauss Seminars in the spring of 1959, and their relationship had expanded. Both men had been awarded their Ph.D.'s, were already instructors in English at Princeton, and planned to focus their research and teaching on the sixteenth and seventeenth centuries. Tom Roche would remain a devoted friend and colleague for the rest of Rosemond's life. In response to their offer, Rosemond wrote a postcard first to Tom, and then to Tom and Sherman. Though the card and letters were ostensibly to make arrangements, her tone revealed her warm feelings toward the young scholars. They were her children; they shared in and supported her scholarly interests; and she would guide and nurture them.

During the fall term at Princeton, Rosemond taught one course— "Studies in Pre-Renaissance and Renaissance Literature." It was limited to advanced graduate students. In addition, as senior fellow of the Council of Humanities, she was involved in meetings and deliberations concerning the development of a new curriculum for Princeton. This gave Rosemond frequent opportunities not only for research, but also for the serious discussion of ideas, the "Exchange of Views," she craved.

Just before Christmas she wrote to her friends the Biebers. Konrad Bieber was professor of French at Connecticut College.

Dear Konni & Tamara,
   AND tom, for you're together I reckon. Many thanks for the dinner invitation—I don't spose I can do it. I hope to be re-packing for a couple days just prior to 8th, but expect to go home that day or Sun. depending on the Dentist. I have a grad.club.lecture coming up the day after and I don't think I dare add another day to the packing ones. I darent say for sure if I'll get to see anybody, depends on how fast I can find my insurance policy, dig out the shoes I didn't think I'd want, replace the books, get the shots and medicines, see the Dr's and dentists and leg and eye and toe and ear and neck men as twere. I'll make it if I can you may be sure—but not the

Mon.party I fear. I guess I'll join up sponsoring the Spain thing hope it is The One To Pick, no time to investigate.

Ever since her increasing involvement with time-consuming research and her myriad academic activities, Rosemond had drifted away from any concern with the political issues of the day. But Konrad Bieber had influenced her to make a donation in support of a group that was giving aid to Spanish refugees. Thus she ended the postcard with these words: "That counts as Xmas card and this does too. MERRY XMAS. I go to bro's for short vac. Love to you all, from Ros"

In January, at the end of her semester at Princeton, Rosemond gave a talk to the Graduate Club, which focused, as most of her speeches did, on allegory. She introduced her lecture by asserting, "One odd thing has happened since I began to teach. (Not to me.) But I've seen a real critical swear-word become a come-on word to try to get into the titles of lectures. The word is Allegory. . . Now this talk is part of a long attempt, twenty years, to read allegory as good WRIT-ERS of it used it. I've been trying to see if we might come at some of the secrets of allegorical writing of the 16thc., some of the *pleasures* men took in them by looking at the late mediaeval writings upon which those later writers were nurtured. Now what WAS this typical-ly mediaeval pleasure they didn't want to give up? I am not trying to make the Renaissance THE SAME THING as the Middle Ages. (I Could try. It wouldn't be.) I wish merely to see if we can learn any-thing by catching some of the same habits from the Middle Ages which Renaissance readers had caught."

As soon as her obligations to Princeton were completed, Rosemond departed, as planned, for England. Shortly after her arrival in Oxford, on January 31, Rosemond wrote long letters, on the same day, to both Tom and Sherman. The first was addressed to "Darling Tom":

I am in a state of extreme bliss and spend my time con-cealing it from the English. Quite aside from their national character bliss is of course awfully unbecoming and you can imagine what it does to the set of My Hats. Everything is cold and poky and murky as I like it best and the soft-coal-mildness of the night air has me utterly drunk when I sail home on the Blatant Beast, that is my superlative Danish bicycle. The men's haircuts are beautiful beyond compare, and the bells clamour all Sunday morning and the Lord God has become superbly comfortably English in that way He has here but He also arranged for them to borrow Vittoria's O magnum mysterium Mass offen the Romans for me to go first to Communion with at the Cathedral last Sunday, et o ces voix d'enfants chantant pas dans le coupole acct. there is none but under that fan-vaulted ceiling I hope you remember; I am so replete with multitudinous gratitudes that it is hard keeping the lids on and the lights out, but the more I offer them up the more get born.

Her letter to Sherman Hawkins was equally ecstatic, if more humorous.

The traffic is a WILD example of Engl. Freedom at its worst; *2* rows of parked cars on the Turl, NewColl. & Qu's lane *solid* with them even on the turn at St.Peter's in the East; STOOpid. I bike d'n Parks Rd. and Longwall and Rose Lane every morning & feed the blue-tits in the meadow; squirrels have taken to crawling up any leg displayed to demand whatever you've got in the sack they hear rustling. Then I buy nuts at the Health-food place & the bags bust as H-place bags naturally would but no squirrels survive on the High so my drips are wasted all the way to the Cat St. turn wh. if you don't dismount to make expect death. I gave yr. best to Katie Lea & she was completely surprised and delighted that you'd think of it.

Sherman had been in England during Rosemond's previous visit and had met her friend Kathleen Lea. Rosemond's own friendship with Lea had come about in a unique way. Following the publication of her book *A Reading of George Herbert,* Lea, who was vice principal of Lady Margaret Hall, had written, quite spontaneously, to Rosemond: "You hardly remember me but we did meet occasionally in Duke Humphrey & once at Miss Spens' when you read from [your] paper on "The Sacrifice": that opened my understanding astonishingly in one evening." Rosemond, as expected, was able to respond shortly to her suggestion that "I hope you will be over here again before too long & that we may meet."

Years later Lea would recall the depth and special quality of their relationship: "But religious she clearly was & in the truest, clearest way. We did not often *talk* of religion in the way of an exchange of ideas but we practised it together with complete harmony of mutual understanding—or so it seemed to me. She loved the Anglican Services . . . I have precious memories of being with her & of seeing how spontaneously & naturally & joyfully she worshipped—not as a duty but a joy.

Her letter continues: "I remember her singing the *Te Deum* at the top of her voice when we went to Matins in a church in Malvern at the end of a happy short holiday together. I remember (even more preciously) the way that as soon as we came to a tiny, *v.* ancient Cotswold Church—Widford) & were alone she went straight to the altar rail & knelt. When we explored churches together in England & France one had to sense (that needed no saying) that she fell in with the time and original purpose of such places & did not only look but also prayed."

On Easter Day, from 3 Crick Road, Oxford, Rosemond responded to a letter from Tom.

Dear Sansloy   [name of a character in the *Fairie Queene*, meaning "lawless"]

I dont really dare call you anything in sp [Spenser] because you know his even inadvertent lines, & what you bet I would make some gaffe, but if ever there was a frank franion you and S. [Sherman] both is them & so I am on safe ground. Dear me I just went to *heavenly* church; those enlightened Xt.Ch.cathedral men sang Victimae paschali bless their thefts forever; and how often have I gone to a Roman church Easter so's to hear dic nobis Maria, Quid vidisti in via? Tell S I sat on the south side down by the organ; and they never sang Palestrina's Missa brevis as they did this morning . . . I have thought of you often; in fact I put a candle for you in the Holy Sepulchre 1½ weeks ago.

You remember I didn't quite want to go to Jerusalem. I didn't want actuality to bowl over reality. To my delight it is quite otherwise. Especially when one has come away. The places are very truly holy, and the sense of the long unrolling of human history is completely overpowering; all the smallness of the human jostling over seizing upon the holy spots (Greeks and Copts and Syrians and Armenians seemed just as right as Westerners to me on Calvary and the Mt. of Olives and the Paternoster hill and Gethsemane—but I went to church Franciscan, they are the only ones with altars everywhere), and the pathetic pointing out of each "exact spot"— the whole result is the strangest sense of the divinity of the protagonist's part in all this. The N.T. could simply not be, but by the Holy Spirit. That little tiny Semitic Jerusalem! you can't believe it. I lived within the walls, by chance; as usual some kind of heavenly Providence just showered things to be grateful for, upon me. No cars are possible.

She continues: There is no "city" as we understand them. I scurried down the alleys reverberating with steps and down the souks and bazaars, like all the others, and passed a dozen times a day the things we have had in our mouths since we were able to speak, scrambled over the brook Kedron with an eager little Mohammedan boy on his way from school, teaching me Arabic, sat by the pool of Bethsaida, in and out of all the named gates we know. The sense of history flowing over one began at Beirut . . .

Goodby, angel face, happy Easter—Pat S. on the nose and I'll see you in Trenton the 17 Sept. at goodness knows what hour of the evening—Love from Ros

In late July, a letter to Tom from Paris revealed an extreme change in Rosemond's handwriting. Although she makes light of the alarming symptoms of an illness as yet undiagnosed, she knew, as she had mentioned to Eleanor, "something is happening to me."

Rosemond's last letter from England to Tom Roche was written just before she flew home.

Sept 3 Monday
Dear Tom,
    I didn't answer your entertaining letter because I was held up by being rushed in a Ambulance to the Edinb. Royal Infirmary WITH NOTHING as it turned out; but I was choking.—Instead of absolutely horrible Heart it turned out to be naught but a special Danish-type Bug which gave me croup as twere. In case you've ever seen a baby with croup they turn blue and must be turnt upside down. Nobody was capable so off I went in Buggy and stayed 9 days or so, delaying all Objectives, in the REI [Royal Edinburgh Infirmary]—which I loved. I had a comical time and was enchanted with the Scots. They tested me backwards & forrards and I had NOTHING. But a cold, which went. [A former student later recalled that Rosemond suspected she might have had a slight stroke.] . . .
    I'll see you about 2 wks from tonight!! . . . all in all I shall be lonesome for Princeton next year I'm afraid. I Like Men. One amusing thing at Edb. before all this drama—I had LOTS of fun with Empson. We are just *naturally* matey. He was at the same univ.hostel as I. Help I cant gossip so much. I shall write a card to Margt. & W. [Thorpe] but I'm sure they expect me the 17th. Love & Respecks,
                    from Ros

    The reference to William Empson is particularly amusing in light of the long letters they exchanged from January to March in 1953, each arguing strenuously, often sarcastically, for their opposing views of Herbert. Rosemond closed her final letter to Empson with these words: "I despair of the printed and typed word. I only know I feel nothing but amiability, will read what you write with attention and willingness, and am mostly impressed with how much gayer it is to differ face to face instead of through these toneless machines!" Most certainly Rosemond charmed him out of any vituperous feelings he still harbored.

12

AFTER A YEAR'S ABSENCE, Rosemond returned to Connecticut College more restless than ever. On her second weekend home, she drove to Northampton to visit Eleanor. On returning to Connecticut she wrote, as always, her "roofer," this time on stationery with the heading AARHUS UNIVERSITY, Institute of English Philology.

> monday [October 1, 1962]
> Dear Eleanor,
> My overflowing Horn of Plenty, my tea and my cookies and my good sendoff and my nice friends, are even more impressive to me this morning on retrospect. Do not you always think we get a WONDERFUL lot into a mere few hours? It seems so varied and so interesting and so full, as I look back! So I had a lovely visit and I do thank you enormously. (I must do some exercises; I have lost typing control).

(It is obvious from the letter that her typing had deteriorated. Undoubtedly it was one of the early indications [along with her illegible handwriting] of the cerebellar disease that would eventually claim her life.)

> It was just right, every move, and now you just turn around & come down here. I'll be still correcting the 38 papers rec'd this a.m. and the 36 due next week, and that will make me sociable and nice. Writing is the ONLY occupation that destroys the Personality. I really love the comfort of having some ordinary duties like papers and submitted essays, unavoidable Juties, merely to Do.

Well *our* trees are pretty *green* still, so lots of good things
to come. I was just knocked over by the beauty of this country, as I always am on return. I guess I like BIG things.

take that any way you please, you little midge-gnat.

[Eleanor was almost as tall as Rosemond] and thank you
& come see me . . .

love & thanks from
Illiterata

The loss of the stimulation of her term at Princeton, enhanced by
exciting new acquaintances; the eight months abroad that included
the exaltations of Oxford; and the sharpened perceptions aroused by
the libraries of London and Europe left Rosemond deflated and
empty. The absence of Rosemary Park, whose resignation had taken
effect that past June, increased her feeling of desolation. In addition,
Dorothy Bethurum had resigned with the condition that she would
teach half time for the next two years, and was now away in Oxford.

Perhaps of equal importance, although little is known of her from
any letters, was the resignation, in 1961, of Lilian Warnshuis, the college physician. Dr. Warnshuis and Rosemond had become close
friends, in part due to Rosemond's many stays in the infirmary, but
also because the doctor was a fascinating and brilliant woman who
shared in the social and intellectual life of Rosemond and her colleagues. Dr. Warnshuis was also disturbed by Rosemond's symptoms
and at one point wrote of her concerns to Merle. Again, at the end of
her life, she wrote to Merle, offering him a bundle of letters from
Rosemond that she had saved. In it she wrote: "Someone simply must
write the book of your wonderful sister. Why she was cornered in little Connecticut College I do not know for she was a woman for much
larger places and I want the world to know about her . . . Roz was a
genius [and] there are many sources which would be glad to give evidence not only of her rich mind but also of the small glimpses of her
unusual glowing 'SPIRIT.'"[1] [Unfortunately, the Warnshuis letters
were lost.]

It was not surprising that Rosemond, in her forlorn state, was vul-
nerable to a letter from Allan G. Chester, chairman of the department

of English at the University of Pennsylvania. It is dated October 22, 1962. Chester wrote: "Sometime during the next year the English Department of the University of Pennsylvania will be searching for a specialist in English literature of the Renaissance to succeed Professor Matthew W. Black, who will shortly retire. It has been suggested to me that Professor Arthur Barker, now at the University of Illinois, might be interested in coming to us. Since administrators are always anxious for outside opinions, I would greatly appreciate any comments concerning Mr. Barker's work which you might feel able to give us. I am of course familiar with his scholarly writings but I should like to know as much as possible of his qualities as a teacher. Since this matter is still in a very early stage of exploration I would prefer, if you do not mind, that the whole matter be kept confidential for the time being."[2]

What we know of Rosemond's reply to Chester's letter is preserved on a piece of pad paper on which she jotted her ideas prior to typing her letter. After praising Barker, she said:

> As I imply above, I will surely not say a word abt yr letter, and I know you'll act the same—as probl Barker doesnt know he came second. [She had suggested him when she turned down Illinois's offer.] You're just lucky I don't turn around and ask for a reversal of the Ill process at Penn [this broad hint is followed by one of her famous smiley faces] but ladies are mostly asked to Western posts, except for Visits! This shd. make you shiver with the dangerous gulf you just missed.
>
> I dont know why I shd have a sense of responsible conscience twd. Ill., but they were so delighted, and the move seems so recent.

Rosemond's depression comes through in this letter to Tom Roche.

Sunday night 4 nov. [1962]
Dear Tawm
    and by extension or implication of contagion I spose I always talk to you both after a fashion.
    I miss you, and I really do *not* quite have sufficient knowl-

edgable spenser and such cronies to have what I call enough conversation. I really am astonished to discover me, the meanie that is always trying to get out of engagements so's I can stay home and read, me I find myself thinking, now it would be nice if those boys went up to New Haven and Boston to see their best girls and stopped overnight to sleep under my piano and I'd ask em if they thought Ellrodt is pretty convincing. [She is referring to *Neoplatonism in the Poetry of Spenser*, by Robert Ellrodt.] Pathetic I call it . . .

As I was saying, I didn't quite feel satisfied after the day I picked my car up, because we didn't have any time to be together and *talk*. I love all the others but I had a million things to ask about Special Topics. Mostly Edmund. [Spenser] And I thought it was a gyp not to see SH [Sherman Hawkins] a tall.

Ai I am in a mis'ry because I mistakenly tried to finish the romances chap. that I was writing on in London & did not get anywhere with. And it writes like GLUE and has to be all done twice more, it is nothing but hen marks showing what I must re-do. So that I am in a slavery, always watching to see that I save me hours-at-a-stretch, and agitated because they do not save . . .

I have to finish my essays but I went to vespers because the BC [Baptist Church] choir from town was doing 5 motets to decorate a visiting Monsignor. All was moving and good and reminded me of you & of all the evensongs I'd see the Black Lord at [Sherman Hawkins].   Ros

A rough draft of another letter, undated, but probably written that fall, was addressed to Bob. It could have been Pratt, or Patton.

I had a note from Dorothy in Oxford (last minutes) and something comical in it made me think I'd tell everybody in the Perfession to scotch the rumour if they hear it, and that you might have and I was too naive to recognize allusion: she said 4 people had written her and asked if RT's heart failure was serious. HA. I was at the Edinburgh Profs conf. when I got a Bug causing bronchial cold, windpipe stuffed up and I went off in High Style in ambulance of the Edinb. Royal Infirmary. They tested everything about 3 times but nothing would persuade my lusty Scandinavian Heart (*or* lungs either) to admit anything was amiss. So they said, "umph Bad Cold; Go Home." But I see rumour took the more melodramatic line. Europe's Bug this year was croup-y; is all. So in Wash. will you snort loudly and say, poof, she was a Fake; when you hear that Dean Swift has died? . . .

With a vacancy created in the English department when Bethurum retired, Rosemond was eager to bring Roche, or Hawkins, to the college as an instructor. That is the topic of her next letter. At the top of the page, under the imprinted words WHITE HALL HOTEL, MONTAGUE STREET, LONDON, Rosemond wrote: "wish I was."

[late November 1962]

Dear Tom, talk about Hot Postal Chutes. But I guess I'd better write, having told Ham Smyser [chairman of the English department] he could, & you might be mystified. He was over to discuss our Present Problem, i.e. that we need a Middling-to-Young 16th C. Man, for a few years if we can't get a permanent blossom, and cannot discover one. Last year they invited that Sidney-man Montgomery (Tex) but before the letter inviting him got there he'd yielded to the extra delights put on at home to keep him.

There's more Ren. than I can do . . . Since we will also have to offer something that is really See-Lect, now we are larger and we have a grad. student here and there. And D.Bethurum leaves soon—she has retired, on leave Oxf. this term, half-time-emeritus-apptment so she'll do full time 2nd sem. this year, and presumably do something next year, but maybe we shd. have a Shak. See-Lect course extra too for her. At any rate she has always done the Shak., though Peter Seng is doing it this term, we do not think of him (SECRET) as the great successor, the 2nd DB and the 2nd RT, and it mustn't happen that he just slides into it. We want a 16th c. man to put the crowns on, and to show our sense of his royal blood would be likely to think up extra crowns—need one more sem. 16-17th c. course, for exmple.

Is there the least chance—I do not think there is for a minit—that you could be siphoned offa Princeton for some time. Maybe to give them a high notion of your Wurrth (tho they have already) or so's to have some change before it's so serious to have it, etc etc etc.

I just thought though you were joking in your phrase in letter, there might be enough openness on subj. to *look* at the matter.

Everything is pleasant. Not even man is vile. Lovely new Pres. (Chas.Shain from P'ton & Carleton). I think it might be less work, i.e. than yr. normal schedule. 3 courses & that is it. Soph. course that we all teach some of is NO punishment as it is all the loveliest works, from 5 wks Chaucer to all P Lost, & Yeats for $2\frac{1}{2}$ weeks. and such tibbits. I think Sherman would be even less amenable to a even temporary like 3 or 4 year move, than you might. I am correct in this suppositn am I not?

I have to WORK this is ter'ble. I go to Penna mts [probably to visit Dutch Burdick] tomorrow & eat raw turkey caught by hand spit out the feathers.

love from R/

Another letter, tentative, but still hopeful, followed:

Dear Tom,

I said Ham Smyser was writing—tho't he was, but he tells me Prexy's latest idea had been that we could "train up" one of our instructors to be renaissance and he didn't wish to seem wilful, by outright moves himself, & hence my writing to sound you out (whether it was entirely a folly to consider you might have an interest) was best.

You're thinking "how shall I put it, to say help-no-would-not-wish-to-discuss-such-a-possibility" unembarrassingly or

else you're going thru' a hundred indecisions betw. a toast and
tea; don't forget that your only decision is now something relatively simple: am I interested to hear about this. I.e., *don't*
worry about commitment—you won't be committed to anything. The nature of the possible (we hope) job is to be determined much as we look; the reason I didn't think you'd care
to discuss possibilities is that of course there isn't enough
Renaissance here to occupy two people's full teaching—I have
always and do now teach other things. It is the first year of my
life (this one) that I have not taught Freshman course at least
a semester; we now have squeezed it to *only* a semester. (1½
required years). I don't have jobs in my hand, even if this one
were surer (I mean surer to be juicy enough financially to
attract), but thought *we* ever should not think of the possibility in case *you'd* not dream of it. But nothing very uncom-
fortable and uprooting faces you at this stage to consider
deciding. Just whether you would admit such a possibility
and wish to have it thought of at this end as "possible" instead
of "out of the question" (which I bet it is).

I hadn't esp. expected to hear soon, but I thought you
might be undergoing too much indecision-mizz'ry, I always
do when people say "would you be willing to be considered
for . . ."

It can be assumed that Rosemond carried on a similar correspondence with Sherman Hawkins but the letters were not saved. She
also expected some of her letters to Tom to be shared with Sherman.
The following postcard is her response to a disappointing reply from
Hawkins.

Dear Lord Edward, also the Fat One:
    . . . shucks, I thought I just might catch one of you in a
morose moment, when the other meadow looked greener but
you're just both always being wooed. My friends are just too
well thought of. I wish I knew a couple of problem boys or
slow blossoms . . . love from Roz

It took less than two months for the University of Pennsylvania to take Rosemond's hint and offer her an appointment. Letters of approval from the faculty there included the following comments: "I think she is clearly one of the two most distinguished female professors of English in the country. She is a most vital, imaginative and enthusiastic person, always full of ideas and giving them off like sparks."[3]

A letter from Robert A. Pratt followed: "I consider her to be the outstanding Renaissance scholar in the country ... [she] has the highest sense of academic standards and fights courageously against every type of watering down. She has sufficient force to prevent any department from being weak-kneed. Her presence would illuminate our University with her learning, with her dignity, and with her sense of the values and joys of the academic life. If Miss Tuve could be persuaded to join our Department, we would have cause for pride and all the other institutions cause for envy."[4]

And finally, from Allan Chester: "Professor Tuve is in my opinion the leading woman scholar in this country in the field of English studies and one of the three or four leading Renaissance scholars (men or women) at present active in the field ... I may add that my colleagues and I feel that it is high time that a distinguished woman be added to our staff. Many of our majors and graduate students are women and Miss Tuve would be for them a kind of model of what can be achieved by a woman in the academic world."[5]

On December 13, 1962, Rosemond wrote a short note to Professor Chester:

> I've written to the REAL ESTATE LADY as I thought it might make things safer if she were posted, and could expect me during the days mentioned, Th–Fri 20–21. If we are still serious by Friday and it gets late, I might rouse up my B.M. friends and stop over to the Sat.
>
> I have asked her to write her address direct to me. But chiefly I have asked her to save me some time, and given a few hints of desired kind of quarters, so that can be a little ready. My chief oddity as a renter is that I like to be near a Library,

and anybody's will do! For I imagine that one's schedule is not likely to take one in every single weekday, and I am a natural-born crawler over book-piles; I just prefer the air.[6]

What the "real estate lady" found was almost perfect. It was a large, handsome, redbrick dwelling, enhanced with white columns and bearing something of a resemblance to an English manor house. More important, it was situated on expansive grounds facing Rockefeller Gate and other Bryn Mawr College buildings beyond. Her apartment, one of four in the building, was unfortunately situated on the second floor, for climbing stairs would soon become a major problem.

It wasn't until May 1963 that President Shain, having failed to receive a written notification, wrote this memorandum for Rosemond's file: "In the absence of a formal note of resignation from Miss Tuve, I am recording that in December, 1962, Miss Tuve told me that regretfully she wanted to resign in order to accept a professorship offered by the University of Pennsylvania, effective at the end of the 1962–3 academic year."[7]

After twenty-nine years of intense devotion to Connecticut College, Rosemond was leaving. Her decision may have seemed abrupt to her colleagues; just one month earlier she was awarded the first Henry B. Plant Professorship. Her good friend Edward Cranz termed it a "bit brash to go but impossible to stay." Leicester Bradner had been urging her to come to Brown, and the president had invited her, but she had rejected their offers. She did, however, give a lecture at Pembroke College on December 3, 1962. Her spur-of-the-moment hint to Allan Chester had come with an unconscious force. Now, having just passed her sixtieth birthday, her reasons for making this wrenching change had been gradually accumulating. Not only had her most intimate friends and colleagues retired, but also her desire to teach graduate students had reached new heights following her experiences at Princeton. In addition, she would be able to teach until the age of seventy. Finally, she would be closer to her brothers. Once she made her decision, and there seems to have been little hesitation, she had few regrets. Only Connecticut College had an adverse response—

there would never be a visible memorial to the fact that perhaps the greatest scholar and teacher of her age had once been a vital force on its campus.

In locating an apartment in Bryn Mawr, Rosemond had, symbolically, come full circle to the spiritual home where she came into being, and where her life would end.

In between postcards to Tom Roche and Sherman Hawkins and book revisions, Rosemond was writing to Professor Chester at the University of Pennsylvania about course titles and formats for the two seminars she would be teaching in September. The annual catalog had already been printed, so her offerings would require a special insert. Although she had only a formal acquaintance with the chairman of the English department at Pennsylvania, she wrote in her usual, unceremonious style.

Fri. 15 Feb. 1963

Dear Dr. Chester,

I write longhand & briefly because I sat at the machine too persistently between terms & got an over-typing shoulder. On lots of scores I'd a bit rather wait till I am in your department (& not in any other) before I'm listed in it; the ordinary way of printing it is next Catalogue after the persons come seems somehow more natural to me. Of course I'm flattered. It would be different if the undergrads needed the knowledge in their business, but just the 300.01 section is affected, so I should think the usual after-I-come is sufficient.

I attach a note I had written before my shoulder kicked up, about office book space (alas I need lots of bookcases requisitioned!) & courses.

Say my name to your Dog, & get him ready for intimacy. If you can't read this just light cigarette with it.

Rosemond

As soon as she received a reply from Chester, Rosemond wrote again.

Dear Prof. Chester,

The afternoon hours have induced much rejoicing, for I

am a 2nd hand (lightly worn) Sir Gawain, and wax mighty from noon, while by four I am literally invincible. [All of her courses were scheduled for Tuesdays and Thursdays, from 2 to 4 in the afternoon.] So they'll get $2\frac{1}{2}$ times as much as they would have, as to brains; in amiability I am fairly constant but it does not seem to illuminate literature . . .

Im sorry it is such bad typing. What you cannot read, colour red.

Rosemond wrote to Allan Chester at least once a month.

She continued to deny her physical problems and in one letter to Dr. Chester she asked him to get tickets to the Philadelphia Orchestra. "If 'amphitheater' is that old *Top* where I stood in line and climbed every living Saturday for two solid years while at BMC, its a dreadful long trek. But good acoustics when you get there."

Rosemond was planning a visit to Princeton during spring vacation to discuss the corrections Tom had suggested for her book; also on her agenda was a stop-over in Philadelphia, to finalize her move to Pennsylvania. The following letter was written in longhand, and although Rosemond joked about her handwriting, she couldn't help but be concerned.

dear Tom,

I'm still not typing (and write just like a Sick Spider) so therell be mistakes.

I write to ask you, apropos of the enclosed: you can see that you neednt go in for the bother of having me. I wd. normally, if possible politely, do one thing atta time, and this time be mewed up with Roche while he tells me advices; run him out to dinner when time comes, and fall on his sofa when exhausted One Sheet Enough. But as you see I can perf'ly well stay at Marg'ts [Thorpe] and get away to spend session with you— had I better do that? I still think I wd. have no engagements to speak of, one Drink where Sherman and those came, prob. Sat. aft. I have to call home, see if Penna stop is req'd (Sun.) and goodness knows what all, but it wd. be Sat. or Sun. our Working Day—& I really wd. like to read piece of you if possible (also where do I have a foot note to your book) and just you hang onto the 2 pp. as getting em legible is always $\frac{1}{2}$ hr. task. I am already v. contrite abt. the amt of your time I've et up. And you with Book to revise I didn't know that.

Be real honest. If it's the slightest weight on you to sleep a fella, you see no need for that weight. I only love simple one-sentence paragraphs as visits, is all.

R

oof *hateful* achey bones. I can't live sans typing.

But Tom was entertaining two friends, and was unable to accommodate Rosemond. She wrote him a postcard to confirm her plans.

Sherman Hawkins notified Rosemond that he would be spending Thursdays in Bryn Mawr—thus this joyful card:

What wonderful news. I think it is absolutely scrumptious. Thurs. IS one of my days in at Penna. all the better, when you aren't seeing the Rich & Great we'll ring all sorts of changes—dinner at Penn Fac. club, even me ride back to Pcton occas. w. you and stay at Corinne Black's [Corinne Manning Black, a former student at Connecticut College] or Margts. etc.; & when you are not tied with others we'll meet at my house across from college (YOU SHALL HAVE A KEY and change your undershirts there) and we'll invite All best People Over & drink bourbon. I teach in town 2–4. I live bang across from Rocky gate: Merion & Yarrow Aves., Bettws-Y-Coed, 2d floor. I'm in NL till I move 14 Aug. so if you go thru or near NL STOP.

Another card to Sherman, with a painting of a yellow grouper on the back, gave him the title of a reference book, then concluded with a story: "I pick this epigraph not only for who-does-it-most-look-like-in-our-group ? but also for Oxford reminiscence; once in the damp cold Ladies in the Camera basement a fishy soft bescarfed aetat. 50 female approached me with 'are You a Grouper, Dear?' I said, Nope. Ever hear of the Oxf'd Group?"   yrs till next time Ros"

Tom Roche's first book had just been accepted for publication by the Princeton University Press. Rosemond wrote to congratulate him.

[Late March or early April 1963]   back at CC   still can't run
my new toy [an electric typewriter] sans errors

Friday

Dear Tom,

I am delighted. Congratulations. Of course they'd have
been all sorts of fools had they not done as they did and
seized upon it—*but* so often publishers *are* that sort. I always
ben turned down coupla places first. I do not think these
smooth paths you wizards have are quite Decent. Well maybe
I had smooth path a couple of times, but not with one's first
book. Now you will be renowned and can publish books any-
time you want to like playing tennis. . . .

Dear Me I am thwarted how to tell you how glad I was
that you would read me. I was stuck. I thought longingly how
I'd like your criticism but I did not work up the audacity to
ask you to read it till well on into the winter. I am so pleased
I did, because the nice Xtian part is that you even made me
feel it was not too out of the way and demanding. But when I
think of the time taken, of the Real Books you Could have
read in same moments, of all the effort and nuisance, I am
really comblé.

I wish I were as generous-minded. I don't think of any
time I've beat off my frens with whips and thorwed their MSS
in the incinerator—but it is true I don't think of an equal
good turn I've donnem either. I have a great ambition to be
good, and would rather be so than anything; therefore when
someone is specially Good, and even good-to-*me*, I am so
impressed. I like Christians as I told you last year. You work
yours into your life better than any young person I've ever
known.* It is extremely comfortable and loveable to me. Then
when it alights special in such a form as the above, I am
delighted at the mere sight, to say nothing of the prudential
results incurred.

I better keep still; I get unreserved toward evening and
tend to say what I think. This is very dangerous (humanrela-
tions). So if you feel over-praised and tend to take out your

disbeliefs on me save til midnight and read.

*Have known couple aged Xtians.

Oh and I got new car. Ravishingly beautiful, "Sahara Mist" and White. Power everything. Seat belts, we use them. Olds again. You can put your whole college education in my trunk. 2-door "Holiday coupe."

I also did my business at Fla. and had a lovely time seeing Harry Morris again. He is bull-doggy scholar and has sense, if he did pick working on Barnfield. It makes one ashamed to see so many people doing good jobs with difficult material in a 1000 places in USA. Did I tell you & SH my address (after abt mid-August): (excuse name of villa, but it is thus): Bettws-Y-Co-ed Yarrow and Merion Aves. Br.Mawr. Baths free.

Thank you angel-face
good-bye. Tell SH abt. new Sioux.

Ros

Harry Morris, the "bull-doggy scholar," was the instigator of an invitation for Rosemond to lecture at Florida State University, in Tallahassee. He was a former student of hers at the University of Minnesota and their relationship had developed beyond the usual teacher/student model. Her presentation followed her customary format—a talk, accompanied by slides, on the uses men of the seventeenth century made of the medieval books and allegorical writing of the sixteenth century.

Sunday [March 24]

Dear Nancy and Harry,

Well it absolutely *made* that trip that I could stay withm you. I haven't had more satisfaction in a long time. I do like to pick up the old broken strands, and I did have such a fondness for everybody in the old Minn. days (I spose partly because it was My Place and I was coming home). Then it is such a pleasure to see everyone doing so well and doing a good job in the world and not pushing the walls apart trying to "GET" somewhere. I was full of respect and admiration and these added to the pleasure of all the old Ghosts—the images of Harry standing in the hall in Folwell, the smell of linseed oil, the old car I first met Nancy in, etc, etc, etc.

So it was all lovely. I don't like to *just* lecture, and I never do it for the income any more (it just makes my bracket terrible, and 40 or 45% goes anyhow). But I *do* like seeing new places, and then the friendship and living with you two days, was just extra gravy. . . .

Ouch I'm getting shoulder again; I guess I have to stop. Evidently my communicating days is over.

love to all live stock [Harry raised peafowl, guineas, and geese, in addition to owning a large collection of snakes]. eating pecans by 100's, thank you for blissful time, Ros

All yr time used up, poor Harry—hope you caught up.

Despite her continuing recognition and her previously acclaimed books, Rosemond still worried about the quality and accuracy of her scholarship. She would never feel totally confident in her abilities and remained truly humble regardless of the extent of her honors, which were soon to be increased.

Part of Rosemond's busy schedule, not mentioned in letters, was an excursion to Syracuse University along the picturesque roads of upstate New York, with all its gingerbread houses that she so loved. There, on June 2, she received an honorary degree, Doctor of Humane Letters. The citation, delivered by William P. Tolley, chancellor of the university, included these remarks. "Rosemond Tuve, distinguished scholar of the English Renaissance . . . your critical discernment and illuminating insights have contributed immensely to the humanities in this age of science. . . . An extraordinarily gifted teacher, you have had a deep and continuing influence on your students."

Rosemond's difficulty walking (she sometimes lost her balance), or writing, as was obvious from her letters, had alarmed her brothers. They insisted that she have a complete physical exam before leaving for Pennsylvania. In compliance with their wishes, her second "short absence" from New London, mentioned in a letter to Tom, was a trip to the Lahey Clinic, in Boston. Although outwardly she denied the facts of her continuing debilitation with droll remarks, and blocked out her physical problems by channeling her mind into her work, assuredly there were many anxious times. The doctors at the Lahey Clinic failed to diagnose the cause of her symptoms. She repeatedly told friends, "They don't know."

Rosemond's international reputation didn't prevent her from being honored in her own backyard. Williams Memorial Institute, a college preparatory school for girls, tucked into a corner of the Connecticut College campus, invited her to give its commencement address in June. Rosemond's irritation with the current crop of college students spiced her remarks, but she never allowed herself to become pessimistic. This is part of her speech: "I think things have gone down, and I conjure you to get them back up again. I intend to let you in on a chief worry of my professional life, and it is not confined to me: faculties in state after state and country after country have talked about it to me . . . It concerns Passivity and "Not-My-Business" in very odd places. Have students stopped caring about whether things are true or not?

"This is the place where I want to say how it *seems*. I don't know how it *is*. That is why I talk about it. And here are some of the things that *seem:* students watch me and see that I care whether Chaucer meant THIS or THAT. And they care about pleasing ME but they do not care WHICH Chaucer meant. They care about Doing Well, about staying in college. They care about Pleasing their Parents. They care about doing something that makes their Parents' sacrifice-to-send-them-to-college *seem worthwhile to the Parents.* (They care less that it *is* worthwhile than that it *seems* worthwhile to the Parents.) . . . Students care whether I am interesting or not. But they do not care whether the interesting things I say are True or not. Now some things are true or not true; they happened or they didn't happen; and it doesn't matter a hoot whether they are interesting or not. They have to interest you by virtue of being TRUE, and if they don't it's YOU that must change.

". . . I would plead with you: next year see whether you can bring—each of you—ONE American college woman back to the original reason women had for learning things when they first got the privilege of going to college, as men could. They went because they wanted to get in touch with the knowledge and experience men had been able to pile up, and to *use* it for the needs they *saw*.

". . . That's the only real reason for studying, and it is awfully like the only real reason for living: to get ready to fill some need that's worth filling, and to do it *right*, the best way men know so far. *Then*, you see, it makes a desperate difference whether you are being taught what's true or not. . . . The years when we study are dedicated to the most civilized and hopeful and humane of all human principles: that we want to know truth from falsehood—just on principle!

". . . You are joining a most august company: it stretches back to include Erasmus and Socrates, St. Paul and St. Augustine, Aristotle and Milton. But you haven't to do what they did, or be up to their measure. You have only to *want what they wanted:* to find and take hold of and hang onto and pass on true things, not false ones—and they didn't care whether or not they impressed others as being good at it. The only reward they expected was *to know*.

". . . You'll see: dare go at it for the sake of the THING Itself, and you will join IMMEDIATELY, however young, however much a Freshman, the Secret Company of Those Who Serve Whatever Is True. They are happy. They have a reason for having been created."

Warrine Eastburn, secretary to President Shain, wrote this note to Rosemond at the University of Pennsylvania the following November, enclosing excerpts from her speech: "It has occurred to me to wonder if anyone sent you a copy of the enclosed. Mr. Shain asked me to get your remarks printed for WMI [Williams Memorial Institute] and I just want you to know that I think even in 'Excerpt' form, they should be read by every secondary and college student in the country. . . ."

Eastburn later commented that she felt Rosemond was "underrated" and never received recognition for her value to Connecticut College.

What was a more moving event that June was a surprise visit from Geoffrey and Mary Waldegrave. Apparently they were in this country on business, and made the trip to New London to see her.

Mary remembered Rosemond's explanation for her decision to leave Connecticut College: "She said she was greatly looking forward to her new position as she was heartily tired of teaching 'the children' and now wanted to 'teach the teachers.'"

Before leaving Connecticut, Rosemond sent her last written communication to Eleanor Lincoln—a postcard that had been picked up during a trip to the White Mountains in New Hampshire. It depicts the first snow of the season on the Presidential Range and in retrospect it is deeply poignant. In the face of continuing physical problems, there was no let-up in her joie de vivre or in her plans for the future. Eleanor had already left for a holiday abroad and was staying, as usual, at the Whitehall Hotel, to which Rosemond addressed her card. Dated July 3 [1963], followed by "Down w. British," she affixed a printed label to the top of the card indicating her new address in Bryn Mawr.

> NOW FILE IT in your raincoat pocket
> Dear Eleanor, what a holiday beyond compare. If I'd only been on it. I'm not coming abroad at all this summer, as Pa. starts Sept 9 & moving has me buffaloed inspite of all they say, how one does Nothing but Nothing.

Around the borders of this card Rosemond wrote the following messages: "Please do give my serious best wishes to Jn Esther Al. & Miss Wright"; [long-time employees of the Whitehall Hotel] "of course if any English inquire U of Penn, Eng. Dept. is safe"; and finally, "Stay Well. Come See Me." Eleanor did visit Rosemond just once in Bryn Mawr. She found her weak, "fey," and insecure. Rosemond urged her to stay overnight, "in case anything happens."

To help her during the complications and stress of her move, her friends the Brodericks urged Rosemond to stay with them for two nights. Prior to being invited to teach at Bryn Mawr College, Jim Broderick had been an instructor in the English department at Connecticut and was something of a protégé to Rosemond. He and his wife, Louise, recalled their experiences of her with humor and warmth: "She had a lot of trouble feeling she was part of Connecticut College, or that the college was going to utilize her best. The Goucher and Vassar experiences made her unsure of herself, and CC had done little to reassure her. Rosemary Park did reassure her.

"She left CC because of that sense that graduate students were interested in the same things she was interested in and they looked to her as a kind of relative. She was so enamored of teaching graduate students at Harvard, and so wounded by the failure of Harvard to appoint her when they should have, that she realized that she had to in some way make the move herself. Harvard wasn't going to appoint a woman, and they weren't going to appoint Roz. Roz was vigorous and decisive, a controversial figure, at Harvard. Douglas Bush said of her: 'After an hour of talking with Miss Tuve I feel like I'm suffering from pernicious anemia.'

"She had a barrel of energy and enormous vitality. It was sort of a Girl Scout manner in a way. She had an open, direct, giggly, very girlish manner. Yet, so incisive, so wonderful. She always preferred to ask the simple, the school-girl type of question, about all sorts of things, to play the neophyte. Her intelligence was extraordinarily well trained and she could get to the central, school-girl type of question, right away. It was sort of puzzling. It wasn't the sort of thing that went down with male scholars in learned meetings. She was often thought of as having knocked people about in those meetings. She would cut through things in a way which often seemed to disregard the person, which I don't think she intended, but the effect was the same. The individual was often quite bruised. She wasn't a saint but she was not mean-spirited. She could make wise cracks like anybody else but she wasn't mean-spirited about people."

As Rosemond's health declined, she realized that if she was going to teach graduate students, she had to move on. "I'm ready to leave," she said to Konrad Bieber, a close friend on the faculty. Broderick commented on her departure: "She was really quite brave, kept up a front. Dorothy Bethurum thought her illness was what influenced her to leave. It was a knocking at the door. She was going to be summoned soon. It would have been enough had she made that decision at that age, anyway, but the illness simply made it clear to her that she should not wait for another visiting chair. If she wanted what she wanted she better go and get it and her illness made it clear to her that time was running out. She never went downhill intellectually.

"Dorothy was terribly competitive. You were in the presence of a grand dame all the time. We would have major meetings of the English department out at Dorothy's place and they were sort of a summons in a way. Ros would get down on the floor and roll around with the cat, a huge cat, while Dorothy, who was so completely decorous, kept saying what a good predatory animal the cat was and Ros would roll around in front of the fireplace, this huge woman, rolling around in the most indecorous way. In some senses it was a little bit aggressive. People were extraordinarily stuffy to begin with. At Harvard and Princeton she would *act up* in their presence occasionally. She wanted to be one of the gang—she didn't want to be one of the girls. It was not masculine, it was girlish. The kind of thing you could get away with. She was uninhibited, and she knew better. She whooped when she laughed, she was noisy. She was big. She didn't make herself inconspicuous. She was always somewhat conspicuous.

"She had a way of speaking which was quite measured. I don't know where it came from. It wasn't fake. It was very deliberate and she could use it in the office with students. Dignified and quiet, too. She was also fun-loving and liked to joke. She was genuine fun to be with. She thought people were kookier than they admitted. She'd come by and stay and have dinner and talk. She'd sew her girdle, or underpants, that she'd pull out of her bag and sit there and say, 'Don't be embarrassed. I like to talk with people but I have to get my chores done too.'"

Elizabeth Turner Pochoda (Betsy), who graduated from Connecticut College in 1963 and followed Rosemond to Pennsylvania, also spoke of her capriciousness: "In a man it's much more tolerable. But in a woman it meant that she was putting herself forward. Bad enough that she was so bright; but that she should carry along these bits of expressiveness and mannerisms, I suppose was too much."

Rosemond's move to Pennsylvania was in two parts. First was her move to her office in room 207C, College Hall, at the University of Pennsylvania, on August 13. There were her typewriter, posture chair, files, their contents, and academic clothes. In addition, Rosemond had requisitioned four bookcases, seven or eight feet high, which, when the movers had unpacked her books, were filled completely. When they had finished, she noticed that the books had been placed on the shelves upside down. She turned to one of the movers and said, "Young man, how did you happen to choose this profession?"

The following day she moved into her new home, Bettws-Y-Coed. Ann Mendelssohn-Iger, a student aide from Bryn Mawr, said that it was "very symbolic, living opposite the gates of Bryn Mawr." Kathleen Swaim, a graduate student at Penn, felt that Rosemond passionately wished to teach at Bryn Mawr. "That was a kind of coming home. That was the place she wanted to be." Although she was a graduate of Bryn Mawr, the college had essentially ignored her professional career. Betsy Pochoda recognized the jealousy and rejection she suffered: "She was probably one of their most distinguished graduates ever; she mentioned to me one time that the alumnae magazine, as far as she knew, never mentioned her name or any of her accomplishments, ever. It sounded vain when she said it. It wasn't vanity. It was sadness." Although unconfirmed, it is believed that her name was considered twice for a possible appointment, but was blackballed by the older faculty, who did not want such a powerful and famous woman in their department.

~ 13 ~

ROSEMOND TUVE WAS THE FIRST WOMAN to be appointed professor of English at the University of Pennsylvania. Due in part to the large size of the department, her colleagues expressed a skepticism and indifference similar to that she received from the administration at Bryn Mawr. "Ros would never complain about an institution she was working for," Jim Broderick observed. "It was part of her training. There were enormous deficiencies in their treatment of her at Pennsylvania, and I don't think it was merely the fault of any individual. It was the fault of a larger department that couldn't ever focus on her."

During her first semester, Rosemond's classes were small. Bill Ingram, one of her graduate students, who went on to become a professor of Elizabethan drama at the University of Michigan, observed some ambivalence on the part of some of the faculty. When he told his graduate adviser that he wanted to take her Spenser seminar, the adviser's reply was, "Well sure, it's the standard Tuve stuff. The same thing she's been doing for twenty years, but you probably ought to have it." Ingram's reaction was: "I thought that was curious. I just don't know how much enthusiasm there was in the department for her presence. That kind of diffidence on the part of some of the other faculty probably communicated itself to students." Obviously some professors were delighted to have her, but others were wary and often envious. Rumor has it that one faculty member remarked: "Nice old duck, but not much cerebration."

Shortly after being settled in her apartment, Rosemond wrote to Roche.

Angel Thos (it'll be a crowded name)

FIRST act: tear off the outside sticker, or else the above nime and give to Mrs Birch. Allus assuming you RIP open my pistells in the office incontinently and do not put in pocket & read when on Trains.

In an almost illegible hand she wrote: "Tho' of course the no memory, always forwardable, address for Mrs Birch (or you all) is Univ Penna. English Phila."

The letter went on:

LOOK. I'm moved I expect to be very amused. It is more my style to have a different thing to do in autumn; I am wanderer.

NAW. There isn't anything to rumour of being sick. WHAT HAVE I GOT COULD YOU ASCERTAIN AND LET ME KNOW.

It is just that old Dean Swift killed Partridge deal I guess. I honestly do hate to hear the rumor from so many sources—or are they mostly Princeton; COULD you ask Bob Patton where he thinks it arose from and scotch it at *source*? I would hate them to think at Penna they were getting a damaged package yesterday's corn. I think it must be because, talky me, I tell every joke I know. Merle wanted me to have check up before leaving New England (He is married to Dr.—they are so nervus) and had notion I had worse balance spring vac or what was it—(I have always steered erratic act. hearing aid and trifocals) so they are daft about people going to Lahey every so often. I spose I brandished it about like a flag—because of course there was not a spot anywhere to be seen on me when I DID go to please Merle to old Lahey & see my Cbge friends and have 3 parties and dinner out and sich.

It was comical the doctor reading off this test that test "and this is fine" "this is negative, no trouble" "no heart" "no chest" "no this no that"—he as much as said you old girls stay home and dont bother the busy. I'm in the pink of condition even if I did just find it out by chance. . . . . Nothing hurts anywhere.

So please do see if you can find out where it all steams up and make that little fountain dry up. . . .

I am a mere FLUFF. I am going to libry tomorrow. And READ. You were a darling to offer help.   Love from Rosemond

Despite the increasing familiarity in the tone of Rosemond's last letters to Tom Roche, a vein of insecurity, a lack of assurance, persisted. She recognized her dependence on him for emotional support and intellectual companionship, and was defending against becoming a burden. In him she found a true disciple, although she never would have used the term, and a colleague to carry on her work in the same devout spirit. When Roche complained to her that there were only twelve students in his first class, she quickly replied, "There was once another Man who had only twelve."

Kathleen Swaim, who was completing her doctoral work in the eighteenth century, remembered that the faculty atmosphere at that time was "not happy." There tended to be too many in one field. Fortunately for Swaim, her graduate director recommended Rosemond's Milton course instead of another eighteenth-century course she had planned: "I had been pushed into this course. I just remember the first day. I had been sitting out in the hall waiting to do my graduate registration, and various people who had wanted to take the course came out and said, 'Whoooo, he wouldn't let me sign up for it. Do you have medieval Latin? Do you have old French? He wouldn't let me sign up for it.' And I went in and he didn't ask me those questions. He said I was to go in there. 'You take that course,' he said, 'you'll be good for her and she'll be good for you.' So I just did it."

She went on: "So the first day I walked into class after all these experiences, and there's a male in the class named Kent Christiansen, and the first words out of her mouth are something in Danish—a question. He dropped the course somewhat later. She knew this and never modified herself in any way. Well, it worked."

Because of this course, Swaim left the eighteenth century and went on to become the eminent Milton scholar she is today. "It was just kind of an accident," she said. "The course just rattled my socks. I never worked so extremely hard for a course before. I knew that everything she said seemed to be directed to me, reshaping my whole life. I begrudgingly finished my eighteenth-century dissertation, but, as I say, I'm a Miltonist."

Swaim explained the power of Rosemond's teaching: "[There were] two very great differences she made to me. I was in my last year of graduate study and I'd been studying and studying with great concentration and she was the first and only teacher I ever had who seemed to me to study literature because she loved it. I could tell when she read a book that wholly different things happened in her head than happened in my head and I wanted some of those things to happen in my head. Like other teachers at Penn, if they were teaching Milton they would rattle off about 80 books about Milton and the dates and stuff. When she was teaching Milton, here's Uriel sliding down a sunbeam, and she would say 'wheeeee.' It's just a whole different thing. She lived it. And that made me realize that there is an epistemology and a pedagogy founded on love.

"The second difference she made to me was seeing her function made me feel it was possible to attain a greater freedom as a teacher. That is, it would be possible to do that, and that there was nothing wrong with sharing love of literature. In fact, that's very likely the best thing you can do for students." There is an echo here of Helen Vendler. Like Vendler, Kathy Swaim received from Tuve an affirmation for her love of literature.

Grace Billings Bress, a former student at Harvard, described her thought as concentric: "seeing ideas as pebbles thrown in water, circling out and influencing and colliding with other circles of thought." Bress described assignment sheets as "hard to follow—blocks of subjects, tangentially related instead of clear-cut assignments listed for each class." Bill Ingram remembered this "embarrassing session in her office: I came in to discuss an approach to a topic and said, I'll do this and I'll do that, and I'll do this, and then I said, Is that what you want? And she fixed me with that look, you know, that she can do, and said, 'It isn't what *I* want, Mr. Ingram, it's what the topic requires.'

"That was a shock for me, that little conversation. The idea that I was doing it to please her, pained her. In fact, in an essay Rosemond wrote, she said that the important thing for her was that her teachers didn't care about her. I've almost memorized that sentence: 'I owe my chance to learn what they [my teachers] could not tell me, or did not believe, to their reticence and disinterested passion; thank heaven their allegiance was to their authors and to learning, and not to my welfare, for this is the condition of freedom.' I have it pinned on my wall."

Betsy Pochoda was also grateful for the same rigorous treatment: "I think the most valuable thing I ever learned from Miss Tuve was how to educate myself. Nobody flattered or stroked me. I liked that and it was useful, but it didn't always go down well with other students. She also wrote really stringent comments on our papers, but they were very instructive. She believed in humility; she was humble before the texts; and students should be humble before the texts and their own inabilities."

Bill Ingram related more of his difficulties: "Her chaotic and disorganized teaching used to drive me up the wall. She would make assignments and one thing we had to do—I hated it—I do it now in my own teaching—was to hand in a paper every week, in which we summarized the week, the week in our head, as it were. And we would keep saying to her, what do you want on these papers? And she wouldn't answer us. We would hand them in and get back, scrawled comments—'No, this isn't what I want.' We'd say, what do you want? And she wouldn't answer."

He continued: "Some of the people in the class, like my wife, saw the value of this. I didn't. I got so frustrated. It was almost Kafkaesque. It was doing something for me. It was forcing me. If she had put it into words she would have said I'm going to get you so confused you've got to stop and figure out what you really think. And that's different from most of the other teachers at Penn who told you what the main ideas were and how you might respond to them. What she taught me was a methodology and an attitude and an approach. So that what I learned from her is all intangible.

"When the father of one of the men in her class died, the student came to Miss Tuve and asked her if he could have a little extra time with his paper, which was due a week later. She said, 'No, do the paper. Life goes on. Do your paper.' That was enough to promote conversation for a couple of days. Betty [Ingram's wife], who is a great and devoted apologist for Miss Tuve, explained that you attach yourself to the permanent Ideas, not the transitory people who happen to embody them at any given moment. When Miss Tuve's father died, life went on, so she internalized that." (Betty Ingram now works in the early sixteenth century because of Rosemond's influence.)

Ingram went on: "She would giggle in class—make silly jokes—and giggle at them. She was intrigued with the name of Pope Pius XI. Papae Pius onze—Pap P Onze—Papillons. Every time she would say it, she may have forgotten, she would giggle. Pope Pius the eleventh in French, is Papillon. This papal butterfly flying around.

"One day, about ten minutes before the end of class, she said, 'Now all you boys get out of here. I want to have a word with the girls.' So we left. I later asked Betty what had gone on. She told me that she gave them a stern lecture about being women scholars. How you had to stick to the truth and not allow yourself to get deflected by boys and things like that, even marriage. She apparently cared very much about that, enough to lecture the women students. Keep your eye on the ball."

Pochoda also recalled her admonitions that day: " 'This is what's going to happen to you. These are the pressures that you're going to have to face in trying to maintain a life as a scholar.' She told us not to get married. 'Imagine what it would be like to sit and face the same person over a breakfast table for twenty-five years.'"

Rosemond apparently insulated herself from any hostility or negative feelings from the faculty at Pennsylvania. Assuredly, her primary concerns were with her students. In November 1963, she wrote to Harry Levin:

> I like it here better every way—climate amusement and classes. The gals were getting quite ruined. [In the margin she inserts a sad face.] It is the recent image of what is necessary for them: they don't dare ignore it. I have too many girls here in my sems (2); both kinds at Penn. & we have the coop. arr. so I've some BMC [Bryn Mawr College] ones. I am wondering if there were 2 mistakes we made: gals don't want educa-

tion but prefer as advertised, an innocent witless charm, and 2. there is no discipline of Engl. studies. Isn't it full of eyewash lately? Oof. PoohPerplex is quite right. Have one undergrad. sem. of honors men, more fun but very arrogant. But they bite bettern the graduate students. Hvd and Pcton were both more fun for that reason, but I am willing to teach anybody that is going to teach young America.

I wish I could see you. Last night I saw the Mpls. people I like so much, John Clark hunting Men. It is not as hard to think of you as a little mpls. boy as to remember my long snowy S. Dak. childhood. I still passionately love it. . . . I am on a Hy [Henry] James binge re reading in default of finding any new; the recent novels are so *unenjoyable.* Take away Malamud Roth Styron Murdock and numerous such fry. YOUR BOOK WAS LOVELY.

Don't do anything now. Rest Back. It is all lies they tell about moving; mine got me tired & I haven't typed the 40 pp. I had left on Aug.13.

I love ilena and only wait for her to have to spend time at BM while you are down at Hopkins talking or something.

At the top of the page of this next letter to Hawkins, probably written early in 1964, she wrote: "I love Henry James. Just read 2 more bks."

Dear Sherman,

Your umbrella! that magnifique appurtenance. I got Jim B. [Jim Broderick] to put it in your office, being so snowy you mightn't come over or have your key. You're sposed to ast anybody you want over, e.g. for drink or tea, and me come in upon from town, later to my great delight; I love to find people here. I think we should ask over both I. McC. [Isabel MacCaffrey, a Miltonist who taught at Bryn Mawr, and the wife of Wallace MacCaffrey, later a professor of history at Harvard] and K.R. [Katherine Rodgers] soon . . .

The letter concluded with reactions to his paper, mostly positive but always honest. There were many references in Rosemond's letters, and other writings, that reveal the depth of her feelings toward her students. They were her "offspring." Almost ten years earlier she had written: "A scholar is only a student; he likes all true fellow-students— those are whom he should like. He will nourish them in his bosom, feed them of his dish, and give them of his drink. The present tendency to ask him to nourish everybody in his bosom, fellow-students or not, is only going to result in crowded bosoms, and no ewe lamb in the end . . . That is only, in Wordsworth's phrase, to become, as a teacher (that is, a senior student) 'the witless shepherd who persists to drive . . . A flock that thirsts not to a pool disliked.'"[1] In return, she enjoyed a special kind of fulfillment knowing that her "children" were serving the cause of literature, in her own strict manner, throughout the world.

By suggesting, in her recent note to Hawkins, that they dine at an inn, in preference to trying to manage a buffet, she acknowledged her increasing physical limitations. In addition, a new tone of weariness, almost peevishness, appeared in her introduction to a lecture to the Pennsylvania Graduate Club, in February:

"There's 2 things you do at the beginning of a speech: 1st thg is, say you're glad to be there. Now this is a big fib. I don't have any special feelings either way. I'm not particularly glad.

"You can be glad I'm here if you want to, I'm not especially noticeably Glad.

"2nd thing is, you change your subject and title. Now I'm just going to let it go, don't know what the cards said, as I hate their crucial air & never look at them, but I'm talking as I think was said, on Eliz. or Spenserian Allegory and some Picture Books—late mediaeval, those.

"I'll substitute remark—same slides as Pcton & the Rutgers club, so if took anr. previous ph.d. THERE and belonged to those doughnut societies, seen same slides & their relevant points (cant change talks and arguments much if tied to slides).

"Be dark here in 4 mins., such people that have heard these ideas, slip out have Free Unexpected evening."

In her last letter to Hawkins, in late April, she continued to urge him to use her apartment more frequently for entertaining. As her disabilities escalated, her loneliness and longing for stimulating companions increased.

Rosemond was planning another trip to Princeton at the end of April. She was going to see her editor at the Princeton University Press with the manuscript of *Allegorical Imagery*. There were also some meetings she wanted to attend. Earlier, Tom Roche had sent her a self-addressed, stamped postcard. The only writing on the card is three boxes drawn next to the names of places to stay during her visit. The choices were "Crimpy Cottage," in which she drew a smiley face; Lowrie, and the Inn. On what space on the card remains she wrote:

> Oh luscious, cant imagine better luck than to spend all the edges in your abode, and Real Careless. I am you try & see a Poifick guest asking no foods only Drinks, and Disposable. Only thing: Dick say I have begun to Snore ERRATIC & WILD SO IF INCARCERATION NOT POSSIBLE & a shut door on that side of the couch (or chaise; I sleep on anything) tell me & I'll go to Lowrie. *Inn* too elegant. Is L. a dorm. You oughta come down w. SH to see things ONCE (I'm sure you are teased to) I'd sleep 1 in study 1 in L rm. and drive you up next day. We will talk RE EVERYTHING. And go & work. I do not aim for anybody to have more than bkfst. and bedmaking added to thr Life. It REALLY would be a chance to drive SH up—doesn't he need a Evening here by April.

In the midst of all these exchanges, Roche's first book, *The Kindly Flame: A Study of the 3rd and 4th Books of Spenser's* Fairie Queene, was published. On the dedication page is this quotation from Shakespeare's *The Tempest*:

> "To Rosemond Tuve:
> She will outstrip all praise
> And make it halt behind her."

Rosemond acknowledged this moving tribute with light-hearted sincerity in a letter to Roche. Emotions on both sides reached deeper than they wished to express. She wrote from her brother's home in Cleveland, where she had gone, as she hinted in her letter to Hawkins, for a family conference on the state of her health. At the top of the page of her letter Rosemond wrote: "Your first Book! Doesn't your Mama mind? Or yr typist?" Then she inserted her address: 3211 Green Road, Cleveland.

Dear Tom,

I'm enchanted. S.H. left me &n I found on table that very Th. I had posted you a card, a copy of the Book—the physical Book. I thot it was a condition in the mind—and he said read front & I immediately did and could not get out the door again that I came in by. Puft Up. Was this what I was getting that dagger for to thrust into anyone who stirred the arras? And never lifted up a single stone. I just purr, I do not have the least impulse toward destruction. There isn't any Xtn humility in this world. I take a quite careless view of whether things said are true or not, I just like to see um. Isn't that unregenerate.

And it is so GOOD. The book, so truly said, the part abt. reading allegory in intr. is quite Perfect, I shall refer to it right away. Imagine being able to read something & say Yes yes to it and not Oh Dear. I have said oh dear ever since Roosevelt died. Luxury, to agree and admire. Oh it's splendid. I am blushing like Shamefastnesse as I say thanks so I guess I will just say thing MUST be true that 2 smart ones like You and Me believe, and I believe every word so far. Don't you feel ebullient, and paternal, and you see this kind will lie quietly and not roll off the crib & not torment you when you begin to disapprove of it.

I am at Lew's my oldest brother—(8 yrs older, the archangel Michael of my childhood). It is luxurious, I am thought to be an enhancement of life, it is so false but agreeable. My nat. selfishness does not show out here, no Beauty is required, I can get up late, I am morgain le fay. I think the Sister relation SHOULD be ezactly like this, & do not mind whatever origin it has, freudian or a spot of incest or anything they fancy. The End justifies the Means. I showed off my Dedic. immed. & Lew I noticed was seen passing on the Show. What are you going to do now the baby is born. It is a lonely moment till you get another offspring started. But I dare say you HAVE. I look forward treimounjously to seeing you lazily and no bells ringing or doors locking in April; consider the remark (jaunt) I prefaced my acceptance with.

Lew is like you and Sherman. I like Christians and I also like Loving Natures that don't count what they've got left all the time. Lew also is like that. Oh all things it was in that bad old Xtine her Ceres, such a dumb figure but the word, *abandon*, is the required thing so few have. It comes with Grace as we know but even trying to get those 7—or so I find—gifts by *name* is obstructed by remains of Apple sitting in one's throat. I stop.I flit.I flee. Bless you. There was such a sweetness about how the act was done, it quite vanquished me with Beauty as Sidney says, COULD we but look upon. . . . Goodbye to you.   Ros

Writing up the side of the page she added: "oh won't it be delightful. . . . we will talk over EVERYTHING. We'll find a Good Book. I am very Quiet and go to bed early and don't need ANY attention, just sofa."

After returning to Bryn Mawr, Rosemond wrote her last extant letter to Tom. It was badly typed on Rosemond's new stationery, with her name and address (Bettws-Y-Coed. Yarrow & Merion Aves., Bryn Mawr, Pennsylvania) imprinted at the top. She was confirming what she had indicated on the earlier postcard, and squeezed into the end of her last letter, that she would be staying with him while she was in Princeton for a brief visit to see her editor.

Dear Tom,

I'm still ever such a Dedicated Spirit, it is quite luscious, like marrying into royalty.

Unless you feel called upon to use the chance to repay old debts with invit.'s, Me I should be so pleased to sit quietly &

get *our* talk really talked, about our own century & our own gossip, that I won't be looking about for any of the famed Rochean hospitality—I won't even attempt to get the rounds of my acquaintanceship, in this fleeting stop; not seeing the older hallowed ones after all but will only sometime drop past Margaret [Thorpe, wife of Willard Thorpe] and tug at her pyjama tops otherwise let even that crowd go too. I have to go in & see Herb Bailey with MS, and show him I'm at the beginning of the end. On Friday before I ever show up. He'll want to get some reading started maybe, as soon as I'm neat enough. I just thought I better write in case you took it for granted you'd got to make an ado over my appearance. I do think it will be splendid to hear your ideas on all subjects and am letting the people go for those. You count as A Idea not a person isn't that interesting, you didn't know you were *that* thin & peaked from loss of weight. Unbodied.

Rosemond's inability to walk was becoming increasingly hazardous. Her anxiety about falling and possibly breaking a hip was mounting. For this reason, as her brothers noticed during her visit to Lew's home in Cleveland, she was spending a growing amount of time in bed. Her speech recently had become slurred, less audible, and Merle was able to design a special microphone for her to use. Her brothers tried to persuade her to find student aides from Bryn Mawr to assist her with meals and transportation. No longer was she able to drive Siouxie. Reluctantly, Rosemond acquiesced. It was obvious that she needed help with all aspects of daily living. Frederica "Ricky" Wolf, later Konolige, one of the graduate students at Bryn Mawr who offered to help her, remembered that her speech was affected, "but she was able to be heard until she died. I'm sure some students couldn't hear every word she said, but the words we heard were better than what we heard from anyone else."

At age sixty, Rosemond's body had given out. Her nephew Rik Tuve remarked that "she burned herself out." The disease from which she suffered was progressive, and in the last few months had become alarming. Shortly after arriving home, she was seen by her regular doctor in Bryn Mawr, John Fisher, who referred her to Dr. Bernard Alpers, a neurologist in Philadelphia, and just coincidentally Paul Alpers's father.

Dr. Alpers admitted her to the hospital for an arteriogram and pneumogram, to rule out any possibility of a tumor. On May 15 he talked with Merle by telephone to discuss his findings. He told him that she had bilateral and progressive cerebellar disease; her unsteadiness was due to cerebellar ataxia, not dizziness. This was a quite common form of unsteadiness, frequently the result of the occlusion of one of the arteries (probably the basal artery) at the base of the brain. Because this had no effect on her mental clarity, Dr. Alpers expected to tell her to "sit down and teach." Rosemond was able to do seminar and thesis work, but no lecturing. Merle was also concerned about the amount of time she spent in bed, and wondered if she was depressed. Alpers assured him that since she was afraid of falling, she felt safer in bed.

Merle quickly took action. He put out several feelers for hotels where she might stay during the summer vacation, if student help was not available, and made inquiries into the possibility of finding students at Bryn Mawr to help her with meals and driving during the semester. Ricky Wolf remembered the first time she saw Rosemond: "I got to know her because she needed a driver to take her from Bryn Mawr to Penn. She really needed a nurse. But she was the kind of woman who could not have had a full-time nurse, she would not have brooked that. I was sitting in a room in the old library at BMC during the summer, shortly before the semester was to begin, when a woman who looked to be about 130 (I'm exaggerating), but very old, was trying to get in the door. I stood up to try to help the woman get into the library. I thought it was some lovely old Main Line lady. She had her walker at that time and it was very cumbersome for her. She thanked me and I sat back down and continued my work." Rosemond was unable to stand or walk without a walker. She put up with it grudgingly. When it was cumbersome, she called it a "poke"; when she could tolerate it, it became a "noble chariot."

Ricky Wolf went on: "Then, about one half hour later, I looked up and saw the same woman coming toward me. She introduced herself as Rosemond Tuve. She had just talked to Isabel MacCaffrey and Isabel had recommended I drive her from BM to Penn. I thought, 'What a delight.' When she said her name, I knew who she was. I also was quite shocked that the lady who was making her way into the library was Tuve. I would have given up, I'm sure."

In August, at the recommendation of Dr. Alpers, Rosemond visited Dr. John Hodges, an internist and professor of medicine at Jefferson Medical College. Dr. Hodges remembered her as a "gracious patient," noting that she was "tall, slender, poorly nourished." His impression was that she had "asthmatic bronchitis, early heart failure and emphysema." She was a heavy smoker, and that was the source of her chronic bronchitis and emphysema. (One of her student aides recalls that "she threw her cigarettes out the window one day and never looked at them again.") Walking to her car, following her visit with Dr. Hodges, she confided his diagnosis to her driver, Kathleen Swaim: "He says I have a tired heart." Swaim added: "You just know that her interpretation of this was 'because I cared so much about people.' It's the heart. It wasn't as if it was something physical, it was allegorized, mythicized. It was just that, that's what I mean by vision."

By September there were several graduate students who were available to assist Rosemond with meals and transportation. Ann Mendelssohn-Iger recalled that "her brothers arranged for someone to care for her—they were not going to let her rattle around on her own after coming out of hospital in May. She resented it like hell. I was there cooking for her and being general companion and nursemaid." Ann remembered sitting down at her "old beat-up piano" (it was her mother's, preserved from the Canton days) and playing from a beautiful book of Danish Lutheran hymns—"a lovely, scholarly edition." She was also struck by Rosemond's pride in her Lutheran, midwestern background and in her participation in the Bryn Mawr Summer School for Women Workers. Rosemond felt that teaching in the summer school was something truly worthwhile. Ann also recalled "murdering Bach for her, on the piano." Rosemond's fingers were so arthritic she could no longer play. She loved Bach; she said, 'Bach just is. He's there.' "

It was about this time that Rosemond learned of Dorothy

Bethurum's marriage to Roger Loomis, a renowned medieval scholar. Although her feelings toward Bethurum were chiefly admiration and warmth, she could also be caustic. When she heard the news about her former colleague she quipped: "Roger Loomis? He's been through three medievalists already."

In late August Rosemond had written to Ricky Wolf. She was apprehensive and wanted to meet her on the fourth of September, a week before the university opened, in order to have a trial run to her office. She wrote: "I think it worth coming in for the know-the-ropes aspect. It will be strange enough for you. . . . Call me the minute you are in town, won't you? It would be too bad to make grandma's life any more miserable." During one of their drives, Rosemond recited "Lycidas" to Ricky, then asked her what she thought of it. Ricky answered, "It's beautiful." Rosemond gazed "mysteriously" out the window and responded, "It's beautiful because it's true." Ricky acknowledged that it was the closest she ever came to being converted.

Another Bryn Mawr student, Susan Gamer, was also recruited to assist Rosemond. Susan was not a student of Rosemond's and so, perhaps, had a different reaction to her "patient." She found her peevish, complaining, demanding that everything on her tray be put in its exact place. Obviously there was no rapport between the two women.

A more satisfying moment was the appearance, a few months earlier, of her essay "Spenserus," the article she had taken with her to Florida to work on during the long plane ride and to show to Harry Morris. It was published in *Essays in English Literature from the Renaissance to the Victorian Age, Presented to A.S.P. Woodhouse*. It is, as the title suggests, an exhaustive exploration of a signature, "Spenserus," which she had discovered years ago in a fifteenth-century manuscript. In more than twenty-three pages involving the most painstaking research, she explains her reasons for suspecting that the signature is indeed Spenser's. She recorded the moment in her diary on February 15, 1933, and had been gnawing at this bone ever since. She wrote: "Perhaps really he. Very exciting, (if the pale lamenting young man in the library *doesn't* think so—! . . ." Although in the end she conceded that she could not prove beyond a doubt that the signature was Spenser's, she expected it would open up avenues for further research. Remarkably, this is the same method she used with her students, throwing out ideas and concepts for them to explore.

The essay "Spenserus" begins: "On the last page of a Bodleian manuscript of Gower's *Confessio Amantis* written in a clear early fifteenth-century hand . . . we encounter the following Ovidian album-sentiment, written in an Italian hand too ordinary to identify as Spenser's or not Spenser's." She inserts the five lines in question, which are bracketed with the signature "Spenserus."[2]

Paul Alpers commented on "Spenserus" as the most "poignant" single moment in Rosemond's writing. "It's tracking down what this signature meant, in an Elizabethan book. It's an elaborate study of commemoration and it's about a commemorative poem of Spenser's and she weaves this extraordinarily, and really brings out the kind of human awareness that Ros brought to the poetry. In some ways, more than anything else she wrote, because it's the least formidable poem she wrote about. You really can see her bringing to it why people write poems in commemoration; they were re-creating a whole culture. She really wrote this as a contribution to a festschrift for A.S.P. Woodhouse. At the end of the essay she has a wonderful sense, she turns it in a way: although Spenser was lamenting his dead friends, it is fortunately not the circumstance which she engaged in in celebrating this occasion. Within a year of that essay both she and Woodhouse were dead. It was really an incredible fatality." Later, one of her student aides recalled how extremely upset Rosemond was when, on October 31, 1964, the news of Woodhouse's death reached her.

Surely Rosemond's spirits were lifted when the *Journal of the Warburg and Courtauld Institutes* came out that fall. The second half of a long article, "Notes on the Virtues and Vices," which she had been working on during her half-year abroad in 1962, appeared in the journal. The first part had been published in 1963. This two-part article was "initiated by a desire to understand better Spenser's use of the virtues in the *Faerie Queene*—their structural role [and] inherited conceptions of them which affected their allegorical power . . ."[3] Much of her interest in this imagery lay in the multidimensional meanings they acquired over time.

Rosemond had discovered another kindred spirit at the journal, Frances A. Yates. She was a scholar, a specialist on Giordano Bruno, and also a mystery writer, of, notably, *The Valois Tapestries.* In early November 1958, writing about editorial concerns with her George Herbert article, Rosemond had finished off a long letter to Yates with jocular comments:

> I've had frisky fall. Too many thousand miles in Sioux my ottermobile. But as you know I love to drive. I went home to my brothers outside Wash. within 3 days of setting foot in this Continent—a 1000 mile drive but the boys are such DUCKS. They came from hither and yon, one lives in Ohio, and nephews down from the university in Penna., etc etc., and we'd fatted calfs and bourbon by the quart and everybody loves Sister.

In August 1964, she wrote a postcard to Frances Yates:

> Dear Frances, SUCH a good book the Bruno. I have just laid it down after reading the last word; was induced to a pious careful and earnest re-reading of the whole by perceiving and getting taken with Perkin's [sic] delectable HELL book, a prize. So I enjoyed GB [Giordano Bruno] so uninterruptedly I seize this card to say so; it is such a satisfaction to ENJOY books. There were references in notes to a thing or two I can still read, for I see I just *like* to read Yates and am going to read every word she has writ even if I find it is on dishwashing . . . I thot I'd stay this side when my eldest bro. last November lost his wife, the wheelchair one (I have all types) but he is going to solace himself with a new one he can exhaust hisself for, so my becoming an Available sister was unneeded, but I did not remake my plans since then I got awkwarder about locomotion and admired the laziness of an Amer. Summer. The climate is however Barbaric—a Quaker mistake, should have gone farther. We start so early at Penn, like schoolchildren, early September. Your scholarship is so satisfying! so fine and hot and interesting. I didn't send you a

Vices & V. reprint bec. you see only too much of the Home
Paper, I th't Coals to Newc.

Sometime before the fall semester started, Rosemond asked
Kathy Swaim if she would rent an apartment with an extra bedroom
so that she (Rosemond) might stay overnight between her Monday
class and her graduate seminar on Tuesday. Rosemond seemed drawn
to Kathy. When asked why, Kathy said, "I'm not sure. She was a strange
duck—a wonderful, magnificent creature, and certainly batty. But she
gave me a vision of several sorts."

Kathy remembered that "she had everything wrong with her, just
everything. She had quite bad arthritis in her knees and her hands.
She couldn't write; she couldn't button buttons. I often changed the
batteries in her hearing aids. One time—starting from nowhere, she
offered: 'He says it won't affect my mind or my eyes.' I didn't press
her." Rosemond wouldn't discuss her problems.

Rosemond became more and more solitary. Mackie Jarrell, her
colleague at Connecticut, observed that "when people know they are
going to die there is a kind of withdrawal. She may have quoted Yeats
about 'making her soul.'" She was headed in the direction of a mystic.
Ricky referred to her as a "hermit scholar," whose closest relationship
was with her book *Allegorical Imagery*. When Dorothy Bethurum
came to the Philadelphia area and telephoned, Rosemond wouldn't
see her. Rosemond said to Kathy, "You'd think when people leave a
place that they'd understand you just leave." It was a very cold statement that emphasized her need to withdraw. When Konrad Bieber
visited her in Bryn Mawr, she saw him briefly. She asked Bieber, "Do I
look awful?" You look awful, all right, but I hope you feel better," was
Bieber's reply. She said, "Let's not talk about feelings." Bieber remembered that she was bedridden, "not in good shape, but not much
changed. She was *very* unhappy."

Beverley Chadwick, later Sherry, was the last of the Bryn Mawr
students to be enlisted to assist Rosemond. She had come from
Australia to complete her studies for a Ph.D. at Bryn Mawr and to take
Rosemond's Milton and Spenser courses at Penn. She knew of her
from her studies and teaching in Australia, and remembered vividly

the times she spent with her as both student and companion: "She had a greater influence on me than any other teacher. She set us an example for life in her tireless pursuit of truth, her exacting expectations of us, her not standing for any bluff or laziness, her own wit and charm and modesty. Her classes—how shall I put this—I am not sure whether we were more stimulated or chastened, certainly they were harrowing sometimes—she demanded a report of work-in-progress every week when we did the *Faerie Queene* to be presented orally in class. I remember on more than one occasion feeling mortified. "Get on with it, you coots," I remember her saying once. There were things she got across so simply—she made me understand for life the sense of the question in *Lycidas*, 'Where were ye, Nymphs . . .?'—that the whole poem is an agonized 'Why?' It was the consummate expression of the acceptance of that in life which we find unacceptable. She had this marvelous combination of a great wealth and authority of learning and a kind of ingenuousness.

"Towards the end she was very aware of the tragic brevity of life—'I wish we had more time,' she said, meaning we have so little time to get things done. And yet she lived so hard herself at her work that she burnt herself out before her time. The doctor tried to fool her," Beverley said, "urging her to go to Washington for a holiday, and yet he told me that everything was breaking down—and I don't think he did fool her. I *think* she was unsure of what was to come. She used to ask me to play some German hymns and especially liked "Jesu joy of man's desiring." She liked to read St. Paul at that time—the bit about 'this corruptible must put on incorruption, and this mortal must put on immortality' (I. Cor.15:53)—I think she certainly *wanted* to believe it.

"Something I always remember about those last days too is her saying that what we need more of is—trust. And another thing—her amazing independence and courage. She knew she was dying I am sure yet she wasn't going to be a burden to anyone. All I did for her was get her some food and my culinary abilities were minimal. Which reminds me she had a tea towel with, 'Cool was her kitchen but her brains were hot!' (borrowed from Dryden's description of Shimei). You know I'm sure she had a beautiful sense of humor. No doubt she has had an inestimable influence, since everyone she taught will have taken something from her which was then passed on to their students."

Beverley also felt that Rosemond's importance to literary scholarship may be seen more clearly now, forty years later. After all the fads in critical theory, good, solid, historical scholarship has become important because it is not dated; she felt that Rosemond was the preeminent historical scholar of her time.

In late September, Beverley went with Rosemond and a few of her friends to Valley Forge for a picnic. It was a difficult but rewarding outing. Somewhere Rosemond found the strength to continue her obligations to the end of the semester. She was hanging on, working against time.

Jim Broderick felt that Rosemond did *not* burn herself out. "She was fulfilling herself through her work and was not going to let other things get in the way. There is a long Bryn Mawr tradition of ignoring physical impediments. There was no way of talking about the ordinary human disasters and pains that make up one's life. One didn't go into that sort of thing. If one is living the life of the mind, one was talking about serious things. Ros was dismissive [of her illness]." Broderick recalled going to her office in College Hall to get her and drive her home. "Her office was on what is in effect a European first floor," he said, "a second floor. It was a Victorian building with very high ceilings and an enormous flight of stairs, zigzagging up. I got some things out of her office and as we were going downstairs she said, 'You just go on ahead, carry them down, I have to hang on to the rail to get down.' When I saw what she had to do and that she was literally crawling along the wall with her hands to get down, she said, 'I don't want you ever to come to get me again; I want the kids to do it. They don't react the way you do. It's too hard on you.' And it was. I thought it was terrible to see what she had to go through."

Thursday before Christmas was Rosemond's final day of classes at the University of Pennsylvania. She did not meet with her seminar that day, but she did turn in her final grades. When Kathy Swaim came to pick her up, she remembered that "she was just sitting there, absolutely gray." Surely she had a premonition that her teaching days were over. A friend remembered her saying, "What can I do if I can't teach? Teaching is my life." Swaim drove her back to Bryn Mawr, then helped her into bed, where she undoubtedly remained in order to gather her strength for a dinner engagement with Isabel and Wallace MacCaffrey the following evening. Fortunately, she was unaware that the University of Pennsylvania had taken her courses away from her. And what she may or may not have known was that Merle was on his way to Bryn Mawr to put her in a nursing home. This made the anticipated evening with the MacCaffreys that much more pleasurable.

Isabel MacCaffrey was a Miltonist who taught at Bryn Mawr; she also looked up to Rosemond as a model for the kind of thing she wanted to do as a literary scholar. Her husband, Wallace MacCaffrey, a historian, later went to Harvard to teach. He recalled that Saturday evening when she came to their home for dinner, and how she had looked forward to coming: "We went and got her and since we lived in an apartment on the second floor, it was a terrible problem because she could hardly walk. When we spoke afterwards of that evening we remembered that although she was physically suffering from great disabilities, her mind was just as sharp and clear as it had ever been. We talked about all kinds of things, important things, not just chit chat. My wife and she talked about problems that interested them, what Isabel was writing, and so on. Her mind was just as clear as a bell and she was operating on all cylinders. Isabel reflected afterwards: 'What an affliction to retain the use of your mind, and she had a first rate mind, but not be able to carry on the rest of one's functions.' We had an enjoyable evening, and I think she enjoyed herself. After taking her home we sat in her apartment and chatted a bit. Then Isabel helped her into bed. We had no premonition, we were shocked."

Wallace MacCaffrey knew Rosemond only socially, but he had an intuitive insight into her special appeal; he also had a historian's response to her work. He recalled: "She was the kind of person who drew people around her. She had a kind of vitality and warmth that made people admire her, and fall in love with her, in a sense. The people who became her close friends and were entertaining her were often people a good bit younger than she and were drawn to her. She was the center of attraction. She would be in a chair and people would be sitting on the floor around her, everybody sort of half listening, even though they weren't involved in the conversation, revolving about her, coming back to her. Everything gravitated around her, not because she was an egotist, and wanted to dominate things, but because she was the center of vitality, of talk and laughter and warmth. I didn't know her and yet I soon looked forward to seeing her. She just reached out to other people. There wasn't anything deliberate about it, it wasn't as though she made an effort to do it, it was just the kind of person she was. [Tom Roche had the perception that what attracted people to her orbit was that "she exuded holiness."]

"She had a very unusual talent which I've seen in a few other instances. The kind of thing she was dealing with was the imagination of men and women who lived three or four hundred years ago. She knew how to get inside their minds, so to speak, to know how they perceived the world, how they imaginatively looked at the world around them and how that imagination reflected itself in their literature. It is an extremely difficult thing to do.

"Music is always a clue. If you listen with any seriousness to sixteenth-century music, you realize its extreme complexity and sophistication, and so was the world of their imagination, and particularly when it was applied to great works of literature. Lots of scholars can get outside, give you a kind of description, as though they were standing outside a building and saying it has three windows on the left, a cornice here, etc.—but it's external. And she was one of the rare scholars, and they're mostly women, who did get inside the minds of the past and look out, and see the world as Spenser, Milton, or any of the great writers of the period saw it. And it's an unusual kind of intuitive ability and it transcends the scholarly abilities. She had an intuitive understanding of the world of the past that only a few ever have. And I think that's one of the reasons she was a great teacher and a great scholar: I think it had something to do with the same kind of personality that warmed and cheered and attracted twentieth-century human beings.

"She understood religion, not simply doctrinal features of sixteenth-century Calvinism, but I think she had a kind of piety which participated in *their* inward feelings. I think her understanding of religion was like theirs was, a mixture of learning but a deep sensitivity of the kind of sensitivity which is very rare in the twentieth century. She had a sense of the other, I think, that was one of the keys to her understanding because the literature she studied was literature written by people who did have that keen sense all the time. It was part of the world in which they lived—an awareness of another dimension which I think is now a very uncommon kind of awareness. She had it. It enabled her to bridge the gap of four hundred years. She shared with them their deep religious faith, a very sophisticated kind of religious faith, a sensitive and subtle one. That enabled her to understand their literature as I think contemporaries understood it. And I think the kind of choices she made in her scholarly life were very intimately related to her own religious sense. You can't get very far in studying Milton unless you have a sense of a man with a deep religious faith. You respond, there is a chord struck there. And that would be why she struck a chord in some students, because they could also be led into that world she was trying to teach.

"I think poetry for her was an entry into the exploration of reality. It wasn't just an academic exercise. Allegory mediates reality. It's something you can't approach directly, but through the allegorical mode you can get a 'it is as if the world were this way.' I think the kinds of concepts she was dealing with aren't the kinds of concepts you can put into crisp, clear, sort of one, two, three arguments. It was a world of the imagination, not a world of logic, which she's dealing with. I think one of the things that clearly makes it difficult for us to read her, as it's difficult for most of us to read the poets of the sixteenth and seventeenth centuries, is not just the language in the technical sense of difficult, archaic language, but their minds were very complex and you can't describe complex phenomena without using complex language.

"She was not the kind of scholar who just trudged along doing the obvious sort of thing. There was a tremendous sense of joy and pleasure and personal return for her. It was a deeply personal involvement for her. Some people do their scholarship sort of off here and their personal life is over there. This wasn't the case with her. Her scholarship was at the very center of her personal life."

Usually, Rosemond had one of her student aides spend the night, but recently Ricky Wolf had begged off. She said, "I had decided to cut my ties with her a little bit because she was such a powerful personality, and I was so in love with her that I was beginning to think if I didn't watch myself, she would swallow me up. Not intentionally, but that would happen." Ricky's final tribute was expressed in these words: "Before anything else it was the utter *brilliance* manifested in wit, humor, and awed serenity of a beleaguered spirit in a world about to kill."

Beverley recalled that Ricky was very impressionable, spent a lot of time with Rosemond, and had dreams of her being crucified. In December, Beverley replaced Ricky and stayed with Rosemond at night. But Rosemond's noisy breathing was beginning to disturb Beverley's sleep, and she needed more rest in order to finish her thesis. Thus, after helping her to get ready to go out for dinner with the MacCaffreys, she left to stay at the graduate dorm. That is why there was no one there when the MacCaffreys brought her home. In a sense, they were the last to see her alive.

During the night, Rosemond got out of bed, was stricken, and fell heavily. Her fall, together with the strange and frightening sounds of her breathing, awakened the woman across the hall. She telephoned to Margaret Collins, who owned Bettws-Y-Coed and rented the apartments; she in turn called the doctor. When the doctor arrived, he and the neighbor got her into bed and covered her with a blanket. She was not entirely conscious, nor did she seem in pain, but she was very far gone. After giving her a shot, the doctor said it would be best to let her go, to let her die in her own bed with dignity.

Rosemond Tuve died early in the morning of December 20, 1964 a few hours following her stroke. It was less than one month after her sixty-first birthday. She had "just everything wrong with her"— arthritis, emphysema, heart failure, chronic bronchitis, and occlusion of the basal artery—the cause of her death. She had completed her semester at the University of Pennsylvania; the manuscript of her final book, *Allegorical Imagery,* which she had kept stashed in a suitcase under her bed, had just been delivered to her editor at the Princeton University Press.

The funeral took place the following Tuesday, at 1:30 P.M., at the Oliver Blair funeral home in downtown Philadelphia. The shock for Beverley Chadwick, who went in to make her breakfast that Sunday morning and found her dead, was compounded by the secular, impersonal atmosphere of the funeral home. And there was Rosemond, looking very old and frail, dressed in a lavender dress with ruffled sleeves. Beverley winced when she heard Rosemond's beloved Lutheran hymns, and particularly Bach's "Jesus joy of man's desiring," played much too fast on poor recordings. The commercial atmosphere of a large, city funeral home was a travesty. One student remembers that the service was well attended, with her brothers looking like "zombies." No doubt they were in shock. Dorothy Bethurum and Hamilton Smyser were two of the people from Connecticut College who came.

Interment was in Canton. There, in the earth she loved, she is buried beside her mother and father. Merle, visibly upset, placed on top of her casket just before it was lowered into the ground a copy of the recent *Life* magazine double issue on the Bible. Rosemond and Merle remained united in their views of life—"the tissue of existence" was how they described it. Five years previously Merle had published an article entitled "Physics and the Humanities: The Verification of Complementarity." Meditating on Bohr's principal of complementarity (the electron must be regarded both as a wave and as a particle—according to its context) as the great contribution of physics to the thought of our epoch, Merle wrote: "Things of the mind and spirit of man have a reality all their own, parallel with, but not the same as, our participation in the physical world."[4] Bohr's principle is analogous to Rosemond's development of her theory of allegory—an image is the particle; its extension is the infinite wave. Merle mirrored his sister's poetic theory: "No man can claim that a description of the physical processes which are simultaneous with a thought or an emotion are fully and identically the *same* as that thought or emotion."[5] These are complementary views of reality that defy classification and cannot be reduced to axioms, logic, measurement. Modern physics and literary critical theory have demonstrated that more than "one set of ideas must be used if our finite minds are to view and comprehend in some increasing measure of completeness the fabulous complexity and beauty of the awareness which is the central mystery of life for each of us."[6] Can there be any difference between truth at the core of an atom and truth at the heart of a poetic image?

Laurence Stavig, then president of Augustana College, was present at the burial with his wife and son, Mark. Mark Stavig recalled meeting Rosemond when she was in Oxford, and the "lively and fascinating session" they enjoyed; also, he remembered how "friendly and gracious" she had been when she invited him to attend the Gauss seminars. He referred to a quotation from Milton used by Merle in a talk at Princeton: "The end, then, of learning is to repair the ruins of our first parents by regaining to know God aright, and out of that knowledge to love him, to imitate him, to be like him, as we may the nearest by possessing our souls of true virtue." Rosemond, in her life and in her writing, echoed Milton's thought.

After Rosemond's death, Harry Morris, her former student who had invited her to lecture at Florida State University, wrote a poem that expressed his personal and specific understanding of her:

> With Twain He Covered His Face
> For Rosemond Tuve
> 1903–1964
> Attain to the knowledge of Him,
> that you may love Him also.
> —St. Bernard
> One of the world's roses is pressed now in
> Her book. She was much thorn and scant of bud,
> But in the thorn is much beauty. Thin
> Petals, bright leaf let spirit; the thorn lets blood.
>
> Rose with wisdom of the thorn
> Enter now the forehead torn,
> Pierce the head with knowledge of him,
> Transfixed yourself with love of him.[7]

14

FOLLOWING THE FUNERAL, Merle discussed with Tom Roche the problem of getting Rosemond's manuscript published. It needed considerable editing; there was no title; pieces of paper with changes had been pasted over some of the paragraphs: and corrections in her illegible handwriting had been crowded between the triple-spaced lines of type. When Roche offered to undertake the final editing and see the book through the press, Merle exclaimed, "Praise Allah!"

Roche's timely and devoted efforts resulted in publication by the Princeton University Press in 1966. The book has gone through several hardcover and paperback editions. In an early review of the 436-page testament, R. E. Kaske, professor at Cornell University, wrote: "This is the posthumously published book of a great scholar and an unforgettable personality; how close it comes to being a life's work is hinted by her own remark that parts of it were begun as early as 1929 ['The Red Crosse Knight and Mediaeval Demon Stories,' *PMLA*, vol. 44, 1929]. Deep as was our previous debt to the learning and industry of Professor Tuve, it will be increased many times over by this last contribution . . . Professor Tuve's style—which, despite a scattering of unusually well-turned sentences and clearly developed paragraphs, has been generally regarded with a kind of affectionate exasperation—loses none of its formidability in the present volume." Kaske remembered her with a quotation from Milton's "Lycidas":

> So sinks the day-star in the Ocean bed,
> And yet anon repairs his drooping head,
> And tricks his beams, and with new-spangled Ore,
> Flames in the forehead of the morning sky.[1]

D. C. Allen confirmed Kaske's belief: "It was doubtless as her *magnum opus* that Miss Tuve conceived this book, and its publication only after her death prevented her from the author's final privilege of review. We must be grateful to Professor Thomas Roche for undertaking its editing and final verification of sources . . . her work is a double fugue, whose major theme is allegory generally during the Late Medieval and Renaissance periods, whose second subject is a romance-oriented view of Spenser . . . [and shows] the evolution of the myth of Magnificence, a myth finally embodied in Spenser's Arthur."

Allen leaves us with another insightful, and entertaining, comment: "One last impression of *Allegorical Imagery:* it is as if one had wandered into the author's classroom, and were beguiled into the rest of the lengthy seminar. In some of her pedagogical moods there is something crotchety about Miss Tuve; sometimes she affects a toughness of tone that rather seeks to undercut a girlishness of manner. Often she seems to be putting the question to us, attending our efforts to follow her argument, stopping to anticipate our doubts, spelling things out, and not always happy with the degree of our attention or the depth of our preparation. She is always the teacher, though sometimes she is pupil as well . . . Miss Tuve's manner, her hopes, weaknesses, enthusiasms, care, and fervor, these give her work a genuine character."[2]

R. M. Adams, writing in the *New York Review of Books* in June 1968, wonders why "the discussion of Edmund Spenser and his poetry has proliferated in the 1960's. . . . Why? There are probably some interesting sociological reasons, such as the prevalent interest in fictive worlds and autonomous structure of myth: for some of the brethren, one suspects. Spenser is a Tolkien off whom it's respectable to make a living." Adams then turns his attention to *Allegorical Imagery:* "The last volume of this great lady comes to hand to make us sensible of our loss . . . she shows the possibilities of allegory for flexible and free interplay between narrative and abstraction, character and prototype . . . Readers acquainted with Miss Tuve's previous work will not have to be told how knotty and knowing and frequently funny she could be . . . its jocose narrative episodes are retold with

warmth and wit. No doubt it's a bit special, the taste for medieval allegorical humor on the subject of the virtues and the vices—but high
scholarship should and can have literary rewards and Miss Tuve's
never failed to. Her wit was wry and dry; all sorts of wise sayings and
abrupt cross-generalizations got packed into her books . . . Miss Tuve's
investigations into what allegory actually was for real readers and
writers in the palmy days of the mode will lend plenitude and humanity to what is all too easily dismissed as a rigid and mechanical structure of abstractions."[3]

Modern psychologists believe people's lives exemplify archetypes
and every individual lives out his or her own myth. Rosemond's life
was guided by a legend of chivalry, animated in her childhood years
by her life on the prairies of South Dakota when she saw distances she
couldn't reach. While reading tales of King Arthur, she may well have
fantasized about a knight's quest for noble deeds and holiness, and
like Arthur her quest for magnificence was attainable only after death.
Later, a college paper expresses her delight with ballad characters and
their virtues, and reinforces her connection to medieval times. Her
first book looks at the origins of seasons and months as artistic and
literary symbols that later become Christianized.

Always in pursuit of sources, her earliest published works, "The
Red Crosse Knight and Mediaeval Demon Stories" followed by
"Guillaume's Pilgrim and the House of Fame," served as the founda-
tion of her life's work, culminating in her final book, *Allegorical
Imagery.* As she moved to the sixteenth century her scholarly articles
concentrate on Spenser, until *Elizabethan and Metaphysical Imagery*
startled the academic world. In this work she describes the myriad
functions of imagery, stressing the importance of "significancy" to the
Renaissance writer: Images both teach and move readers to right
action and belief.

In *A Reading of George Herbert,* she responds with a moving and
prayerful rejoinder to Empson's Freudian interpretations of Herbert's
poetry. She believed profoundly in the implication of her subject matter. James Baird, a colleague at Connecticut College, recalled that during a reading of her paper on Herbert's "Sacrifice," she was on the
verge of tears. He commented, "It was a statement of faith, which we

all needed." Once more, she spoke of the power of poetry to bring to our awareness ancient and affecting symbols.

Rosemond delivered a paper on "Lycidas," which later appeared in her book on Milton, at a meeting of the Modern Language Association in New York. Baird remembered her "famous reprimand" just prior to reading the essay: "The back doors of this room will now be closed. I'm here for my pound of flesh. Those of you who want to make cocktail engagements will now absent themselves." In her essay on Milton's "Comus," and in her classroom teaching, Rosemond repeatedly stressed the struggle between the figure of vice (Comus) and virtue, presented by the Lady. She shows us how the Lady in "Comus," in harmony with nature, preserves her virginity, one type of chastity, but also the figurative chastity of the untouchable soul. What Rosemond stressed was that Comus never does touch the freedom of the Lady's mind, which "is *exactly* what he wished to take possession of." Chastity is inviolable fidelity to God.

All of Rosemond's research and writings led to her final book, *Allegorical Imagery*—the climax of her work and her life. Years of scholarship and teaching, coupled with her profound spiritual beliefs, culminated in what can be read as an allegory of her own life. In this book she enlarges on the meaning of imagery by extending it to allegory: Spenser's knights present more than the virtues they embody. Their conflicts are not just moral struggles; they are faced with the death of the soul or learning what its freedom depends on. The book is a brilliant achievement to which scholars today turn for both sources of information and topics requiring further investigation. She remained didactic, always proselytizing for significancy—ultimate concerns. Allegory has the power to teach us true belief, and in writing this book its author is attempting nothing less. She lived in the world of being, allegory and metaphor her only language, one that discursive reasoning cannot provide. She spoke that language.

In the years following her death, colleagues continued to praise her. Willard Thorpe enclosed a note along with his contribution to the Renaissance book fund that was established in her memory at Connecticut College, observing: "What a silence she left behind." Kathleen Lea felt as though a "light had gone out." Rosemond Tuve was one of four scholars to appear in *Notable American Women* when it was published in 1980.

In 1984, in the foreword to his book, *Chaucer and the Imagery of Narrative*, V. A. Kolve wrote, "Something hereditary may even be involved: though I never met her, I learned on a visit to my ancestral Norway that Rosemond Tuve was a cousin twice-removed. Whatever the logic of such a history may be, what began as an incidental pleasure has become no small part of my profession. It has led to the kind of book this is, a book in which pictures and texts are seen to cast a mutual light." Later he refers to her work as a "model for this study."[4]

Rosemond's achievements in the academic world are the visible, quantifiable part of her heritage. If she didn't quite "save a century of poetry from the new critics," as one student proclaimed, she did make an undeniable advance in historical criticism. She struggled against the prejudice endured by women scholars; the bitter jealously of some of her Connecticut colleagues; the loneliness assuaged only by friends who spoke her language and by "her poets," as she liked to refer to Spenser, Milton and Herbert. What she left behind, for those who heard her, and were "galvanized for life," was her pilgrimage—the story of a human being who maintained throughout her life an inviolable chastity— integrity—and her freedom.

— Bibliography —

Childs, Herbert E. P. *An American Genius*. New York: Dutton & Co., 1968.

Daniélou, Jean. *Origin*. New York: Sheed & Ward, 1955.

Dinsmore, Charles Allen. *Aids to the Study of Dante*. New York: Houghton, Mifflin & Company, 1903.

Dodds, E. R., editor. *The Journal and Letters of Stephen Mackenna*. New York: William Morrow and Company (n.d.).

Eliot, T. S. *Selected Essays* (New Edition). New York: Harcourt, Brace and Company, 1950.

Finch, Edith. *Carey Thomas of Bryn Mawr*. New York: Harper Brothers, 1947.

Gilson, Etienne. *The Spirit of Mediaeval Philosophy* (Gifford Lectures, 1931–32), translated by A. H. C. Downes. New York: Charles Scribners Sons, 1936.

Honan, Park. *Matthew Arnold: A Life*. New York: McGraw-Hill Book Co., 1981.

Kolve, V. A. *Chaucer and the Imagery of Narrative*. Stanford, CA: Stanford University Press, 1984.

Kunitz, Stanley J. *Twentieth Century Authors*. New York: The H. W. Wilson Co., 1955.

Langer, Susanne K. *Philosophy in a New Key*. New York: A Mentor Book, The American Library, 1951.

Lewis, C. S. *The Allegory of Love*. New York: Oxford University Press, 1958.

Morris, Harry. *Birth and Copulation and Death*, Tallahassee: Florida State University Press, 1969,

Ong, Walter J. "Metaphor and the Twinned Vision," *Sewanee Review*, April 1955.

Roche, Thomas P., Jr. *Essays by Rosemond Tuve: Spenser; Herbert; Milton*. Edited by Thomas P. Roche Jr. Princeton, NJ: Princeton University Press, 1970.

Rölvaag, O. E. *Giants in the Earth*. New York: Harper & Brothers, 1927.

Seeger, Raymond J. "Scientist and Poet," in *American Scientist*, vol. 47, no. 5, September 1959, 350–360.

Tuve, Merle. "Physics and the Humanities—The Verification of Complementarity," in *The Search for Understanding*. Edited by Caryl P. Haskins. Washington: Carnegie Institution, 1967.

Tuve, Rosemond. *Allegorical Imagery.* Princeton, NJ: Princeton University Press, 1966.

—. *Elizabethan and Metaphysical Imagery.* Chicago: The University of Chicago Press, 1947.

—. *Images and Themes in Five Poems by Milton.* Cambridge, MA: Harvard University Press, 1957.

—. *Palingenius's Zodiake of Life.* Facsimile edition with critical introduction. New York: Scholars' Facsimiles and Reprints, 1947.

—. *A Reading of George Herbert.* Chicago: The University of Chicago Press, 1952.

—. *Seasons and Months: Studies in a Tradition of Middle English Poetry.* Paris: Librairie Universitaire S. A., 1933.

ESSAYS AND REVIEWS
By Rosemond Tuve

"The Red Crosse Knight and Mediaeval Demon Stories," *PMLA* 44 (1929), 706–714.

"Guillaume's Pilgrim & the *Hous of Fame*," *MLN* 45 (December 1930), 518–522.

Marion Crane Carroll & Rosemond Tuve, "Two Manuscripts of the Middle English *Anonymous Riming Chronicle*," *PMLA* 46 (1931), 115–154.

"A Mediaeval Commonplace in Spenser's Cosmology," *Studies in Philology,* vol. 30, (1933), 133–147.

"Spenser and the Zodiake of Life." *Journal of English and Germanic Philology,* vol. 34, (January 1935), 1–19.

"Spenser's Readings: *The De Claris Mulieribus*," *Studies in Philology,* vol. 33 (April 1936), 147–165.

"Spring in Chaucer and before Him," *MLN,* vol. 52 (January 1937), 9–16.

"Spenser and Mediaeval Mazers: with a Note on Jason in Ivory," *Studies in Philology,* vol. 34 (April 1937), 138–147.

"Ancients, Moderns and Saxons," *ELH,* vol. 6 (September 1939), 165–190.

"Spenser and Some Pictorial Conventions: with Particular Reference to Illuminated Manuscripts," *Studies in Philology,* vol. 37 (April 1940), 149–176.

Review of Cleanth Brooks, *Modern Poetry and the Tradition,* 1939. In *Modern Language Quarterly,* vol. 2 (March 1941), 147–150.

"Imagery and Logic: Ramus and Metaphysical Poetics," *Journal of the History of Ideas,* vol. 3 (October 1942), 365–400.

"A Critical Survey of Scholarship in the Field of English Literature of the Renaissance," *Studies in Philology*, vol. 40 (April 1943), 204–255. Published under the direction of the Committee on Renaissance Studies of the American Council of Learned Societies; written at their request as one of a series covering all fields of study in the Renaissance.

Review of Eric Bentley's *The Playwright as Thinker: A Study of Drama in Modern Times*. In *Journal of Aesthetics and Art Criticism*, vol. 5 (June 1947), 326–327.

"More Battle than Books," in a Symposium: The Teaching of Literature. *Sewanee Review*, vol. 55 (October–December 1947), 571–585.

Review of E. Catherine Dunn's *Concept of Ingratitude in Renaissance English Moral Philosophy*. In *MLN*, vol. 63 (1948), 427–428.

Review of Moody Prior's *Language of Tragedy*. In *Journal of Aesthetics and Art Criticism*, vol. 6 (1948), 349–352.

"On Herbert's *Sacrifice*." *Kenyon Review*, vol. 12 (Winter 1950), 511–575.

Review of Josephine Miles's *The Primary Language of Poetry in the 1640's*. In *MLN*, vol. 65 (January 1950), 60–62.

"A.A.U.W. Fellows and Their Survival." *Journal of the American Association of University Women*, vol. 44 (1951), 201–208.

Review of R. Kirk's *Joseph Hall's "Heaven upon Earth"* and *"Characters of Vertues and Vices."* In *MLQ*, vol. 12 (September 1951), 364–366.

Review of Milton Crane's *Shakespeare's Prose*. In *Journal of Aesthetics and Art Criticism*, vol. 10 (December 1951), 181–183.

Review of George Williamson's *The Senecan Amble*. In *Journal of English and Germanic Philology*, vol. 52 (January 1953), 112–115.

Review of E. M. W. Tillyard's *The English Renaissance: Fact or Fiction?* In *MLN*, vol. 68 (June 1953), 421–423.

Review of Erich Auerbach's *Mimesis: The Representation of Reality in Western Literature*. In *Yale Review*, vol. 43 (Summer 1954), 619–622.

Review of J. H. Summers's *George Herbert: His Religion and Art*. In *The Journal of English and Germanic Philology*, vol. 54 (April 1955), 284–285.

"The Race Not to the Swift," *Journal of the American Association of University Women*, vol. 49 (1955), 23–27.

Review of Louis Martz's *The Poetry of Meditation*. In *Modern Philology*, vol. 53 (1956), 204–207.

"Rosemond Tuve on John Milton." Reprint of most of a talk in the Third Programme, British Broadcasting Corporation. In *The Listener*, vol. 60 (August 28, 1958), 312–313.

Review of W. S. Howell's *Logic and Rhetoric in England, 1500–1700*. In *MLN*, vol. 73 (March 1958), 206–211.

"George Herbert and *Caritas*," In *Journal of the Warburg and Courtauld Institutes*, vol. 22 (July–December 1959), 303–331.

"Sacred 'Parody' of Love Poetry, and Herbert." In *Studies in the Renaissance,* vol. 8 (1961), 249–290.

"Baroque and Mannerist Milton?" In *Milton Studies: in Honor of F. H. Fletcher.* (Urbana: 1961), 209–225; and *Journal of English and Germanic Philology,* vol. 60 (1961), 817–833.

Excerpts from Commencement Address at Williams Memorial Institute. New London, Connecticut, June 10, 1963.

"Notes on the Virtues and Vices." *Journal of the Warburg and Courtauld Institutes,* vols. 26–27 (1963–1964), 264–303, 42–72.

"Spenserus." In *Essays in English Literature from the Renaissance to the Victorian Age, Presented to A. S. P. Woodhouse.* Edited by Millar MacLure and F. W. Watt (Toronto, 1964), 1–25.

～ *End Notes* ～

Acknowledgments

1. Tuve, Rosemond. *A Reading of George Herbert.* London: Faber and Faber; Chicago: University of Chicago Press, 1952, 99.

Chapter 1

1. Letter from Park Honan to the author.
2. Rölvaag, O. E. *Giants in the Earth.* New York: Harper & Brothers, Publishers, 1927, xvii.
3. Introduction to a speech given at Augustana College, Sioux Falls, S.D., 1961.
4. Kunitz, Stanley J. *Twentieth Century Authors.* New York: The H. W. Wilson Co., 1955, 1011.
5. Ibid.
6. Tuve, Rosemond, "The Race Not to the Swift," in *Journal of the American Association of University Women,* vol. 40 (1955), 23–27.
7. Kunitz, 1011.
8. Letter to the author. June, 1945.
9. Kunitz, 1011.
10. Erpestad, Emil. "Augustana College: A Venture in Christian Education." Dissertation presented to the faculty of the graduate school of Yale University in candidacy for the degree of doctor of philosophy, 1956, 119.

Chapter 2

1. Kunitz, 1011
2. Ibid.
3. Ibid.
4. Reproduced from the Manuscript Division of the Library of Congress. Merle A. Tuve papers.
5. Ibid.
6. Ibid.
7. Ibid.

8. Ibid.
9. Ibid.
10. Ibid.
11. Ibid.
12. Ibid.
13. Ibid.
14. Ibid.
15. Ibid.
16. Ibid.
17. Ibid.
18. Ibid.
19. Ibid.
20. Ibid.
21. Ibid.
22. Kunitz, 1012.
23. Ibid. 1011–1012.
24. Library of Congress.
25. Ibid.
26. Ibid.
27. Ibid.
28. Ibid.
29. Ibid.
30. Kunitz, 1012.

Chapter 3

1. Library of Congress.
2. Ibid.
3. Ibid.
4. Ibid.
5. Ibid.
6. Kunitz, 1012.
7. Library of Congress.
8. Ibid.
9. Ibid.
10. Ibid.
11. Ibid.
12. Ibid.
13. Ibid.
14. Ibid.
15. Tuve, Rosemond. *Seasons and Months: Studies in a Tradition of Middle English Poetry.* Paris: Libraire Universitaire S. A., 1933, 4–5.
16. Ibid. 126.

17. Letter to the author. June, 1945.

18. Tuve, 98.

19. Finch, Edith. *Carey Thomas of Bryn Mawr.* New York: Harper Brothers, 1947, 273.

20. Ibid. 275.

21. Ibid. 276.

22. Kunitz, 1012.

23. Library of Congress.

24. Tuve, Rosemond, "The Red Crosse Knight and Mediaeval Demon Stories," in *PMLA*, 46 (1929), 706.

25. Ibid. 714.

26. ALES Papers (The American Labor Educational Service), Labor Management Documentation Center, M. P. Catherwood Library, Cornell University.

Chapter 4

1. Kunitz, 1012.

2. Library of Congress.

3. *Fritillary,* Magazine of the Oxford Women's Colleges, March 9, 1929, 17.

4. Ibid.

5. Ibid.

6. Tuve, Rosemond, "A Mediaeval Commonplace in Spenser's Cosmology," in *Studies in Philology,* 30, (1933), 133.

7. Kunitz, 1012.

8. ALES Papers.

9. Reproduced from the archives of the Charles E. Shain Library, Connecticut College.

10. Ibid.

11. Library of Congress.

12. Tuve, Rosemond, "Spenser and Mediaeval Mazers," in *Studies in Philology,* 34 (1937), 138–147.

13. Ibid.

14. Library of Congress.

15. Ibid.

16. *The Book Collector,* vol. 29, no. 2, (Summer 1980), 243-244.

17. Connecticut College Archives.

18. Ibid.

19. Ibid.

20. Ibid.

Chapter 5

1. Library of Congress.
2. Tuve, Rosemond, "Spring in Chaucer and Before Him," in *Modern Language Notes,* (January 1937), 9–16.
3. Ibid.
4. Tuve, "Spenser and Mediaeval Mazers."
5. Tuve, Rosemond, "Spenser's Reading: The De Claris Mulieribus," in *Studies in Philology,* 33 (1936), 147.
6. Connecticut College Archives.
7. Ibid.

Chapter 6

1. Tuve, "The Race Not to the Swift," 32–33.
2. Connecticut College Archives.
3. Ibid.
4. Ibid.
5. Reproduced from the Archives of the Johns Hopkins University.
6. Connecticut College Archives.
7. Tuve, Rosemond, "A Critical Survey of Scholarship in the Field of English Literature of the Renaissance," in *Studies in Philology,* vol. 40 (April 1943), 253.
8. Ibid. 243.
9. Ibid. 255.
10. Ibid. 255.
11. Library of Congress.
12. Ibid.
13. Ibid.
14. Connecticut College Archives.
15. Ibid.
16. Connecticut College *Bulletin,* September 30, 1945.
17. Tuve, Rosemond. *Elizabethan and Metaphysical Imagery.* Chicago: The University of Chicago Press, 1947, 183.
18. Ibid.
19. Tuve, Rosemond, "More Battle Than Books," in a symposium: The Teaching of Literature. *Sewanee Review,* vol. 55 (October–December 1947), 572–574.
20. Ibid. 578.
21. Ibid. 578-582.
22. Ibid. 583-585.
23. Library of Congress.

Chapter 7

1. Connecticut College Archives.
2. Tuve, Rosemond. "On Herbert's Sacrifice," in *Kenyon Review,* vol. 12 (Winter 1950), (51–75.)
3. Tuve, Rosemond. "A.A.U.W. Fellows and Their Survival," in *Journal of the American Association of University Women,* vol. 44 (1951), (**201–208.**)
4. The Richmond, Virginia *News Leader,* April 14, 1951. 5. JAAUW, 201-208.
5. *JAAUW,* 201-208.
6. Reproduced from the files of the English department at the University of Minnesota.
7. Ibid.
8. Ibid.
9. Ibid.
10. Ibid.
11. Ibid.
12. Ibid.
13. Connecticut College Archives.
14. Ibid.
15. Tuve, Rosemond. *A Reading of George Herbert.* 111.
16. Ibid. 203.
17. Library of Congress.
18. Reproduced from the files of the English department of the University of Minnesota.
19. Connecticut College Archives.

Chapter 8

1. Library of Congress.
2. Quoted by Paul Alpers.
3. Connecticut College Archives.
4. Ibid.
5. Ibid.
6. Letter to the author. June, 1945.
7. *Journal and Letters of Stephen Mackenna,* edited by E. R. Dodds, New York: William Morrow & Company, n.d., p. 69.
8. Ibid. 239.
9. Ibid. 239.
10. Ibid. 239–240.
11. Connecticut College Archives.
12. Library of Congress.
13. Ibid.

14. Ibid.
15. Ibid.
16. Ibid.
17. *Hartford Courant,* July 1, 1955.
18. Tuve, "Race Not to the Swift," 31.
19. Ibid. 35.

Chapter 9

1. Library of Congress.
2. Ibid.
3. Ibid.
4. Ibid.
5. Connecticut College Archives.
6. *Harvard Crimson,* September 25, 1956.
7. Connecticut College Archives.
8. Report of President Park to the board of trustees, 1955.
9. "George Herbert and *Caritas,*" in *Journal of the Warburg and Courtauld Institutes,* vol. 22 (July–December 1959), 303–331.
10. Ibid. 314, 315

Chapter 10

1. Library of Congress.
2. "Rosemond Tuve on John Milton," *The Listener,* August 28, 1958, vol. LX, no. 1535, 312–313.
3. Reproduced from the Archives of the Seeley G. Mudd Manuscript Library, Princeton University.
4. Ibid.
5. Ibid.
6. Ibid.
7. Ibid.
8. Connecticut College Archives.
9. Ibid.
10. Ibid.
11. Ibid.
12. Ibid.
13. Library of Congress.
14. Ibid.
15. *Goucher Weekly,* November 10, 1959.
16. Bryn Mawr *College News,* November, 1959.
17. *ACLS Newsletter,* 1960.
18. Connecticut College Archives.

Chapter 11

1. D. C. Allen in the *Journal of English and Germanic Philology,* January, 1967, 118.
2. Library of Congress.
3. Connecticut College Archives.
4. *Conn Census,* January 12, 1961.
5. Connecticut College Archives.
6. Ibid.
7. Reed Whittemore in *The Voice of the Carleton College Alumni,* July 1961.

Chapter 12

1. Library of Congress.
2. Reproduced from the files in the English department of the University of Pennsylvania.
3. Ibid.
4. Ibid.
5. Ibid.
6. Ibid.
7. Connecticut College Archives.

Chapter 13

1. Tuve, "Race Not to the Swift," 26–27.
2. Tuve, Rosemond. "Spenserus," in *Essays in English Literature from the Renaissance to the Victorian Age, Presented to A. S. P. Woodhouse,* ed. Millar MacLure and F. W. Watt (Toronto, 1964), 3.
3. Tuve, Rosemond, "Notes on the Virtues and Vices," in *Journal of the Warburg and Courtauld Institutes,* 26–27 (1963–64), 265–303, 42–72.
4. Tuve, Merle. "Physics and the Humanities: The Verification of Complementarity," in *The Search for Understanding,* ed. Caryl P. Haskins. Washington: Carnegie Institute, 1967, 50.
5. Ibid. 49.
6. Ibid. 52.
7. Morris, Harry. *Birth and Copulation and Death,* Tallahassee: Florida State University Press, 1969, 55.

Chapter 14

1. R. E. Kaske, *Speculum,* vol. 42 (January 1967), 196.
2. D. C. Allen, 118.
3. R. M. Adams, *New York Review of Books,* June 6, 1968, 32.
4. Kolve V. A. *Chaucer and the Imagery of Narrative.* Stanford: Stanford University Press, 1984, vii.

❯ *About the Author* ❮

Margaret Evans was born in New York City and grew up in New Rochelle, New York. After graduating from Connecticut College she attended Columbia University, receiving a Masters Degree in Renaissance Literature. At B. Altman & Co. she wrote advertising for New York newspapers and later served as acting editor of the *Clinton Courier* in Clinton, New York, contributing weekly columns. Her first published article, "The Luminous Life of Rosemond Tuve," appeared in the *Connecticut College Alumni Magazine*, Fall, 1980. As a professional horsewoman, she taught equitation and trained hunters and jumpers. She has four grown children and lives in Hartland, Vermont.